Skitka

A BEGINNER'S GUIDE
TO STRUCTURAL
EQUATION MODELING

A BEGINNER'S GUIDE TO STRUCTURAL EQUATION MODELING

Randall E. Schumacker
University of North Texas

Richard G. Lomax
Northern Illinois University

LEA LAWRENCE ERLBAUM ASSOCIATES, PUBLISHERS
1996 Mahwah, New Jersey

Lawrence Erlbaum Associates, Inc., Publishers
10 Industrial Avenue
Mahwah, New Jersey 07430

Library of Congress Cataloging-in-Publication Data

Schumacker, Randall E.
    A beginner's guide to structural equation modeling / Randall E.
Schumacker, Richard G. Lomax
        p.   cm.
    Includes bibliographical references and index.
    ISBN 0-8058-1766-2 (cloth : alk. paper). — ISBN 0-8058-1767-0
(pbk. : alk. paper).
        1. Multivariate analysis. 2. Social sciences—Statistical
methods. I. Lomax, Richard G. II. Title.
    QA278.S36 1996
    519.5'35—dc20   95-5868
                                                                          CIP

Books published by Lawrence Erlbaum Associates are printed on acid-free paper,
and their bindings are chosen for strength and durability.

Printed in the United States of America
10 9 8 7 6 5 4 3 2 1

Dedicated to our Mentors

Dennis W. Leitner
Southern Illinois University

Earl L. McCallon
University of North Texas

and

Jamie Algina
University of Florida

Jim Carlson
Educational Testing Service

Bill Cooley
University of Pittsburgh

Neil Timm
University of Pittsburgh

CONTENTS

PREFACE

———◇◇◇———

This volume presents a basic elementary introduction to structural equation modeling. The reader is provided a review of correlation and covariance among variables followed by multiple regression and path analysis techniques to better understand the building blocks of structural equation modeling. The concepts behind measurement models are introduced to illustrate how measurement error impacts our statistical analyses, and structural models are presented that indicate how latent variable relationships can be established. Examples are included in the book to make the concepts clearer to the reader. The structural equation modeling examples are presented using either EQS5.0 or LISREL8–SIMPLIS programming language. Both software packages have an eas-to-use set of commands to specify measurement and structural models. No complicated programming is required, nor does the reader need an advanced understanding of statistics or matrix algebra. Basically, if you can diagram a theoretical model, you will be able to analyze it after reading this book.

Faculty, students, and researchers should be well equipped with the resources and references contained in the book to enhance their working knowledge of structural equation modeling. This book is not intended to provide an indepth presentation of statistics, factor analysis, or structural equation modeling. Rather, we assume that the reader has a basic understanding of correlation, and we build upon this understanding to present the basic ideas and principles behind structural equation modeling. A goal in writing the book was to focus conceptually on the steps one takes in analyzing theoretical models. These steps encompass specifying a model based upon theory or prior research, determining whether the model can be identified to have unique estimates for variables in the model, selecting an appropriate estimation method based on the distributional assumptions of the variables, testing the model and interpreting fit indices, and finally respecifying a model, based on suggested modification indices, which involves adding or dropping paths in the model to obtain a better model fit.

Our approach to presenting the basic concepts and principles that form the building blocks of structural equation modeling are presented logically in the chapters. Chapter 1 discusses the terminology used in this approach and a general perspective regarding measurement and statistics, which includes the handling of missing data, outliers, and normality of variables. This chapter also lists available software which can be used for structural equation modeling, and provides additional references on the subject (books, journals, and quantitative series paperbacks). Chapter 2 covers an overview of correlation. This includes the various types of correlation coefficients, factors affecting correlation, covariance, and causality issues in modeling. Chapter 3 presents the structural equation modeling approach to multiple regression, path analysis, and factor analysis (measurement models). This chapter provides the first introduction to the EQS5.0 and LISREL8–SIMPLIS software programs. Chapters 4 and 5 provide an overview of measurement and structural models, and includes an example to illustrate the basic concepts. It covers the two-step approach to modeling, how to diagram models, and how to interpret direct, indirect, and total "effects" in a model. Chapter 6 discusses model specification, identification, and estimation. Chapter 7 discusses and presents the various fit indices output in EQS5.0 and LISREL8–SIMPLIS. Chapter 8 presents the EQS5.0 and LISREL8–SIMPLIS computer output for the main example used in the book. The chapter also provides comparisons of their computer output and assists the reader in interpreting the results. Chapter 9 serves to illustrate how the diagramming of a model, as a first step, can be translated into either an EQS5.0 or LISREL8–SIMPLIS program. Several different types of regression, path, factor, and structural models are presented to enable the reader to understand how the equations are written in the software programs. Chapter 10 provides a basic understanding of how to program more advanced applications in either EQS5.0 or LISREL8–SIMPLIS. These advanced topics include cross-validation, simulation, bootstrapping, jackknifing, multiple sample comparisons of model estimates, and interaction "effects" in structural models. Chapter 11 contains LISREL matrix programs for some of the examples in the book. This Technical Section was provided so the reader could make a comparison between the matrix notation language used in LISREL8 to the easier SIMPLIS command language used in our examples. We also felt this comparison was important because the SIMPLIS program can output results in a matrix format upon request and the 8 matrices help to further our understanding of the modeling process. A beginning reader can skip this chapter without any loss in understanding of the basic concepts and principles underlying structural equation modeling.

Theoretical models are present in almost every discipline, and therefore can be formulated and tested. The contents of this book should provide a helpful beginning to structural equation modeling for any student, faculty, or researcher in medicine, political science, sociology, education, psychology, business, or the biological sciences, to name only a few. The modeling concepts and principles presented here are general in nature and therefore can be widely applied in any of these disciplines. We hope you begin, as we have in our own research, to understand and apply structural equation modeling techniques.

Randall E. Schumacker
Richard G. Lomax

ACKNOWLEDGMENTS

This book took shape over several years of interacting with our colleagues and new users of structural equation modeling software. Our experience has taught us that we are forever grateful to the pioneers in the field who initially developed the software and later guided our experiences in analyzing data. To Drs. Karl Jöreskog, Dag Sörbom, and Peter M. Bentler we owe a debt of gratitude. We hope this book helps to further the interest in structural equation modeling.

We would like to especially thank Dr. Karl Jöreskog for kindly reviewing the draft of the book, as well as, his associates Stefan Mattsson and Fan Yang. They detected numerous errors and suggested several additions to the content. We have hopefully addressed all of their concerns. After their thorough review, any errors or omissions are uniquely ours.

This book was made possible by the support and encouragement from Mr. Lawrence Erlbaum. His remarkable belief in our book, understanding, patience, and guidance are deeply respected and appreciated. We also would like to thank Judith Amsel, Kathy Dolan, and Sondra Guideman for helping us through the difficult process of revisions, galleys, and getting the book into print. They put forth a tremendous effort on our behalf.

PROLOGUE

The idea for this book had an interesting beginning. In 1981, Richard presented a paper at the American Educational Research Association annual meeting which was later published in 1982 entitled, "A guide to LISREL-type structural equation modeling." Several years later in 1993, an AERA presentation by Richard, entitled, "A beginner's guide to structural equation modeling," led to the name we chose for the book.

A few years prior to 1993, Randall created a LISREL newsletter (later changed to Structural Equation Modeling Newsletter). The newsletter was created in response to requests from his workshop participants to keep better informed about structural equation modeling techniques. Shortly thereafter, several colleagues inquired about a special interest group. This eventually led to his development of a special interest group at the American Educational Research Association annual conference (Structural Equation Modeling/SIG).

Once the special interest group at AERA became established, Randall initiated the structural equation modeling journal so that issues, applications, and theoretical developments across multiple disciplines could be published. The first issue of *Structural Equation Modeling: A Multidisciplinary Journal* was printed in 1994. Around this same time (February 1993), a SEMNET electronic bulletin board was created at The University of Alabama by Dr. Carl Ferguson, Jr. to permit further dialogue and assistance among researchers.

Subscribers to the newsletter, participants at the workshops, members of the AERA SEM/SIG, subscribers to the journal, and SEMNET users eventually suggested that an introductory level text on structural equation modeling was needed for beginners. They encouraged us to consider writing the text from a correlation, regression, and path analysis perspective. Our goal in writing the book was therefore to provide an easy to understand beginning to structural equation modeling. We have taken that approach by building upon the reader's background in correlation, regression, and path analysis to provide a much better understanding of how to use latent variable models. Moreover, with the new SIMPLIS (SIMPle LISrel) command language in LISREL8 and EQS 5 features, measurement models (confirmatory factor analysis) and structural equation models can be easily hypothesized, tested, and diagrammed. We have made every effort in the book to demonstrate both SIMPLIS and EQS program syntax so that the reader can become familiar with their software. In addition, if you purchase either SIMPLIS or EQS software, other easy to follow examples are included.

We have provided examples throughout the text to make the basic concepts easier to understand. Every effort has been made to keep the content at an introductory level. Additional references are provided so that the reader, if interested, can further research a given topic of interest. Our goal for the text was to provide the essential elements to make structural equation modeling easier to understand and apply in research. We hope this beginner's guide helps you get started.

R.E.S.
R.G.L.

1

INTRODUCTION

Chapter Outline:

1.1 The Basics
    Terminology
    Variable scale and statistics
    Missing data
    Outliers and normality
    Conclusion

1.2 Structural Equation Modeling Software Programs

1.3 Additional Sources of Information
    Journals
    Books
    Quantitative series paperbacks

1.4 Organization of the book

1.5 Summary

References

Key Concepts:

Measures of skewness and kurtosis
Methods for handling missing data
Outliers
Normality

Structural equation modeling can be easily understood if the researcher has an understanding of basic statistics and of correlation, regression, and path analysis. The first three chapters of this book were written to provide the reader with a brief introduction to basic statistics and to the concepts of correlation, regression, and path analysis. This basic understanding will provide the framework necessary for understanding the material presented in later chapters on confirmatory factor-analytic models (measurement models) and structural equation models (latent variable relationships). First, however, we need to present the terminology used in structural equation modeling, measurement, and statistical concepts, and problems caused by missing data, outliers, and lack of variable normality.

1.1 THE BASICS

Terminology

It is not uncommon to find that scientific disciplines generate their own terminology. This is no different in structural equation modeling. In years past, the structural equation modeling approach has been described in many ways, and to some extent the varied usage continues today. Several terms that are commonly found in use today include *latent variable modeling, covariance structure analysis, confirmatory factor analysis*, and *linear structural relationships*. These terms in one way or another describe varying aspects of the measurement models and latent variable relationships that make up structural equation modeling. Our use of the term *structural equation modeling* embodies each of these terms. The term *structural equations* has its roots in econometrics but has also been applied elsewhere, for example, in psychology, sociology, political science, and education.

Variable Scale and Statistics

Structural equation modeling, like other statistical methods, involves the measuring of both independent and dependent observed variables. These variables are used to define both independent and dependent latent variables that cannot be directly measured but are instead inferred or hypothesized from the observed variables. Most observed variables used in structural equation models are defined as being measured on a linear continuous scale. This, however, does not preclude ordinal or nominal measured variables. In fact, some structural equation modeling programs have been written to handle ordinal and categorical variables, for example, EQS5, LISCOMP, and COSAN.

It is important to understand how your variables are being measured (i.e., scaled), how to treat missing data, and how to compute means, standard deviations, variances, and covariances among the sets of observed variables. In structural equation modeling programs, sets of measured (observed) variables form a variance/covariance matrix that is used in testing a theoretical model. Problems can occur in structural equation modeling analyses if a variance/covariance matrix is made up of a mixture of scaled variables that are categorical (dichotomized, ordinal) with others that are interval- or ratio-scaled. With the LISREL8 program, a preprocessor program named PRELIS2 is used to condition such matrices and produce an asymptotic variance/covariance matrix for input.

We have assumed that the reader is somewhat knowledgeable about scaling, linear transformations, and the computing of basic statistical values. If not, it is recommended that the reader review Hinkle, Wiersma, and Jurs (1994) for basic statistics and permissible linear transformations; Alreck and Settle (1995) or DeVellis (1991) for scaling; and Cohen and Cohen (1975) or Cohen (1988) for a review of basic correlation, regression, and variance/covariance methods. We feel that understanding the basic descriptive statistics and adhering to sound data editing and missing-value handling will prevent many unforeseen problems in running any of the structural equation modeling programs.

Missing Data

A problem that researchers often confront is how to treat missing data, that is, the absence or unavailability of data on one or more measured (observed) variables for one or more cases (subjects or individuals). Of course, missing data are a problem in all areas of statistical analysis, not only in structural equation modeling. Much of the general statistical literature is devoted to estimation problems in the presence of missing data with linear models, for example, analysis of variance and regression models (Afifi & Elashoff, 1966; Anderson, 1958; Browne, 1983; Haitovsky, 1968; Orchard & Woodbury, 1970; Rubin, 1976; Timm, 1970).

Several methods have been developed to deal with missing data in structural equation modeling. These include the following:

1. The complete-data method, where cases with any missing data are not included (known as *listwise deletion*).

2. The complete-pair-only method, where all cases are included and each covariance between variables is computed solely on the basis of available pairs of observations (known as *pairwise deletion*; Wilks, 1932). This may lead to a non-positive definite covariance matrix. Sample size is also ambiguous, and the use of different sample sizes for computing covariance terms in the matrix is not recommended.

3. The *mean replacement* method, where means are used to replace missing values (Afifi & Elashoff, 1966).

4. The *regression replacement* method and the *principal components* method, where missing values are replaced using regression and principal components analyses, respectively (Gleason & Staelin, 1975). This method as well as Method 3 may lead to heteroscedastic error variances or to nonnormal distributions of the now complete data despite normally distributed incomplete data.

5. *Maximum likelihood* (ML) estimation (Rubin, 1976; Wilks, 1932), including the situation where missing data are modeled as additional groups, one group for each distinct pattern of missing data (Allison, 1987; Baker & Fulker, 1983; Lee, 1986; Muthén, Kaplan, & Hollis, 1987; Werts, Rock, & Grandy, 1979).

6. The *EM method* for ML estimation (Dempster, Laird, & Rubin, 1977; Rubin & Thayer, 1982).

7. The *similar response pattern imputation* (Jöreskog & Sörbom, 1993b, example 7D) method, which is based on matched variable similarity by using a vector of variables with incomplete data and a vector of variables with complete data to impute the missing values.

A more complete discussion and additional references on these direct and indirect approaches to missing data can be found in Arbuckle (1996), Bollen (1989), and Brown (1994), who compared the efficacy of some of these approaches for estimating parameters in a structural equation model with various levels of missing data.

These missing-data approaches all involve assumptions about the mechanism that caused the missing data. These include the assumption of data missing completely at random (where some cases have missing data on all variables, which most of the aforementioned procedures make) and data missing at random (where some cases have missing data on only some variables, which the ML multiple group procedure makes). Jöreskog and Sörbom (1993a, example 10.3) demonstrated how to estimate a correlation coefficient when data are missing at random. In either case, the failure to meet one of these two missing-data assumptions requires the use of models of selectivity bias (see Berk, 1983; Bielby, 1981; Muthén & Jöreskog, 1983).

Many of these approaches to treating missing data are now available in the structural equation modeling software. PRELIS2 (Jöreskog & Sörbom, 1993b) includes pairwise, listwise, and imputation procedures for several different types of correlations depending upon the types of variables used, while LISREL8 (Jöreskog & Sörbom, 1993a) includes a listwise deletion procedure. Previous EQS manuals (Bentler, 1989, 1992; Bentler & Wu, 1993) included a discussion of how to handle missing data and implement the ML method using the multiple group procedure. The new EQS for Windows software provides missing-data options, including the regression imputation option. Preliminary research by Finkbeiner (1979) for factor analysis and by Muthén, Kaplan, and Hollis (1987) for structural equation models indicates that the ML method might be the most advantageous. This was recently verified by Arbuckle (1996). However, further research similar to that by Brown (1994) still remains to determine which methods are most appropriate under what conditions. In practice, one could compare a model both with and without the missing data, or compare the model using several of the missing-data approaches.

Outliers and Normality

Oftentimes the sample data may be unduly influenced by one or more extreme observations that are quite different from the rest of the data. These extreme values, known as *outliers*, often alter the covariance matrix and can seriously impact the results in structural equation modeling. For example, the parameter estimates and associated standard errors, as well as fit indices, may be biased in the presence of outliers.

An observation may be an outlier for one of the following reasons: (a) there was a recording or data entry error, (b) an error was made in observation, (c) an instrument functioned improperly, (d) instrument administration instructions were used improperly, or (e) a true outlier existed. An outlier that is the result of an error should be corrected, if at all possible, and the analysis redone. If an obvious error cannot be corrected, then consideration should be given to the deletion of the observation. If the outlier is an accurate observation, then this observation should probably be retained, because it contains important information even though no similar observations were collected.

There are several methods for the detection of outliers. In the univariate case—that is, for a single observed variable—one should consider the following: (a) examine the distribution of the observed variables using a histogram, frequency distribution, stem-and-leaf display, or boxplot; and (b) examine skewness and kurtosis statistics for deviations from univariate normality. In the multivariate case—that is, for multiple observed variables—one should consider the following: (a) examine scatterplots of the observed variables (this can now be done in more than two dimensions using multivariate graphics software); (b) examine multivariate skewness and kurtosis statistics (see, e.g., Mardia, 1970, 1974) for deviations from multivariate normality; and (c) examine a statistical test of deviation from multivariate normality. However, multivariate outliers are more difficult to detect, because they may differ from the remaining data in many ways.

To determine the effect of a single outlier, a simple initial procedure is to compute the sample covariance matrix with and without the outlier included. This will provide some indication of the effect of the outlier on the input data. A simple follow-up procedure is to conduct the model analysis, both with and without the outlier included. A comparison of the results can then be made to examine the outlier's impact. If the results are not comparable, then the outlier should probably be deleted.

When outliers cannot justifiably be removed and skewness and kurtosis statistics indicate non-normality, several solutions are available. One strategy is to find transformations that will normalize the data and then analyze the transformed data—for example, $\log X$, $\sqrt{X}$, or $1/X$. Another strategy is to use some other method of estimation described in chapter 6.

Finally, consider what is available in the structural equation modeling software packages for the outlier problem. The PRELIS2 program (a) allows for numerous data transformations; (b) enables the selection of cases for analysis; (c) provides univariate and multivariate skewness and kurtosis statistics (Mardia's [1970] measure of multivariate kurtosis); (d) provides other descriptive statistics, such as the mean, standard deviation, minimum, maximum, and frequency distribution (for noncontinuous variables); and (e) includes a bivariate normal chi-square test. The EQS5 program (a) includes a test for multivariate outliers using a normalized multivariate kurtosis measure (EQS5 prints out the five cases contributing the most to the measure); (b) enables the deletion of the offending outliers (up to 20 cases); and (c) provides univariate skewness and kurtosis measures, and various measures of multivariate kurtosis (i.e., normalized estimate, Mardia's measure, and several elliptical estimates). The EQS5 program for Windows also provides an integrated statistical package for the analysis of data.

Conclusion

The common problems mentioned in this section tend to be at the root of many errors that prevent the software from properly analyzing structural equation models. The problem of missing data, its effect in structural equation models, and the methods for dealing with missing data should be better understood by the researcher. As mentioned in this chapter, there are ways to cope with this situation. The problem of outliers—what causes an outlier, how one can detect an outlier statistically, and the methods available for remediating this problem—further points out the need to really "know" your data before conducting any statistical analysis. The references provided in the chapter should give the reader additional sources with program examples and a discussion of these topics.

1.2 STRUCTURAL EQUATION MODELING SOFTWARE PROGRAMS

A researcher who is just starting to use structural equation modeling software will find several new, user-friendly, Microsoft Windows-compatible personal computer programs to choose from. Many of the new versions provide statistical analysis of raw data (means, correlations, missing data conventions, etc.), provide routines for handling missing data and detecting outliers, generate the program's syntax language, diagram or graph the model, and provide for the import and export of data and figures. Also, many of the programs come with sets of data and program examples that are clearly explained in their user guides. Given these newer software packages, we felt it important to provide a list of the software packages and where to obtain them. Many of these software packages have been reviewed in the *Structural Equation Modeling* journal. We have deliberately not included pricing information, because it varies depending on individual, group, or site license arrangements; corporate or educational settings; and even whether you are a student or faculty member. Furthermore, newer versions and updates necessitate changes in pricing. Most of the software programs will run in either the DOS or Windows environment; some run on Macintosh personal computers (e.g., EQS5). They are presented in alphabetical order, rather than in any order of preference.

- **AMOS/AMOSDraw**

  Developed by:

  Dr. James Arbuckle
  Department of Psychology
  Temple University
  Philadelphia, PA 19122

  Distributed by:

  Dr. Werner Wothke
  SmallWaters Corporation
  1507 East 53rd Street, #452
  Chicago, IL 60615
  TELEPHONE: (312) 667-8635
  FAX: (312) 955-6252
  INTERNET: smallwaters@acm.org

- **CALIS**

  Developed by:

  SAS Institute Inc.
  SAS Circle, Box 8000
  Cary, NC 27512-8000

  Distributed by:

  SAS Institute Inc.
  SAS Circle, Box 8000

Cary, NC 27512-8000
TELEPHONE: (919) 677-8000
FAX: (919) 677-4444
INTERNET: software@unx.sas.com

- **EQS5**

Developed by:

Dr. Peter M. Bentler
Department of Psychology
University of California, Los Angeles
Los Angeles, CA 90025

Distributed by:

Multivariate Software, Inc.
4924 Balboa Blvd., #368
Encino, CA 91316
TELEPHONE: (818) 906-0740
FAX: (818) 906-8205
ORDERS: (800) 301-4456
INTERNET: eqs@netcom.com

- **LISREL8-SIMPLIS, LISREL8/PRELIS2**

Developed by:

Dr. Karl Jöreskog and Dr. Dag Sörbom
Department of Statistics
Uppsala University
P.O. Box 513
S-75120 Uppsala
Sweden

Distributed by:

Scientific Software International, Inc.
1525 East 53rd Street, Suite 530
Chicago, IL 60615
TELEPHONE: (800) 247-6113
FAX: (312) 684-4979
INTERNET: iessg25@uchimvs.uchicago.edu

or

Lawrence Erlbaum Associates, Inc., Publishers
10 Industrial Avenue
Mahwah, NJ 07430-2262
TELEPHONE: (201) 236-9500
FAX: (201) 236-0072
ORDERS: (800) 926-6579
INTERNET: orders@leahq.mhs.compuserve.com

or

iec ProGAMMA
P.O. Box 841, 9700 AV
Groningen, Netherlands
TELEPHONE: +31 50 636900
FAX: +31 50 636687
INTERNET: gamma.post@gamma.rug.nl

- **LISCOMP**

Developed by:

Dr. Bengt O. Muthén
Department of Education
University of California, Los Angeles
Los Angeles, CA 90025

Distributed by:

Scientific Software International, Inc.
1525 East 53rd Street, Suite 906
Chicago, IL 60615
TELEPHONE: (800) 247-6113
FAX: (312) 684-4979
INTERNET: iessg25@uchimvs1.uchicago.edu

- **Mx: Statistical Modeling**

Developed by:

Dr. Michael C. Neale
Department of Psychiatry
Medical College of Virginia
Virginia Commonwealth University
1200 East Broad Street, 9 North
P.O. Box 980710
Richmond, VA 23298-0710

Distributed by:

Dr. Michael C. Neale
Department of Psychiatry
Medical College of Virginia
Virginia Commonwealth University
1200 East Broad Street, 9 North
P.O. Box 980710
Richmond, VA 23298-0710
TELEPHONE: (804) 828-8590
FAX: (804) 828-1471
INTERNET: neale@ruby.vcu.edu

• **SEPATH**

Developed by:

Dr. James H. Steiger
Department of Psychology
University of British Columbia
Vancouver, B.C.
Canada V6T 1Z4

Distributed by:

StatSoft
2325 East 13th Street
Tulsa, OK 74104
TELEPHONE: (918) 583-4149
FAX: (918) 583-4376
INTERNET: steiger@unixg.ubc.ca

1.3 ADDITIONAL SOURCES OF INFORMATION

There are other excellent sources of information about structural equation modeling in addition to the user-friendly software programs, data set examples, and user guides. These other sources represent books, journals, and series paperbacks, some more advanced than others. We have chosen to include this information so that once you feel more comfortable with the methodology after reading this text, you can take advantage of it. Once again, we have alphabetized these sources.

The lists of books, journals, and series paperbacks are in no way intended to be comprehensive; rather, they are listed to provide a starting point for finding many of the articles that examine either applications of structural equation modeling or present methodological developments, issues, or concerns. Austin and Wolfle (1991) and Austin and Calderón (1996) provided the most recent annotated bibliography of structural equation modeling articles. You may wish to review their articles first.

Books

Bartholemew, D. J. (1987). *Latent variable models and factor analysis*. London: Oxford University Press.

Bollen, K. A. (1989). *Structural equations with latent variables*. New York: Wiley.

Bollen, K. A., & Long, J. S. (Eds.). (1993). *Testing structural equation models*. Newbury Park, CA: Sage.

Byrne, B. M. (1989). *A primer of LISREL: Basic applications and programming for confirmatory factor analytic models*. New York: Springer-Verlag.

Byrne, B. M. (1994). *Structural equation modeling with EQS and EQS/Windows: Basic concepts, applications, and programming*. Thousand Oaks, CA: Sage.

Collins, L. M., & Horn, J. L. (Eds.). (1991). *Best methods for the analysis of change: Recent advances, unanswered questions, and future directions*. Washington, DC: American Psychological Association.

Dunn, G., Everitt, B., & Pickles, A. (1993). *Modelling covariances and latent variables using EQS*. London: Chapman & Hall.

Eye, A. V., & Clogg, C. C. (Eds.). (1994). *Latent variable analysis*. Newbury Park, CA: Sage.

Goldberger, A. S., & Duncan, O. D. (1973). *Structural equation models in the social sciences*. New York: Seminar Press.

Hatcher, L. (1994). *A step-by-step approach to using the SAS system for factor analysis and structural equation modeling*. Cary, NC: SAS Institute.

Hayduk, L. A. (1987). *Structural equation modeling with LISREL: Essentials and advances*. Baltimore: Johns Hopkins University Press.

Hoyle, R. H. (Ed.). (1995). *Structural equation modeling: Concepts, issues, and applications*. Newbury Park, CA: Sage.

Jöreskog, K. G., & Sörbom, D. (1993). *LISREL 8: Structural equation modeling with the SIMPLIS command language*. Hillsdale, NJ: Lawrence Erlbaum Associates.

Loehlin, J. C. (1992). *Latent variable models: An introduction to factor, path, and structural analysis* (2nd ed). Hillsdale, NJ: Lawrence Erlbaum Associates.

Marcoulides, G., & Schumacker, R. E. (Eds.). (1996). *Advanced structural equation modeling: Issues and techniques*. Mahwah, NJ: Lawrence Erlbaum Associates.

Pedhazur, E. J., & Schmelkin, L. P. (1992). *Measurement, design, and analysis: An integrated approach*. Hillsdale, NJ: Lawrence Erlbaum Associates.

Paperbacks in the Sage Quantitative Series

Asher, H. B. (1976). *Causal modeling*. Quantitative Applications in the Social Sciences, Vol. 3. Beverly Hills, CA: Sage.

Kim, J., & Mueller, C. W. (1978). *Introduction to factor analysis: What it is and how to do it*. Quantitative Applications in the Social Sciences, Vol. 13. Beverly Hills, CA: Sage.

Kim, J., & Mueller, C. W. (1978). *Factor analysis: Statistical methods and practical issues*. Quantitative Applications in the Social Sciences, Vol. 14. Beverly Hills, CA: Sage.

Long, J. S. (1983). *Confirmatory factor analysis*. Quantitative Applications in the Social Sciences, Vol. 33. Beverly Hills, CA: Sage.

Long, J. S. (1983). *Covariance structure models: An introduction to LISREL*. Quantitative Applications in the Social Sciences, Vol. 34. Beverly Hills, CA: Sage.

Journals

Academy of Management Journal
American Educational Research Journal
American Journal of Sociology
American Political Science Review
American Sociological Review
Annual Review of Psychology
Anxiety Research
Applied Psychological Measurement
British Journal of Mathematical and Statistical Psychology
Econometrica
Educational and Psychological Measurement
Health Education Quarterly
Health Psychology
Journal of Applied Psychology
Journal of Business Research
Journal of Consulting and Clinical Psychology
Journal of Econometrics
Journal of Educational Psychology
Journal of Management and Business
Journal of Marketing Research
Journal of Occupational Psychology
Journal of Organizational Behavior
Journal of Personality and Social Psychology
Journal of Social Psychology
Journal of Sport and Exercise Psychology
Journal of the Academy of Marketing Science
Journal of the American Statistical Association
Language Learning
Learning and Instruction
Multivariate Behavioral Research
Political Methodology
Psychological Bulletin
Psychometrika
Quality and Quantity
Research Quarterly of Exercise Science
Sociological Methods and Research
Structural Equation Modeling: A Multidisciplinary Journal

1.4 ORGANIZATION OF THE BOOK

This book has been organized to provide the reader with a better understanding of structural equation modeling techniques. Chapters 1 and 2 provide important information concerning basic data collection, data editing,
correlation, and covariance that affect most statistical methods. We highly
recommend that these basics not be overlooked; otherwise they can cause
serious problems in structural equation modeling.

Chapter 3 presents the structural equation modeling approach to regression, path, and factor analyses. The examples in the chapter provide the

reader with a clearer understanding of how regression, path, and factor analyses can be programmed using EQS5 and LISREL8-SIMPLIS. The concept of measurement error in statistics is also discussed in this chapter.

Chapters 4 to 7 form the core of the book. Chapter 4 builds a conceptual understanding of measurement and structural models. Chapter 5 presents a more advanced presentation of the modeling approach with an example, including a discussion of total, direct, and indirect "effects." Chapter 6 describes model specification, identification, and estimation concerns. Chapter 7 describes the several fit criteria used in testing a model, hypothesis testing, power, and sample size concerns. Consequently, in Chapters 4 to 7, we present the steps one takes in structural equation modeling: model specification, identification, estimation, testing, and respecification.

Chapter 8 compares the EQS5 and LISREL8-SIMPLIS programs and their associated output. We recommend using the new Windows versions of EQS5 and LISREL8, which have many useful features, including diagramming. Chapter 9 presents several basic models and diagrams with accompanying program examples. It is anticipated that if one can diagram a hypothesized model, then it can be easily written in either an EQS5 or a SIMPLIS program. This is something you should try after reviewing the chapter.

Chapter 10 provides a brief introduction to more advanced topics. We do not attempt to fully describe or present these, but hope that in giving some basic information and program examples, the reader will be better informed of some current applications in structural equation modeling. We hope these new applications help to further your understanding of structural equation modeling. Chapter 11 provides technical information about the matrix approach in LISREL8.

1.5 SUMMARY

In this chapter we have discussed basic terminology, variable scale and statistics, missing data, and outliers and variable normality. In addition, we have recommended ways to cope with these problems often encountered in statistics, and hence structural equation modeling. This chapter also provided valuable information about where to obtain structural equation modeling software and additional references and sources of information on structural equation modeling.

REFERENCES

Afifi, A. A., & Elashoff, R. M. (1966). Missing observations in multivariate statistics. Part 1. Review of the literature. *Journal of the American Statistical Association, 61*, 595–604.

Allison, P. D. (1987). Estimation of linear incomplete data. In C. C. Clogg (Ed.), *Sociological methodology* (pp. 71–103). Washington, DC: American Sociological Association.

Alreck, P. L., & Settle, R. B. (1995). *The survey research handbook* (2nd ed.). Bensenville, IL: Irwin Press.

Anderson, T. W. (1958). *An introduction to multivariate statistical analysis*. New York: Wiley.

Arbuckle, J. L. (1996). Full information estimation in the presence of incomplete data. In G. A. Marcoulides & R. E. Schumacker (Eds.), *Advanced structural equation modeling: Issues and techniques* (pp. 243–277). Mahwah, NJ: Lawrence Erlbaum Associates.

Austin, J. T., & Calderón, R. F. (1996). Theoretical and technical contributions to structural equation modeling: An updated annotated bibliography. *Structural Equation Modeling, 3,* 105–175.

Austin, J. T., & Wolfle, L. M. (1991). Annotated bibliography of structural equation modeling: Technical work. *British Journal of Mathematical and Statistical Psychology, 44,* 93–132.

Baker, L. A., & Fulker, D. W. (1983). Incomplete covariance matrices and LISREL. *Data Analyst, 1,* 3–5.

Bentler, P. M. (1989). *Theory and implementation of EQS: A structural equations program.* Los Angeles: BMDP Statistical Software, Inc.

Bentler, P. M. (1992). *EQS structural equations program manual.* Los Angeles: BMDP Statistical Software, Inc.

Bentler, P. M., & Wu, J. C. E. (1993). *EQS/Windows user's guide.* Los Angeles: BMDP Statistical Software, Inc.

Berk, R. A. (1983). An introduction to sample selection bias in sociological data. *American Sociological Review, 48,* 386–398.

Bielby, W. T. (1981). Neighborhood effects: A LISREL model for clustered samples. *Sociological Methods and Research, 10,* 82–111.

Bollen, K. A. (1989). *Structural equations with latent variables.* New York: Wiley.

Brown, R. L. (1994). Efficacy of the indirect approach for estimating structural equation models with missing data: A comparison of five methods. *Structural Equation Modeling, 1*(4), 287–316.

Browne, C. H. (1983). Asymptotic comparison of missing data procedures for estimating factor loadings. *Psychometrika, 48,* 269–291.

Cohen, J. (1988). *Statistical power analysis for the behavioral sciences* (2nd ed.). Hillsdale, NJ: Lawrence Erlbaum Associates.

Cohen, J., & Cohen, P. (1975). *Applied multiple regression/correlation analysis for the behavioral sciences.* Hillsdale, NJ: Lawrence Erlbaum Associates.

Dempster, A., Laird, N., & Rubin, D. (1977). Maximum likelihood from incomplete data via the EM algorithm (with discussion). *Journal of the Royal Statistical Society, Series B, 39,* 1–18.

DeVellis, R. F. (1991). *Scale development: Theory and applications.* Applied Social Research Methods Series, vol. 26. Newbury Park, CA: Sage.

Finkbeiner, C. (1979). Estimation for the multiple factor model when data are missing. *Psychometrika, 44,* 409–420.

Gleason, T. C., & Staelin, R. (1975). A proposal for handling missing data. *Psychometrika, 40,* 229–252.

Haitovsky, Y. (1968). Missing data in regression analysis. *Journal of the Royal Statistical Society, Series B, 30,* 67–82.

Hinkle, D. E., Wiersma, W., & Jurs, S. G. (1994). *Applied statistics for the behavioral sciences* (3rd ed.). Boston: Houghton Mifflin.

Jöreskog, K. G., & Sörbom, D. (1993a). *LISREL8 user's reference guide.* Chicago: Scientific Software International, Inc.

Jöreskog, K. G., & Sörbom, D. (1993b). *PRELIS2 user's reference guide.* Chicago: Scientific Software International, Inc.

Lee, S.-Y. (1986). Estimation for structural equation models with missing data. *Psychometrika, 51,* 93–99.

Mardia, K. V. (1970). Measures of multivariate skewness and kurtosis with applications. *Biometrika, 57,* 519–530.

Mardia, K. V. (1974). Applications of some measures of multivariate skewness and kurtosis in testing normality and robustness studies. *Sankhya, Series B, 36,* 115–128.

Muthén, B., & Jöreskog, K. G. (1983). Selectivity problems in quasi-experimental studies. *Evaluation Review, 7,* 139–174.

Muthén, B., Kaplan, D., & Hollis, M. (1987). On structural equation modeling with data that are not missing completely at random. *Psychometrika, 52,* 431–462.

Orchard, T., & Woodbury, M. A. (1970). A missing information principle: Theory and applications. *Proceedings of the Sixth Berkeley Symposium on Mathematical Statistics and Probability,* 697–715.

Rubin, D. B. (1976). Inference and missing data. *Biometrika, 63,* 581–592.

Rubin, D. B., & Thayer, D. T. (1982). EM algorithms for ML factor analysis. *Psychometrika, 47,* 69–76.

Timm, N. H. (1970). The estimation of variance-covariance and correlation matrices from incomplete data. *Psychometrika, 35,* 417–437.

Werts, C. E., Rock, D. A., & Grandy, J. (1979). Confirmatory factor analysis applications: Missing data problems and comparisons of path models between populations. *Multivariate Behavioral Research, 14,* 199–213.

Wilks, S. S. (1932). Moments and distributions of estimates of population parameters from fragmented samples. *Annals of Mathematical Statistics, 3,* 163–195.

2

CORRELATION

Chapter Outline:

2.1 Types of Correlation Coefficients

2.2 Factors Affecting Correlation Coefficients
Type of scale and range of values
Linearity
Sample size (accuracy or representativeness), effect size, significance, and power

2.3 Bivariate Correlation, Part, and Partial Correlation

2.4 Correlation Versus Covariance

2.5 Non-positive Definite Covariance Matrices

2.6 Variable Metrics (standardized vs. unstandardized)

2.7 Causation Assumptions and Limitations

2.8 Summary

Exercises
References
Answers to Exercises

Key Concepts:

Bivariate, part, and partial correlation
Correlation, covariance, and variable metric
Non-positive definite covariance matrices

2.1 TYPES OF CORRELATION COEFFICIENTS

Sir Francis Galton conceptualized the correlation procedure for examining covariation in two or more traits, and Karl Pearson developed the statistical formula for the correlation coefficient in 1896 (Pearson, 1896) based on his suggestion (Crocker & Algina, 1986; Ferguson & Takane, 1989, pp. 7–8). Shortly thereafter, Charles Spearman used the correlational procedure to develop the factor analysis technique (Spearman, 1904). The correlation and factor analysis techniques have for several decades formed the basis for generating tests and defining constructs. Today, researchers are expanding their understanding of the role correlation and factor analysis play in construct formation to include latent-variable, covariance-structure, or confirmatory-factor measurement models.

The contributions of Galton, Pearson, and Spearman to the field of statistics, especially correlation and factor analysis, are well known. In fact, the basis of association between two variables—correlation or covariance—has played a major role in statistics. The Pearson correlation coefficient provides the basis for point estimation (test of significance), explanation (variance accounted for in a dependent variable by an independent variable), prediction (one variable's scores through linear regression), reliability estimates (test–retest; equivalence), and validity (factorial, predictive, concurrent).

The Pearson correlation coefficient also provides the basis for establishing and testing models among measured and/or latent variables. The partial and part correlations further permit the identification of specific relationships between variables and allow for the specification of unique variance shared between two variables. These correlations can also be tested for significance (see Table A.3 in the Appendix).

Although the Pearson correlation coefficient has had a major impact in the field of statistics, other correlation coefficients have emerged depending upon the level of variable measurement. Stevens (1968) provided the properties of scales of measurement that have become known as nominal, ordinal, interval, and ratio. The types of correlation coefficients developed for these various levels of measurement are categorized in Table 2.1. Many popular computer programs—among them SAS, SPSS, and BMDP—typically do not compute all of these correlational types. Therefore, you may need to check a popular statistics book or look around for a computer program that will compute the type of correlation coefficient you need if, for example, you are looking for the phi or the point-biserial coefficient. In practice, the Pearson coefficient, the tetrachoric (polychoric) coefficient, and the biserial (polyserial) coefficient are typically used (see *PRELIS2* for the use of Kendall's tau-c or tau-b, and canonical correlation; or *LISCOMP* user's guide for further explanation of other types of correlations used with categorical and otherwise non-normally distributed variables).

TABLE 2.1
Types of Correlation Coefficients

Correlation Coefficient	Level of Measurement
Pearson product–moment	Both variables interval
Spearman rank	Both variables ordinal
Phi	Both variables nominal
Point-biserial	One variable interval, one variable dichotomous
Gamma	One variable ordinal, one variable nominal
Contingency	Both variables nominal
Biserial	One variable interval, one variable artificial[a]
Polyserial	Correlation between an observed variable and a latent variable
Tetrachoric	Both variables dichotomy (nominal-artificial)
Polychoric	Correlation between two latent variables

[a]*Artificial* refers to recoding variable values into a dichotomy.

In this chapter, we describe the important role that correlation (covariance) plays in structural equation modeling. We include a discussion of factors that affect correlation coefficients, the problem of non-positive definite covariance matrices, variable metrics, and the assumptions and limitations of correlational methods in determining causation.

2.2 FACTORS AFFECTING CORRELATION COEFFICIENTS

Given the important role that correlation plays in structural equation modeling, it is important to understand the factors that affect it. The key factors are type of scale and range of values (homogeneity, skew, kurtosis); linearity; and sample size (accuracy or representativeness), effect size, significance, and power.

Type of Scale and Range of Values

Four types or levels of measurement typically define whether the characteristic or scale interpretation of a variable is nominal, ordinal, interval, or ratio (Stevens, 1968). In structural equation modeling, each of these types of scaled variables can be used, but it is not recommended that they be included together or mixed in a correlation (covariance) matrix. Since the Pearson product–moment correlation coefficient forms the basis for analysis in regression, path, and factor analysis and structural equation modeling, other types of correlations and combinations are not of particular interest to us just yet. We will discuss them more in later chapters.

We recommend that numerical scales, such as 1 to 7 or 1 to 9, be used to measure variables when possible, to create an interval or ratio level of measurement. The use of the same scale values for variables also helps in the interpretation of results and/or relative comparison of variables.

The interval or ratio scale should also have a sufficient range of score values to introduce variance. If the range of scores is restricted, the magnitude of the correlation value is decreased. Basically, as the homogeneity of a group of subjects increases, score variance decreases, reducing the correlational value between the variables. This points out an interesting concern, namely, that there must be enough variation in scores to allow a correlational relationship to manifest itself.

The meaningfulness of a correlational relationship will depend on the variables employed; hence, your theoretical perspective is very important. You may recall from your basic statistics course that a spurious correlation is possible when two sets of scores correlate significantly but are not meaningful or substantive in nature. Also, two sets of scores can indicate no correlation but have a curvilinear relationship.

If the variances of variables are widely divergent, correlation can also be affected, and so several permissible data transformations are suggested by Ferguson and Takane (1989) to provide a closer approximation to a normal, homogeneous variance for skewed or kurtotic data. The permissible transformations are square root transformation (sqrt X), logarithmic transformation (log X), reciprocal transformation ($1/X$), and arcsine transformation (arcsin X). Consequently, the type of scale used and the range of values for the measured variables can have profound effects on your statistical analysis (in particular, on the mean, variance, and correlation). The scale and range of numerical values affect numerous statistical methods, and the case is no different in structural equation modeling. The PRELIS2 program is available to provide tests of normality, skewness, and kurtosis on variables and to compute an asymptotic variance–covariance matrix for input into LISREL8 if required. Other statistical packages, as previously mentioned, are also available for handling missing data and checking the skewness and kurtosis of scores.

Linearity

The Pearson correlation coefficient indicates the degree of linear relationship between two variables. The extent to which one or both variables deviate from the assumption of a linear relationship will affect the size of the correlation coefficient. It is therefore important to check for linearity of the scores; the common method is to graph the coordinate data points. The linearity assumption should not be confused with recent advances in testing interaction in structural equation models discussed in chapter 10. You should also be familiar with the *eta* coefficient as an index of nonlinear relationship between two variables and with the testing of linear, quadratic, or cubic effects in multiple regression. Consult a standard regression text to review these basic concepts.

Sample Size (Accuracy or Representativeness), Effect Size, Significance, and Power

A common formula used to determine sample size when estimating means of variables was given by McCall (1982): $n = (\sigma Z/\varepsilon)^2$, where n is the sample size needed for the desired level of precision and confidence (with ε the effect size and Z the confidence level; see Table A.1 in the Appendix) given the population standard deviation σ of scores (actual = average values from prior research studies or the population norm; or estimate = range of scores divided by 6). For example, given a random sample of ACT scores from a defined population with a standard deviation of 100, a desired confidence level of 1.96 (which corresponds to a .05 level of significance), and an effect size of 20 (difference between sampled ACT mean and population ACT mean), the sample size needed would be $(100 \cdot 1.96/20)^2 = 96$.

In structural equation modeling, however, the researcher often requires a much larger sample size to maintain the accuracy of estimates and to ensure representativeness. The need for larger sample sizes is also due in part to the program requirements and the multiple observed indicator variables used to define latent variables (degrees of freedom in a measurement model). Hoelter (1983) proposed the *critical N* statistic, which indicates the sample size that would make the obtained chi-square from a structural model significant at the stated level of significance. This sample size provides a reasonable indication of whether your sample size is sufficient to estimate parameters and determine model fit given your specific theoretical relationships among the latent variables.

Ding, Velicer, and Harlow (1995) indicated numerous studies (such as Anderson & Gerbing, 1988) that were in agreement that 100 to 150 subjects is the *minimum* satisfactory sample size when conducting structural equation models. Boomsma (1982, 1983) recommended 400, and Hu, Bentler, and Kano (1992) indicated that in some cases 5,000 is insufficient! Many of us may recall rules of thumb in our statistics texts—10 subjects per variable or 20 subjects per variable. In our examination of the published research, we have found that many articles used from 250 to 500 subjects, although the greater the sample size, the better—especially when you are cross-validating your model (see chap. 10). For example, Bentler and Chou (1987) suggested that a ratio as low as 5 subjects per variable would be sufficient for normal and elliptical distributions when the latent variables have multiple indicators, and that a ratio of at least 10 subjects per variable would be sufficient for other distributions.

2.3 BIVARIATE CORRELATION, PART, AND PARTIAL CORRELATION

The types of correlations indicated in Table 2.1 are considered bivariate correlations, or associations between two variables. Cohen and Cohen (1983), in conducting correlational research, further presented the correlation between two variables controlling for the influence of a third. These correlations are referred to as *part* and *partial* correlations, depending upon how variables are controlled or partialed out. Some of the various ways in which three variables can be depicted are illustrated in Fig. 2.1. The diagrams in the figure illustrate different situations among variables where (a) all the variables are uncorrelated (case 1), (b) only one pair of variables is correlated (cases 2 and 3), (c) two pairs of variables are correlated (cases 4 and 5), and (d) all of the variables are correlated (case 6). It is obvious that with more than three variables the possibilities become overwhelming. It is therefore important to have a theoretical perspective to suggest why certain variables are correlated and/or controlled for. A theoretical perspective is essential in specifying a model and forms the basis for testing a structural equation model.

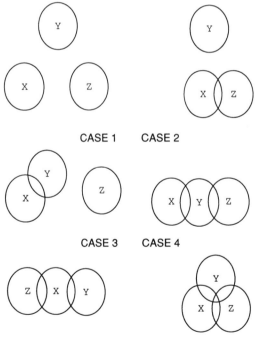

CASE 1   CASE 2

CASE 3   CASE 4

CASE 5   CASE 6

FIG. 2.1. Possible three-variable relationships.

The *partial correlation coefficient* measures the association between two variables while controlling for a third—for example, the association between age and comprehension level, controlling for reading level. Controlling for reading level in the correlation between age and comprehension partials out the correlation of reading level with age and the correlation of reading level with comprehension. *Part correlation*, in contrast, is the correlation between age and comprehension level with reading level controlled for, where only the correlation between comprehension level and reading level is removed before age is correlated with comprehension level.

Whether a part or a partial correlation is used depends on the specific model or research question. Convenient notation helps distinguish these two types of correlations (1 = age, 2 = comprehension, and 3 = reading level): partial correlation, $r_{12.3}$; part correlation, $r_{1(2.3)}$ or $r_{2(1.3)}$. Different correlation values will be computed depending upon which variables are controlled or partialed out. For example, using the correlations in Table 2.2, the partial correlation coefficient $r_{12.3}$ (correlation between age and comprehension, controlling for reading level) is computed as:

$$r_{12.3} = \frac{r_{12} - r_{13}r_{23}}{\sqrt{(1 - r_{13}^2)(1 - r_{23}^2)}}$$

$$= \frac{.45 - (.25)(.80)}{\sqrt{[1 - (.25)^2][1 - (.80)^2]}}$$

$$= .43.$$

Notice that the partial correlation coefficent should be smaller in value than the Pearson product–moment correlation between age and comprehension, which is $r_{12} = .45$. If the partial correlation coefficient is not smaller than the Pearson product–moment correlation, then a suppressor variable may be present (Pedhazur, 1983). A suppressor variable correlates near zero with a dependent variable but correlates significantly with other predictor variables. This correlational situation serves to control for variance shared with predictor variables and not the dependent variable. Once this effect is removed from the correlation between two predictor variables with a crite-

TABLE 2.2
Correlation Matrix ($n = 100$)

Variable	Age	Comprehension	Reading Level
1. Age	1.00		
2. Comprehension	.45	1.00	
3. Reading level	.25	.80	1.00

rion, the correlation (partial) increases. Partial correlations will be greater in magnitude than part correlations, except when independent variables are zero correlated with the dependent variable; then, part correlations are equal to partial correlations.

The part correlation coefficient $r_{1(2.3)}$, or correlation between age and comprehension where reading level is controlled for in comprehension only, is computed as:

$$r_{1(2.3)} = \frac{r_{12} - r_{13}r_{23}}{\sqrt{(1 - r_{23}^2)}}$$

$$= \frac{.45 - (.25)(.80)}{\sqrt{[1 - (.80)^2]}}$$

$$= .42,$$

or, in the case of correlating comprehension with age where reading level is controlled for in age only:

$$r_{2(1.3)} = \frac{r_{12} - r_{13}r_{23}}{\sqrt{(1 - r_{13}^2)}}$$

$$= \frac{.45 - (.25)(.80)}{\sqrt{[1 - (.25)^2]}}$$

$$= .26.$$

The correlation, whether zero-order (bivariate), part, or partial, can be tested for significance (see Table A.3 in the Appendix), interpreted as variance accounted for (explained) by squaring each coefficient, and diagrammed using Venn or Ballentine figures to conceptualize their relationships. In our example, the zero-order relationships between the three variables can be diagrammed as in Fig. 2.2. However, the partial correlation of age with comprehension level controlling for reading level would be $r_{12.3}$ = .43, or area a divided by the combined area of a and e [$a/(a + e)$]; see Fig. 2.3. A part correlation of age with comprehension level while controlling for the correlation between reading level and comprehension level would be $r_{1(2.3)}$ = .42, or just area a; see Fig. 2.4.

These examples consider only controlling for one variable when correlating two other variables (partial), or controlling for the impact of one variable on another before correlating with a third variable (part). Other higher-order part correlations and/or partial correlations are possible (e.g., $r_{12.34}$, $r_{12(3.4)}$) but are beyond the scope of this book. Readers should refer to the references at the end of the chapter for a more detailed discussion of part and partial correlation.

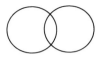

Age and Comprehension

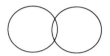

Age and Reading

Reading and Comprehension   FIG. 2.2. Bivariate correlations.

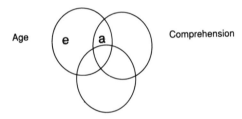

Age   e   a   Comprehension

Reading   FIG. 2.3. Partial correlation area.

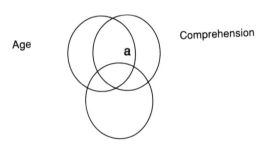

Age   a   Comprehension

Reading   FIG. 2.4. Part correlation area.

2.4 CORRELATION VERSUS COVARIANCE

The data matrix typically used for computations in structural equation modeling programs is a variance–covariance matrix. A variance–covariance matrix is made up of variance terms on the diagonal and covariance terms on the off-diagonal. If a correlation matrix is used as the input data matrix, most of the computer programs convert it to a variance–covariance matrix using the means and standard deviations of the variables, unless specified otherwise. The researcher has the option of inputting raw data, a correlation matrix, or a variance–covariance matrix. The software defaults to using a variance–covariance matrix. The correlation matrix provides the option of using standardized or unstandardized variable input for analysis purposes. If a correlation matrix is inputted with a row of variable means and a row of standard deviations, then unstandardized output is printed. If only a correlation matrix is inputted, the means and standard deviations, by default, are set at 0 and 1, respectively, and standardized output is printed. When raw data are inputted, a variance–covariance matrix is computed.

Boomsma (1983, p. 113) concluded that the analysis of correlation matrices led to imprecise values for the parameter estimates in a structural equation model. He specifically found a problem with the estimation of standard errors for the parameter estimates. Suggested corrections for the standard errors when correlations or standardized coefficients are used have been recommended by Browne (1982), Jennrich and Thayer (1973), and Lawley and Maxwell (1971). However, one structural equation modeling program, SEPATH, permits the inputting of a correlation matrix rather than a variance–covariance matrix and performs a correct analysis, that is, computes the correct standard errors. In general, a variance–covariance matrix should be used in structural equation modeling.

2.5 NON-POSITIVE DEFINITE COVARIANCE MATRICES

A distressing error message to read from the output of a structural equation modeling computer program is that a covariance matrix is *not* positive definite. When you receive this message on the computer printout, you are not given any other information. What is this problem, and what do you do about it? The purpose of this section is to describe non-positive definite (NPD) covariance matrices: what they are, what causes them to occur, and how to deal with them. A more in-depth treatment of this problem and possible solutons are contained in an important article by Wothke (1993), which we strongly recommend reading.

An assumption of many structural equation model estimation procedures (e.g., ML, GLS, but not ULS) is that the sample covariance matrix must be positive definite or nonsingular. In addition, the covariance matrix constructed by the model must also be positive definite, as well as the associated covariance matrices of parameters and associated errors.

What does this problem of non-positive definite matrix mean, technically speaking? If the determinant of a matrix is zero, then the matrix is known as a singular or non-positive definite matrix. This also means that the inverse of the covariance matrix does not exist. Under these conditions, numerous statistics related to covariance matrices either cannot be generated or cannot be trusted, because they are not valid. Statistically speaking, a covariance matrix is positive definite if all of its eigenvalues are greater than zero.

First let us consider the situation where the sample covariance matrix is non-positive definite. This typically occurs when either the pairwise deletion method is used for handling missing data or there is a linear dependency among the observed variables. The pairwise deletion method may result in a covariance matrix that differs from the one generated by those individuals with complete responses. The solutions are to (a) use one of the procedures for dealing with missing data or (b) use a smoothing procedure. The latter option involves altering or smoothing the sample covariance matrix so that it becomes positive definite. For example, in the LISREL8 program, smoothing may be done using the RIDGE option. In ridge estimation, a constant times the diagonal values in the sample covariance matrix S is added to S. The constant is either determined automatically by the program or set by the researcher using the OU command line with the RC and RO options. The RC option specifies a ridge value that is multiplied by 10, and the RO option invokes the ridge option to replace the diagonal values of the S matrix; for example, OU RC = .001 RO. If the new covariance matrix is not positive definite, then the constant value specified by RC is multiplied repeatedly by 10 until this matrix eventually becomes positive definite. You may need to try different values for RC, since .001 is the default. There is little research, however, on how well this smoothing process works in structural equation modeling.

The second reason noted for the sample covariance matrix being non-positive definite was that there exists some linear dependency (known as collinearity) among the observed variables. Collinearity is defined as the situation in which one variable is a linear combination of some other observed variables. Collinearity may be a result one of the following factors: (a) a composite or total score variable that is a sum of two or more component variables, all of which are included in the covariance matrix; (b) outliers or extreme observations; or (c) a sample size that is less than the number of observed variables. One way to determine the cause of the collinearity is by computing the eigenvalues and eigenvectors of the sample covariance matrix using factor analysis. If you find an eigenvalue at or near zero, an examination of its eigenvector will tell you how the variables are involved in the collinearity. An option available in PRELIS2, the RG or Re- Gression command, allows one to regress each variable on any set of variables. Outlier detection procedures in EQS5 can also be used. The solutions to the collinearity problem include (a) removing the redundant variables; (b) removing the offending outliers; (c) reducing the number of observed variables or collecting more observations; (d) using a smoothing procedure such as RIDGE; or (e) using ULS or WLS as the estimation procedure, because neither of these assumes that the sample covariance matrix is positive definite.

The second situation where a non-positive covariance matrix might be a problem is in the estimation of the covariance matrix constructed from the model specified by the researcher. The use of "bad" starting values in the estimation process may cause this matrix to be non-positive definite. To resolve this situation, one can (a) generate ULS estimates and use these starting values as initial estimates; (b) select one's own starting values (a requirement in the early versions of the LISREL program; see Wothke, 1993, for further details); or (c) input starting values for estimates that are obviously out of line (e.g., an estimate that is considerably larger than the rest).

The third situation in which a non-positive definite covariance matrix can occur involves the estimation of covariance matrices for the parameters and measurement errors. In this situation, one might observe the following: (a) negative or zero variances (which will occur when a variance is fixed to zero, such as when there is only a single indicator of a latent variable and its measurement error must also be fixed to zero; in this case, the error message can be ignored); or (b) covariances or correlations that are inconsistent because they are outside a permissible range of values given other covariances or correlations (e.g., if $r_{12} = .70$ and $r_{13} = .80$, then r_{23} must be between .131 and .989).

There are several reasons for the existence of a non-positive definite matrix in the third situation. The sample data may not provide enough information to obtain reasonable estimates. The converse could be true: It may be that the data are being asked to estimate too many parameters. Extreme outliers could exist. The data might be non-normal. There could also be an identification problem, or the model might not be properly specified. Some of the more obvious solutions would include collecting more observations, estimating fewer parameters, using an estimation procedure that is less restrictive in terms of normality (e.g., GLS), removing outliers, using a smoothing procedure, making the model identified, properly specifying the model, or imposing constraints on the variances and/or covariances in order to yield reasonable estimates (see Rindskopf, 1983 and 1984, for more detail). If you fail to consider these factors, your program will surely not run or will yield incorrect results.

2.6 VARIABLE METRICS (STANDARDIZED VS. UNSTANDARDIZED)

Researchers have debated the use of unstandardized or standardized variables (Lomax, 1992). The standardized coefficients are thought to be sample-specific and not stable across different samples because of changes in variance of the variables. The unstandardized coefficients permit an examination of change across different samples. The standardized coefficients are useful, however, in determining the relative importance of each variable to others for a given sample. Other reasons for using standardized variables are that variables are on the same scale of measurement, are more easily interpreted, and can easily be converted back to the raw scale metric. In SIMPLIS, the command LISREL OUTPUT SS SC will provide a standardized solution. The EQS5 program routinely provides a standardized solution.

2.7 CAUSATION ASSUMPTIONS AND LIMITATIONS

As previously discussed, the Pearson correlation coefficient is limited by the range of score values and the assumption of linearity, among other things. In the presence of curvilinearity, the correlation can be zero, yet a relationship can exist, although not linear. Even if the assumptions and limitations of using the Pearson correlation coefficent are met, a cause-and-effect relationship still has not been established. The following conditions are necessary for cause and effect to be inferred between variables X and Y (Tracz, 1992): (a) temporal order (X precedes Y in time), (b) existence of covariance between X and Y, and (c) control for other causes (e.g., Z).

These three conditions may not be present in the research design setting, and in such a case only association rather than causation can be inferred. However, if *manipulative* rather than *attribute* variables are used, a researcher can change or manipulate one variable in a model and examine subsequent effects on other variables, thereby determining cause-and-effect relationships (Resta & Baker, 1972). In structural equation modeling, the amount of influence is determined by direct, indirect, and total "effects" among variables. This is discussed further in chapter 5.

Causal relationships, suffice it to say, require a sound theoretical perspective. Bullock, Harlow, and Mulaik (1994) provided an in-depth discussion of causation issues related to structural equation modeling research; see their article for a more elaborate discussion. We feel that structural equation models will evolve beyond model fit (discussed in chap. 7) into the domain of model testing. Model testing involves the use of manipulative variables, which, when changed, affect the model outcome values, and whose effects

CORRELATION **29**

can hence be assessed. This approach, we believe, best depicts a causal assumption. In addition, structural models in longitudinal research can depict changes in latent variables over time (Collins & Horn, 1992).

2.8 SUMMARY

In this chapter, we have attempted to describe some of the basic concepts underlying structural equation modeling. This discussion included various types of bivariate correlation coefficients, part and partial correlation, problems with non-positive definite covariance matrices, variable metrics, and the assumptions and limitations of causation in models.

Many popular computer programs (SAS, SPSS, BMDP) do not compute all the types of correlation coefficients used in the structural equation modeling programs; for the rarer ones, refer to a standard statistics textbook for computational formulas and understanding (Hinkle, Weirsma, & Jurs, 1994). Additionally, structural equation modeling programs typically use a variance–covariance matrix. In some cases, categorical and/or ordinal variables with underlying continuous latent-variable attributes have been used with tetrachoric or polychoric correlations (Muthén, 1982, 1983, 1984; Muthén & Kaplan, 1985). PRELIS2 was developed to permit a correlation matrix of various types of correlations to be conditioned or converted into an asymptotic covariance matrix for input into structural equation modeling programs (Jöreskog & Sörbom, 1993). The use of various correlation coefficients and subsequent conversion into a variance–covariance matrix will continue to play a major role in structural equation modeling. It is therefore important for you to use variables with the same scale of measurement, or better understand how PRELIS2 works.

EXERCISES

1. Given the following Pearson correlation coefficients, compute the part and partial correlations ($r_{12} = .6$; $r_{13} = .7$; $r_{23} = .4$):

$$r_{12.3} =$$
$$r_{1(2.3)} =$$

2. Compare the variance explained between the bivariate, partial, and part correlations in Exercise 1.

3. Explain causation and provide examples of when a cause-and-effect relationship could exist.

4. Given the following variance–covariance matrix, compute the Pearson correlation coefficients: r_{xy}, r_{xz}, and r_{yz}:

$$
\begin{array}{c}
\\
X \\
Y \\
Z
\end{array}
\left[
\begin{array}{ccc}
X & Y & Z \\
15.80 & & \\
10.16 & 11.02 & \\
12.43 & 9.23 & 15.37
\end{array}
\right]
$$

REFERENCES

Anderson, J. C., & Gerbing, D. W. (1988). Structural equation modeling in practice: A review and recommended two step approach. *Psychological Bulletin, 103*, 411–423.

Bentler, P. M., & Chou, C. (1987). Practical issues in structural modelling. *Sociological Methods and Research, 16*, 78–117.

Boomsma, A. (1982). The robustness of LISREL against small sample sizes in factor analysis models. In K. G. Jöreskog & H. Wold (Eds.), *Systems under indirect observation: Causality, structure, prediction (Part I)*. Amsterdam: North-Holland.

Boomsma, A. (1983). *On the robustness of LISREL against small sample size and nonnormality.* Amsterdam: Sociometric Research Foundation.

Browne, M. W. (1982). Covariance structures. In D. M. Hawkins (Ed.), *Topics in multivariate analysis*. Cambridge, England: Cambridge University Press.

Bullock, H. E., Harlow, L. L., & Mulaik, S. A. (1994). Causation issues in structural equation modeling. *Structural Equation Modeling: A Multidisciplinary Journal, 1*(3), 253–267.

Cohen, J., & Cohen, P. (1983). *Applied multiple regression/correlation analysis for the behavioral sciences* (2nd ed.). Hillsdale, NJ: Lawrence Erlbaum Associates.

Collins, L. M., & Horn, J. L. (Eds.). (1992). *Best methods for the analysis of change: Recent advances, unanswered questions, future directions.* Washington, DC: American Psychological Association.

Crocker, L., & Algina, J. (1986). *Introduction to Classical and Modern Test Theory.* New York: Holt, Rinehart & Winston.

Ding, L., Velicer, W. F., & Harlow, L. L. (1995). Effects of estimation methods, number of indicators per factor, and improper solutions on structural equation modeling fit indices. *Structural Equation Modeling, 2*, 119–143.

Ferguson, G. A., & Takane, Y. (1989). *Statistical analysis in psychology and education* (6th ed.). New York: McGraw-Hill.

Hinkle, D. E., Wiersma, W., & Jurs, S. G. (1994). *Applied statistics for the behavioral sciences* (3rd ed.). Boston: Houghton Mifflin.

Hoelter, J. W. (1983). The analysis of covariance structures: Goodness-of-fit indices. *Sociological Methods and Research, 11*, 325–344.

Hu, L., Bentler, P. M., & Kano, Y. (1992). Can test statistics in covariance structure analysis be trusted? *Psychological Bulletin, 112*, 351–362.

Jennrich, R. I., & Thayer, D. T. (1973). A note on Lawley's formula for standard errors in maximum likelihood factor analysis. *Psychometrika, 38*, 571–580.

Jöreskog, K. G., & Sörbom, D. (1993). *PRELIS2 user's reference guide.* Chicago: Scientific Software International, Inc.

Lawley, D. N., & Maxwell, A. E. (1971). *Factor analysis as a statistical method.* London: Butterworth.

Lomax, R. G. (1992). *Statistical concepts: A second course for education and the behavioral sciences.* White Plains, NY: Longman.

McCall, C. H., Jr. (1982). *Sampling statistics handbook for research.* Ames: Iowa State University Press.

Muthén, B. (1982). A structural probit model with latent variables. *Journal of the American Statistical Association, 74*, 807–811.

Muthén, B. (1983). Latent variable structural equation modeling with categorical data. *Journal of Econometrics, 22*, 43–65.

Muthén, B. (1984). A general structural equation model with dichotomous, ordered categorical, and continuous latent variable indicators. *Psychometrika, 49*, 115–132.

Muthén, B., & Kaplan, D. (1985). A comparison of some methodologies for the factor analysis of non-normal Likert variables. *British Journal of Mathematical and Statistical Psychology, 38*, 171–189.

Pearson, K. (1896). Mathematical contributions to the theory of evolution. Part 3. Regression, heredity and panmixia. *Philosophical Transactions, A, 187*, 253–318.

Pedhazur, E. J. (1982). *Multiple regression in behavioral research: Explanation and prediction* (2nd ed.). New York: Holt, Rinehart & Winston.

Resta, P. E., & Baker, R. L. (1972). *Selecting variables for educational research.* Inglewood, CA: Southwest Regional Laboratory for Educational Research and Development.

Rindskopf, D. (1983). Parameterizing inequality constraints on unique variances in linear structural models. *Psychometrika, 48*, 73–83.

Rindskopf, D. (1984). Using phantom and imaginary variables to parameterize constraints in linear structural models. *Psychometrika, 49*, 37–47.

Spearman, C. (1904). The proof and measurement of association between two things. *American Journal of Psychology, 15*, 72–101.

Stevens, S. S. (1968). Measurement, statistics, and the schempiric view. *Science, 101*, 849–856.

Tracz, S. M. (1992). The interpretation of beta weights in path analysis. *Multiple Linear Regression Viewpoints, 19*(1), 7–15.

Wothke, W. (1993). Nonpositive definite matrices in structural modeling. In K. A. Bollen & J. S. Long (Eds.), *Testing structural equation models.* Newbury Park, CA: Sage.

ANSWERS TO EXERCISES

1. $r_{12.3} = \dfrac{.6 - (.7)(.4)}{[1 - (.7)^2 * 1 - (.4)^2]^{1/2}} = .49$

   $r_{1(2.3)} = \dfrac{.6 - (.7)(.4)}{[1 - (.4)^2]^{1/2}} = .35$

2. Bivariate = area $[a + c] = (.6)^2 = 36\%$
   Partial = area $[a/(a + e)] = (.49)^2 = 24\%$
   Part = area $a = (.35)^2 = 12\%$

3. A meaningful theoretical relationship should be plausible given that:
   1. Variables logically precede each other in time.
   2. Variables covary or correlate together as expected.
   3. Other influences or "causes" are controlled.
   4. Variables should be measured on at least an interval level.
   5. Changes in a preceding variable should affect variables that follow, either directly or indirectly.

4. The formula for calculating the Pearson correlation coefficient from the covariance and variance of variables—for example r_{xy}—is:

$$r = \frac{s_{xy}}{\sqrt{s_x^2 s_y^2}}$$

a. $r_{xy} = 10.16/(15.80 \cdot 11.02)^{1/2} = .77$

b. $r_{xz} = 12.43/(15.80 \cdot 15.37)^{1/2} = .80$

c. $r_{yz} = 9.23/(11.02 \cdot 15.37)^{1/2} = .71$

3

STRUCTURAL EQUATION MODELING APPROACH TO REGRESSION, PATH, AND FACTOR ANALYSIS

Chapter Outline:

Computer Programs
SPSSX regression analysis program
SPSSX path analysis program
SPSSX factor analysis program
EQS5 regression analysis program
EQS5 path analysis program
EQS5 factor analysis program
LISREL8–SIMPLIS regression analysis program
LISREL8–SIMPLIS path analysis program
LISREL8–SIMPLIS factor analysis program

References

Key Concepts:

Standardized partial regression coefficients
Squared multiple correlation coefficient and factor commonality
Original and reproduced correlation coefficients
Conditions necessary for structural equation modeling
Path diagrams and factor models

Multiple regression, or the general linear modeling approach to the analysis of data, has become increasingly popular since 1967 (Bashaw & Findley, 1968). In fact, it has become recognized as an approach that bridges the gap between correlational and analysis-of-variance thought in answering research hypotheses (McNeil, Kelly, & McNeil, 1975). Consequently, many statistical textbooks today often elaborate the relationship between multiple regression and analysis of variance (Draper & Smith, 1966; Edwards, 1979; Lomax, 1992; Roscoe, 1975; Williams, 1974b).

Graduate students who take an advanced statistics course are typically provided with the multiple linear regression framework for data analysis. Given their knowledge of multiple linear regression techniques applied to univariate analysis (one dependent variable), their understanding can be extended to various multivariate statistical techniques (Kelly, Beggs, McNeil, Eichelberger, & Lyon, 1969, pp. 228–248; Newman, 1988). A basic knowledge of multiple regression concepts is therefore important in further understanding path and factor analyses. These *multivariable* methods have in common the least-squares method of achieving an iteratively derived weight or solution to a theoretical model. In many respects, the methods also identify, partition, and control variance, and the weights can be computed on the basis of standardized partial regression coefficients.

This chapter will present how beta weights (standardized partial regression coefficients) are utilized in multiple regression, path, and factor analysis via structural equation models. More specifically, we illustrate how the structural equation modeling approach can be used to compute parameter estimates in multiple regression, path, and factor analyses. Consequently, we begin with a brief overview of multiple regression concepts followed by a discussion of path and factor analysis methods in order to understand their relationship to structural equation modeling.

3.1 MULTIPLE REGRESSION

Multiple regression techniques require a basic understanding of sample statistics (n, mean, and variance), standardized variables, correlation (Pedhazur, 1982, pp. 53–57), and partial correlation (Cohen & Cohen, 1975; Houston & Bolding, 1974). In standard-score form, the simple linear regression equation is:

$$\hat{z}_y = \beta z_x,$$

where β is the standardized regression coefficient. The basic rationale for using the standard-score formula is that variables are converted to the same scale of measurement, that is, the z scale. Conversion back to the raw-score scale is easily accomplished by using the raw-score mean and standard deviation.

The relationship between the Pearson product–moment correlation coefficient, the unstandardized regression coefficient (b), and the standardized regression coefficient (β) is:

$$\beta = \frac{\Sigma z_x z_y}{\Sigma z_x^2} = b \frac{s_x}{s_y} = r_{xy},$$

where the subscripted s_x and s_y are the sample standard deviations for variables X and Y, respectively. For two independent variables, the multiple linear regression equation with standard scores would be:

$$\hat{z}_y = \beta_1 z_1 + \beta_2 z_2$$

and the standardized partial regression coefficients, β_1 and β_2, would be computed by:

$$\beta_1 = \frac{r_{y1} - r_{y2} r_{12}}{1 - r_{12}^2} \quad \text{and} \quad \beta_2 = \frac{r_{y2} - r_{y1} r_{12}}{1 - r_{12}^2}.$$

The correlation between the dependent observed variable (Y) and the predicted scores ($\hat{Y}$) is given the special name *multiple correlation coefficient*. It is indicated by:

$$R_{y\hat{y}} = R_{y.12},$$

where the latter subscripts indicate that the dependent variable Y is being predicted by two independent variables, X_1 and X_2. The *squared multiple correlation coefficient* is computed as:

$$R_{y\hat{y}}^2 = R_{y.12}^2 = \beta_1 r_{y1} + \beta_2 r_{y2}.$$

The squared multiple correlation coefficient indicates the amount of variance explained, predicted, or accounted for by the set of independent predictor variables. It is important to understand the basic concepts of multiple regression and correlation because they provide a better understanding of path, factor, and structural equation modeling techniques. An example might help to further review and clarify these basic multiple regression computations.

Multiple Regression Example

A multiple linear regression program using a correlation matrix as input appears in the computer program section at the end of the chapter. The correlation matrix as data input can be accomplished in most statistics programs (SPSS, SAS, BMDP, MiniTab, etc.). Means and standard deviations can also be inputted along with the correlation matrix, which, if supplied, will compute the unstandardized coefficients. The SPSSX program generated the following results (*SPSSX User's Guide*, 1988):

$$R_{y.123}^2 = \beta_1 r_{y1} + \beta_2 r_{y2} + \beta_3 r_{y3}$$

$$= .423(.507) + .363(.481) + .040(.276)$$

$$= .40.$$

The correlation coefficients are in the parentheses after each standardized partial regression weight. The correlation coefficients are multiplied by their respective standardized partial regression weights and summed to yield the squared multiple regression coefficient using a generalized least-squares solution.

The LISREL8-SIMPLIS regression analysis program (see the computer program section at the end of the chapter) yielded the following output:

```
Y = 0.42*X1 + 0.36*X2 + 0.04*X3, Errorvar.= 0.60,R²=.40
    (.081)     (.099)     (.097)               (.087)
    5.20       3.65        .42                  6.93
```

These results indicated the same R-squared value as the SPSSX program, and the regression weights were rounded to two decimal places by default (note: the SIMPLIS program does allow for changing the number of decimal place values). In addition, the output reports the standard errors in parentheses, and below each standard error value is a t value. The t value is computed as follows: $t = \beta/STD\ ERROR$. For X_1, this would be $.42/.081 = 5.19$ (not 5.20, on account of rounding errors), which is significant at the .05 level ($t = 5.20$ is greater than critical $t = 1.96$). The output also indicated that the model is saturated because all variables have been included with weights estimated for each variable.

Multiple Regression Issues

Variable Selection (Model Specification). A critical issue in multiple regression has been how to determine the "best" set of independent variables for prediction. It is highly recommended that a regression model be based upon some theoretical framework that can be used to guide the decision of what variables to include. Model specification consists of determining both what variables to include in the model, and which variables are independent or dependent. A systematic determination of the most important set of variables can then be accomplished by setting the partial regression weight of a single variable to zero, hence testing full and restricted models for significance. This approach and other alternative methods are presented by Kelly et al. (1969) and Darlington (1968).

In multiple regression, the selection of a wrong set of variables can yield erroneous and inflated R^2 values. The process of determining which set of variables provides the best prediction, given time, cost, and staffing, is often problematic because several methods and criteria are available to choose from. Recent methodological reviews have indicated that stepwise methods are not preferred, and that an "all possible" subset approach is recommended (Huberty, 1989; Thompson, Smith, Miller, & Thomson, 1991). In addition, the Mallows C_P statistic is advocated by some, rather than R^2, for selecting the best set of predictors (Mallows, 1966; Schumacker, 1994; Zuccaro, 1992). Overall, which variables are included in a regression equation will determine how valid the model is.

Since multiple regression techniques have been shown to be robust (Bohrnstedt & Carter, 1971)—applicable to contrast coding (Lewis & Mouw, 1978), dichotomous coding (McNeil et al., 1975), ordinal coding (Lyons, 1971), and criterion scaling (Schumacker & Williams, 1993)—they have been used in many research situations. In fact, multiple regression equations can be used to address several different types of research questions. The model specification issue, however, is paramount in specifying the multiple regression equation. In addition, there are certain other issues related to using the regression method, namely, variable measurement error and the additive nature of the equation.

Measurement Error. The issue of unreliable variable measurements and their effect on multiple regression—and, for that matter, on the field of statistics—has been previously discussed (Cleary, 1969; Cochran, 1968; Fuller & Hidiroglou, 1978; Meredith, 1964; Subkoviak & Levin, 1977; Sutcliffe, 1958). A recommended solution has been to multiply the dependent variable reliability and/or average of the independent variable reliabilities by the R^2 value (Cochran, 1968, 1970). The basic equation is:

$$\hat{R}^2_{y.123} = R^2_{y.123} r_{yy}$$

or:

$$\hat{R}^2_{y.123} = R^2_{y.123} r_{yy} \bar{r}_{xx}.$$

This is not always possible unless the reliabilities of the measures are known, as in the case of test scores. It has intuitive appeal, however, given the definition of classical reliability, namely, the proportion of true score variance accounted for given the observed scores. In our previous example, $R^2 = .40$. If the dependent variable reliability is .80, then only 32% of the variance predicted is true variance. Similarly, if the average of three independent variable reliabilities is .90, then multiplying .40 by .80 by .90 yields only 29% predicted true variance. Obviously, the effect of unreliable variables (measurement error) on statistics can have a dramatic effect. Werts, Rock, Linn, and Jöreskog (1976) further examined correlations, variances, covariances, and regression weights with and without measurement error and developed a program that corrected the regression weights for attenuation. Our basic concern is that unreliable measured variables coupled with a potential model that is not valid do not represent the theory well.

Additive Equation. The multiple regression equation is by definition additive and thereby does not permit any relational specification of variables. This limits the potential for variables to have direct, indirect, and total effects on each other as described in the next section on path analysis. In fact, a researcher's interest should not be so much with Pearson product–moment correlations, but rather with partial or part correlations that reflect the unique additive contribution of each variable. Even with this emphasis, the basic problem is that variables must be added to an equation—a process that functions ideally only if all independent variables are highly correlated with the dependent variable and uncorrelated amongst themselves. Consequently, path analysis emerged to provide models that result in the relational specification of variable relationships in a manner not restricted to additive models, and to permit hypothesized direct and indirect effects among the variables.

3.2 PATH ANALYSIS

Sewall Wright is credited with the development of path analysis as a method for studying the direct and indirect effects of variables (Wright, 1921, 1934, 1960). Path analysis is not actually a method for *discovering causes*; rather, it tests theoretical relationships, which unfortunately has been termed "causal modeling." A specified model might actually establish causal relationships among the variables when:

1. Temporal ordering of variables exists.
2. Covariation or correlation is present among variables.
3. Other causes are controlled for.
4. Variables are measured on at least an interval level.

Obviously, a model that is tested over time and manipulates certain variables to assess the change in other variables more closely approaches our idea of causation. In the social sciences, the issue of causation is not as presentable as in the physical sciences, but it has the potential to be modeled.

Model Specification

Model specification is necessary in examining multiple variable relationships in path models, just as in the case of multiple regression. In the absence of a theoretical basis for a model, many different relationships among variables can be postulated with many different coefficients computed. In a three-variable model, for example, the four path models in Fig. 3.1 could be postulated on the basis of different hypothesized relationships among the three variables.

How can one determine which model is correct? This is the important role that theory plays in justifying (specifying) a model. Path analysis does not provide a way to specify the model, but rather estimates the effects among the variables once the model has been specified a priori on the basis of theoretical considerations.

Path coefficients in path models take on the values of a Pearson product–moment correlation coefficient and/or a standardized partial regression coefficient (Wolfle, 1977). For example, in the path model of Fig. 3.1d, the path coefficients (p) as depicted by arrows from X1 to Y and X2 to Y, respectively, are:

$$\beta_1 = p_{Y,X1}$$

$$\beta_2 = p_{Y,X2}$$

and the curved arrow between X1 and X2 is denoted as:

$$r_{X1,X2} = p_{X1,X2}$$

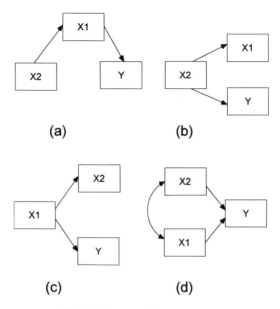

FIG. 3.1. Four possible path models.

The variable relationships, once specified in standard-score form, become standardized partial regression coefficients. In the multiple regression example, the dependent variable was regressed in a single analysis on all the independent variables. In path analysis, one or more multiple regression analyses are performed depending upon the variable relationships in the path model. Path coefficients are therefore computed only on the basis of the particular set of independent variables that lead to the dependent variable under consideration. In the path model—Fig. 3.1d, for example—two standardized partial regression coeffecents (path coefficients) are computed. The curved arrow represents the covariance or correlation between the two independent variables in predicting the dependent variable and does not need to be included in the program. Also, as in regression analysis, path analysis can use dichotomous and ordinal data in the model (Boyle, 1970; Lyons, 1971), and an important issue in path analysis is determining an appropriate index of model fit to the data, which is discussed later in the chapter.

Path Analysis Example

Path models permit diagramming how a particular set of independent variables influence a dependent variable under consideration. How the paths are drawn determines whether the independent variables are correlated causes (unanalyzed; Fig. 3.2a), mediated causes (indirect; Fig. 3.2b), or independent causes (direct; Fig. 3.2c). In a path model, the path coefficients can

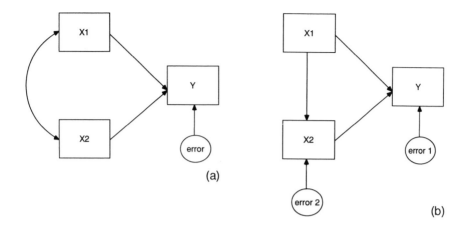

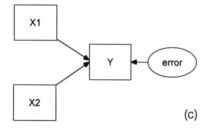

FIG. 3.2. Path model types. (a) Correlated path model. (b) Mediated path model. (c) Independent path model.

be tested for significance (Pedhazur, 1982, pp. 58–62), and a goodness-of-fit criterion (Marascuilo & Levin, 1983, pp. 169–172; Tatsuoka & Lohnes, 1988, pp. 98–100) can reflect the significance between the original and reproduced correlation matrices. The process of comparing the original and reproduced (model implied) correlation matrices is commonly called *decomposing* the correlation matrix (Asher, 1976, pp. 32–34) according to certain rules (Wright, 1934). An example will help to further integrate a basic understanding of multiple regression concepts into the relational model that a path analysis provides.

A four-variable SPSSX path analysis program is in the computer program section at the end of the chapter. In order to calculate the path coefficients for the model, two separate regression equations are solved in the program. The first regression equation computes the path coefficients from variable

X1 to variable X3 (−.071) and from variable X2 to variable X3 (.593) and yields an $R^2 = .34$. The path coefficient indicating residual error for this equation is designated as P_{e1}, and is computed as follows:

$$P_{e1} = \sqrt{1 - R^2_{3.12}} = \sqrt{1 - .34} = \sqrt{.66} = .81.$$

The second regression equation computes the path coefficients from variable X1 to variable Y (.423), from variable X3 to variable Y (.040), and from variable X2 to variable Y (.362) and yields an $R^2 = .40$. You may have noticed that these standardized partial regression coefficients and the R-squared value are the same as those computed in the SPSSX regression program. (Note: The EQS5 and LISREL8-SIMPLIS path analysis programs also permit the calculation of both sets of path coefficients in the same program, and yield identical results.) The path coefficient indicating residual error for this equation is designated as P_{e2} and is computed as follows:

$$P_{e2} = \sqrt{1 - R^2_{y.123}} = \sqrt{1 - .40} = \sqrt{.60} = .77.$$

The curved arrow between X1 and X2 indicates the same correlation as in the correlation matrix, which is $r_{12} = .224$. All of these path coefficients are indicated on the diagrammed path model in Fig. 3.3.

An intuitive method for interpreting path models involves comparing the original correlations with the path coefficients computed (estimated) on the basis of the path model. For example, the original correlation between X1 and X3 is .062; however, when considering their direct effect in the model with X1 and X2 covarying, the path coefficient is −.071. It is interesting to note that the sum of the *direct* relationship between X1 and X3 (−.071) and the *indirect* relationship between X1 and X3 through X2 (.133; computed as .593 × .224) yields the original correlation coefficient—that is, $r_{13} = .062 = −.071 + .133$. Obviously, X1 does not directly affect X3 significantly in the path model.

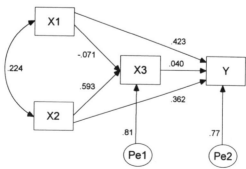

FIG. 3.3. Path model example.

TABLE 3.1
Original and Reproduced Correlations in the Path Model

Variable	Y	X1	X2	X3	
Y	1.000	.507	.480	.275	
X1	.423	1.000	.224	.062	Original
X2	.362	.224	1.000	.577	correlations
X3	.040	−.070	.593	1.000	
		Reproduced correlations			

The original and reproduced correlations are presented in matrix format in Table 3.1. The upper half represents the original correlations, and the lower half indicates the reproduced correlations, which include the regression of paths linking independent variables to the dependent variable in the specified path model.

The original correlations can be completely "reproduced" if all effects— direct (DE), indirect (IE), spurious (S), and correlated (C)—are accounted for, given a specific path model. For our example:

$$r_{12} = p_{12} = .224$$
$$\text{(C)}$$

$$r_{13} = p_{31} + p_{32}p_{21} = -.071 + (.224)(.593) = .062$$
$$\text{(DE)} \quad \text{(IE)}$$

$$r_{23} = p_{32} + p_{31}p_{21} = .593 + (-.071)(.224) = .577$$
$$\text{(DE)} \quad \text{(S)}$$

$$r_{1Y} = p_{Y1} + p_{Y2}p_{21} + p_{Y3}p_{31} + p_{Y3}p_{32}p_{21}$$
$$\quad \text{(DE)} \quad \text{(IE)} \quad \text{(IE)} \quad \text{(IE)}$$
$$= .423 + (.362)(.224) + (.040)(-.071) + (.040)(.593)(.224) = .507$$

$$r_{2Y} = p_{Y2} + p_{Y3}p_{32} + p_{Y1}p_{21} + p_{Y3}p_{31}p_{21}$$
$$\quad \text{(DE)} \quad \text{(IE)} \quad \text{(S)} \quad \text{(S)}$$
$$= .362 + (.040)(.593) + (.423)(.224) + (.040)(-.071)(.224) = .480$$

$$r_{3Y} = p_{Y3} + p_{Y1}p_{31} + p_{Y2}p_{32} + p_{Y1}p_{21}p_{32} + p_{Y2}p_{21}p_{31}$$
$$\quad \text{(DE)} \quad \text{(S)} \quad \text{(S)} \quad \text{(S)} \quad \text{(S)}$$
$$= .040 + (.423)(-.071) + (.362)(.593) + (.423)(.224)(.593)$$
$$+ (.362)(.224)(-.071) = .275$$

Significance Tests

Path Coefficients. Path analysis can obviously be carried out within the context of ordinary regression analysis and does not require the learning of any new analysis techniques (Asher, 1976, p. 32; Williams, 1974a). The advantage of path analysis is that one can specify direct and indirect effects among independent variables and compare these relationships with the original correlations given a hypothesized theoretical model. In addition, path analysis enables us to decompose the correlation between any two variables into simple and complex paths of which some are meaningful.

Path coefficients, like regression weights, can be tested for significance. Path coefficients are tested using the same *t* value as in multiple regression. If the *t* value (path coefficient/standard error) is significant, then the null hypothesis that the path coefficient is equal to 0 is rejected. This indicates that a significant relationship exists between the two specific variables linked by a path in the model. In our example, the paths leading from X1 to X3 (–.071), and from X3 to Y (.040) were nonsignificant at the .05 level. Another approach would be to compare two different path models, the first model with the hypothesized path included, and the second model with the hypothesized path not included.

Model Fit. The relationship between the original and reproduced correlation matrices can be tested for significance (Specht, 1975). This is accomplished by calculating a χ^2 statistic. A *significant* χ^2 value at a predetermined level of α indicates the model *does not* fit the data. If $\chi^2 = 0$, then the original and reproduced correlations in the matrix are identical; in other words, the correlations are perfectly reproduced by the path model. Also, if the residuals (i.e., P_{e1} and P_{e2}) are uncorrelated in the path model, then the sum of the squared residual path coefficients will equal the χ^2 value.

Another test of the overall path model fit to the data can be accomplished by computing the generalized squared multiple correlation (Pedhazur, 1982) as follows:

$$R_m^2 = 1 - (1 - R_1^2)(1 - R_2^2) \dots (1 - R_p^2).$$

The R^2 values are the squared multiple correlation coefficients from each of the separate regression analyses. Each term in the parentheses is equal to a squared residual path coefficient. In the multiple regression example, $R^2 = .40$. In the path model where the two regression analyses were computed, the R^2s were .34 and .40, respectively. The path model R_m^2 in our example would be computed as:

$$R_m^2 = 1 - (1 - .34)(1 - .40) = .604.$$

This is obviously an improvement over the multiple regression model R-squared value of .40 previously reported.

An analogous statistic, M, and a large-sample measure of model fit, Q, are presented in Pedhazur (1982). It is recommended, because χ^2 is affected by sample size, that Q be used; it varies between zero and one and is not a function of sample size. The formula for Q is:

$$Q = \frac{1 - R_m^2}{1 - M},$$

where M is calculated in the same manner as R_m^2, but with nonsignificant path(s) deleted. In our case, we would first drop the path from X1 to X3 because it yielded a nonsignificant path coefficient and therefore M would have a different value from R_m^2 (M values range between zero and R_m^2). In our example, the path from X1 to X3 in the program was dropped by changing the first LISREL8-SIMPLIS equation command line to read: Equation: X3 = X2. The new R^2 value was .33, so $M = 1 - (1 - .33)(1 - .40) = .598$, with $Q = [(1 - .604) / (1 - .598)] = [.396/.402] = .98$! Remember, the closer the value of Q to 1, the better the model fit. Q can be tested for significance using W, which is computed as:

$$W = -(N - d) \log_e Q,$$

where N = sample size, d = number of path coefficients hypothesized to be zero, and $\log_e$ is the natural logarithm (ln). For our example, $W = -(100 - 1) \log_e (.98) = 2.00$. Since W approximates the χ^2 distribution with degrees of freedom equal to d, the tabled critical chi-square value in Table A.2 ($\chi^2 = 3.84$, $d = 1$, .05 level of significance) indicates that our W value is *nonsignificant*, suggesting a *good* model fit. In fact, the W value falls between $p = .80$ ($\chi^2 = 1.64$) and $p = .90$ ($\chi^2 = 2.71$) in Table A.2. The LISREL8-SIMPLIS program output also indicated a good model fit with a nonsignificant $\chi^2 = .71$ ($p = .40$). Several other model fit indices appear on the LISREL8-SIMPLIS output, but they will be discussed later in chapter 7.

3.3 FACTOR ANALYSIS

Factor analysis methods generally attempt to determine which sets of observed (measured) variables sharing common variance–covariance characteristics define constructs. In practice, one collects data on variables and uses factor-analytic techniques to either *confirm* that a set of variables define a construct (factor) or *explore* how variables relate to factors. In this chapter, we present a confirmatory approach to factor analysis in which the researcher hypothesizes and tests a theoretical measurement model.

Path diagrams can be used to display which variables are hypothesized to define which factors. Path diagrams therefore permit representation of the relationships among factors, while also displaying which observed (measured) variables define which factors. The confirmatory approach also permits a set of variables to uniquely define a factor, and/or permits a single variable to share variance on two or more factors. It is also possible to have several orthogonal factors define yet another single higher-order factor known as *second-order factor analysis*.

In general, the first step in confirmatory factor analysis is the theoretical formulation of a measurement model. Once data are collected, interrelationships among the variables in the variance–covariance matrix are analyzed to identify the hypothesized factors (constructs). Confirmatory factor analysis is used to test specific hypotheses regarding which variables correlate with which constructs (Long, 1983). The confirmatory factor-analytic approach has yielded numerous unidimensional (single-factor) tests in several disciplines, especially psychology.

Single-Factor Model

Factor analysis assumes that some factors, which are smaller in number than the number of observed variables, are responsible for the covariation among the observed variables. For example, using our previous correlation matrix from the multiple regression and path analysis programs, a unidimensional trait can be hypothesized using the four variables. The single-factor model is typically diagrammed with F (or Factor) denoting the latent variables, X denoting the observed variables, and U denoting the measurement errors (Kim & Mueller, 1978, p. 35). The single factor model is diagrammed in Fig. 3.4.

The variance of each observed variable is made up of the proportion of variance determined by the common factor (F) and the proportion determined by the unique factor (U_i), which together equal the total variance of each observed variable. Notice that in our example, the factor loadings are standardized partial regression weights in standard-score form, and therefore:

$$S_i^2 = \beta_i^2 + d_i^2 = 1.$$

The correlation between the single common factor and each variable is:

$$r_{F,X_i} = \beta_i.$$

The correlation between the unique (residual) factor and a variable is:

$$r_{U,X_i} = d_i.$$

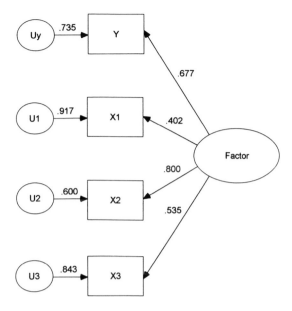

FIG. 3.4. Factor analysis model.

The correlation between the observed (measured) variables sharing the common factor is:

$$r_{X_i, X_j} = \beta_i \beta_j.$$

And finally, the total variance of the factor as a result of the variables sharing common variance is:

$$h^2 = \frac{\Sigma \beta_i^2}{M} = R^2_{F.1234} \, ,$$

where M = number of variables and β_i = factor loadings. An example will help to further elaborate these relationships.

Factor Analysis Example

An SPSSX factor analysis program with four variables in a correlation matrix format is found in the computer program section at the end of the chapter. The program syntax indicates that only one factor is to be defined, the unweighted least-squares method of estimation is used, no rotation method is used, and a scree plot of eigenvalues is requested. The factor path diagram in Fig. 3.4 (Kim & Mueller, 1978, p. 35) indicates the factor loadings, which are as follows: $\beta_Y = .677$, $\beta_1 = .402$, $\beta_2 = .800$, and $\beta_3 = .535$. Multiplying these weights (factor loadings) between pairs of variables yields the correlation coefficients in the matrix in Table 3.2. In confirmatory factor analysis, a

TABLE 3.2
Factor Analysis Model Correlation Matrix

Variable	Y	X1	X2	X3
Y	—			
X1	.27	—		
X2	.54	.32	—	
X3	.36	.22	.43	—

Note. The — indicates no correlation value.

reproduced factor model matrix is compared with the original sample matrix to test model fit. Remember, though, that it is the variance–covariance matrices that are compared; hence, the term *covariance structure analysis* is often used in the research literature.

The total common factor variance defined by the four variables can next be computed by squaring each of the weights (factor loadings), summing them, and then dividing the sum by the number of variables, as follows: $h^2 = R^2_{F.1234} = \Sigma\ \beta_i^2/M = (.46 + .16 + .64 + .29)/4 = .39$. This indicates that only 39% of the factor variance is defined by the four variables. The unique (residual) factor variance is computed as the average of 1 minus these squared factor loadings: $1 - h^2 = 1 - R^2_{F.1234} = \Sigma(1 - \beta_i^2)/M = (.54 + .84 + .36 + .71)/4 = .61$.

The calculation of total factor variance indicates how much of the theoretical construct is explained by the shared common variance in the set of variables loading on the single factor. In contrast, the residual factor variance indicates the amount of variance not explained, and this is due to unique or specific sources of error. One can improve the amount of total factor variance explained by either selecting better variables to define the factor or including more variables. In any case, it is important to have constructs that are well defined by multiple measures (variables). For example, if test scores were used in multiple regression or path analysis, the factor analysis of the items making up the test score would indicate how much of the test construct the test items were measuring. Similarly, the consistency of responses by the subjects across the set of items would indicate the degree of internal consistency or reliability of the scores. Confirmatory factor analysis allows us to test whether our measured variables define a valid construct and assess the reliabilities of the variables. The importance of defining measurement models is further discussed in chapter 4.

Summary

Factor loadings (variable weights) can be interpreted as standardized partial regression coefficients used with an unweighted least-squares method of estimation. In a single unidimensional factor, the weights indicate the correlation between the observed (measured) variables and the single factor (hypothetical construct). If the variables' factor loadings are squared, summed, and divided by the number of variables, they indicate the total factor variance defined. This is traditionally known as an eigenvalue, but termed *communality* in factor analysis.

The confirmatory factor analysis approach is distinguished from regression or path analysis in that observed variable variance and covariance (correlation) define a common factor (hypothetical construct). In factor analysis, the correlation between observed variables is treated as the result of their sharing a common factor, rather than of a variable's being a direct or an indirect effect (as in path analysis) or a predictor of another variable (as in regression analysis).

The validity and reliability issues in measurement have traditionally been handled by first examining the validity and reliability of scores on instruments used in a particular research design. Given an acceptable level of score validity and reliability, the scores are then used in a statistical analysis. The traditional statistical analysis of these scores (multiple regression, path analysis, etc.), however, does not adjust for measurement error; hence, a method that accounts for the measurement error of variables in the statistical analysis was developed. The structural equation modeling approach does permit the specification of measurement errors within the context of relational models.

The impact of measurement error on statistical analyses has been investigated. Fuller (1987) extensively covered structural equation modeling and factor analysis models, and especially extended regression analysis to the case where the variables were measured with error. Wolfle (1979, pp. 48–51) presented the relationship between structural equation modeling, regression, and path analysis, especially in regard to how measurement error affected regression coefficients (path coefficients). Cochran (1968) studied from four different aspects how measurement error affected statistics: (1) types of mathematical models, (2) standard techniques of analysis that take measurement error into account, (3) effect of errors of measurement in producing bias and reduced precision and what remedial procedures are available, and (4) techniques for studying error of measurement. Cochran (1970) also studied the effects of measurement error on the squared multiple correlation coefficient. It is not surprising, therefore, to find that an approach was developed to incorporate measurement error adjustments into statistical analyses.

3.4 STRUCTURAL EQUATION MODELING APPROACH

Structural equation models are often diagrammed by using path models in which the factors (hypothetical contructs) are viewed as latent variables (Jöreskog & Sörbom, 1986, pp. I.5–I.7). These structural equation models typically consist of two parts: the measurement model, and the structural equation model. The measurement model specifies how the latent variables or hypothetical constructs are measured in terms of the observed (measured) variables and describes their measurement properties (reliability and validity). The structural equation model specifies the direct and indirect relationships among the latent variables and is used to describe the amount of explained and unexplained variance.

Structural equation models encompass a wide range of models, for example: univariate or multivariate regression models, confirmatory factor analysis, and path analysis models (Jöreskog & Sörbom, 1986, pp. I.3, I.9–I.12). Cuttance (1983) presented an overview of several of these submodels with diagrams and explanations. Wolfle (1982) also presented an in-depth presentation of a single model to introduce and clarify the structural equation modeling approach. Today, the popularity of testing theoretical models has grown partly because of the new, updated software programs that operate in the MS Windows environment, such as LISREL8-SIMPLIS, EQS5, AMOS/AMOSDraw, and SEPATH. We have included only SPSSX, EQS5, and LISREL8-SIMPLIS software programs at the end of the chapter, but the other programs would provide similar results for multiple regression, path, and factor analyses. The basic program syntax for EQS5 and LISREL8-SIMPLIS is presented next.

EQS5 Program Syntax

The EQS5 program command language syntax defines all variables as being in one of two different categories: observed (measured) variables, or unobserved (latent) variables. The measured variables have the prefix V, and the latent variables have the prefix F. Likewise, the measurement error associated with observed variables has the prefix E, and the measurement error associated with the prediction of a latent variable has the prefix D. All variables using EQS5 syntax are represented as either independent or dependent variables. Only for independent variables (latent or observed) can variances and covariances be estimated, and only for dependent variables can equations be entered.

The EQS5 program is simple to code and easy to understand. A /TITLE command followed by the name of your program run helps to distinguish the computer printout from other program runs. A /SPECIFICATION command is listed next, followed by values on the subcommands: CASES= <number of subjects>, VARIABLES= <number of observed variables>, and METHOD= <estimation method>. A /LABELS command allows you to expand the description of variables beyond the use of the four prefixes (V, F, E, and D). The /EQUATIONS command indicates the type of statistical analysis to perform by specifying variable equations. The expression 1* can be used in front of each variable (observed, latent, measurement error, or prediction error variables) to indicate that a parameter value is to be estimated. A single asterisk can be specified, or a number can precede the asterisk to serve as a start value for estimating the coefficient. The /VARIANCES command indicates which of the variables on the right-hand side of the equation require estimated variances. The /COVARI-ANCES command indicates which variables on the right-hand side of the equation require estimated covariance (correlation). Dependent variables do not appear in this command. The /MATRIX command is followed by a variance–covariance matrix. EQS5 also permits the inputting of raw data or correlation matrices with means and standard deviations. The EQS5 program is stopped by specifying an /END command. Notice that a semicolon is used to separate expressions and subcommands or to end equations, except in the /TITLE command.

EQS5 programs may contain additional commands, subcommands, and options. For example, the /SPECIFICATION command can have subcommands that indicate the type and format of the matrix input for data analysis (MATRIX =COVARIANCE; and FORMAT = `5F1.0';). The EQS5 program can also include an /LMTEST (Lagrange multiplier test) command to help the researcher determine whether certain parameters, if deleted, modified, or added, would lead to a model that better represented the data; a /PRINT command to specify certain computer output; a /CONSTRAINT command to fix values for certain parameters; and a /DIAGRAM command to diagram the model. These and other subcommands are not discussed further here; rather, we suggest that you check the EQS5 manual and accompanying software program examples of EQS5 program setups using these commands.

LISREL8-SIMPLIS Program Syntax

The LISREL8 matrix notation uses up to eight different matrices in the analysis of structural equation models (see chap. 11) and can be difficult to program. Consequently, an easier, new command language called SIMPLIS (SIMPle LISrel) was developed to make it easier for the researcher to specify and analyze structural equation models.

The LISREL8-SIMPLIS program begins on the first line with a title or description of the program run. This does not require any command or use of quotation marks. Next, the Observed Variables: command lists the observed variables included in the raw data file or matrix. Then, either a Raw Data:, a Correlation Matrix:, or a Covariance Matrix: command is entered and followed by the input data or file name. If the Correlation Matrix: command is used and unstandardized coefficients are to be estimated, then observed variable means are specified on a Means: command and the Standard Deviations: command is used to specify corresponding standard deviations. These values for the observed variables are simply listed with blank spaces between them. A `Sample size:` command indicates the number of subjects. If latent variables are to be identified by a set of observed variables (under the measurement model), simply specify a name for the latent variable using up to eight characters on the `Latent Variable:` commmand. The `Relationships:` command specifies the equations and therefore indicates the type of statistical analysis to be performed. The LISREL8-SIMPLIS program is stopped by an `End of Problem` command. Notice that most of the commands are followed by a colon before variable names or values are specified.

Other commands are available to use in LISREL8-SIMPLIS programs. For example, a `LISREL OUTPUT` command just before the end of the program will produce output in matrix format and will optionally permit standardized parameter solutions to be requested. A `PRINT` command can be used to specify certain values to be printed, and an `EQUATION:` command is used when only observed variables are inputted for statistical analysis. No expression is needed to specify a parameter estimate, nor does the LISREL8-SIMPLIS program require that measurement error or prediction error be specified. The LISREL8-SIMPLIS program also provides modification indices to suggest addition, deletion, or modification of paths in the model to obtain a better fit. As before, we recommend that the reader further study the LISREL8-SIMPLIS program examples that accompany the software for programs using these commands.

Multiple Regression, Path, and Factor Analysis Output

Both the EQS5 and LISREL8-SIMPLIS regression programs, with a correlation matrix as input, yielded the same results. The regression model was depicted as:

$$\hat{Y} = \beta_1 X_1 + \beta_2 X_2 + \beta_3 X_3,$$

where Y = dependent variable, β = regression weights, and the X_i = independent variables. These results are the same as in the SPSSX regression program, namely:

$$R^2_{y.123} = \beta_1 r_{y1} + \beta_2 r_{y2} + \beta_3 r_{y3}$$

$$= (.423).507 + (.363).481 + (.040).276$$

$$= .40.$$

Both the EQS5 and LISREL8-SIMPLIS path analysis programs permit separate regression equations that define the relationships (paths) among the variables in the path model. The estimated path coefficients and model fit were the same for both programs, namely, $R^2_m = .604$. The Q and associated W statistic, however, are not printed as part of the output and must be calculated by hand. The EQS5 and LISREL8-SIMPLIS structural equation modeling programs, however, do provide several fit indices and modification indices, which are discussed in later chapters.

The EQS5 and LISREL8-SIMPLIS factor analysis programs computed the same results as the SPSSX factor analysis program. The factor loadings, unique residuals, and common factor variance for each variable were the same, namely:

1. Factor loadings:
   $Y = .677$ $X_1 = .402$ $X_2 = .800$ $X_3 = .535$
2. Unique factor variance:
   $Y = .54$ $X_1 = .84$ $X_2 = .36$ $X_3 = .71$
3. Common factor variance:
   $Y = .46$ $X_1 = .16$ $X_2 = .64$ $X_3 = .29$

3.5 SUMMARY

This section contains a summary both of this chapter and of the field, in general. Structural equation modeling, in this chapter and elsewhere (Loehlin, 1992; Schumacker, 1991), has been shown to be related to multiple regression, path analysis, and factor analysis techniques. The appropriate statistical method to use, however, is often an issue of debate. It sometimes requires more than one approach to analyzing data. The rationale for choosing among the alternative methods of analysis is usually guided by research hypotheses or questions. The multivariable methods presented in this chapter have different applications. Multiple regression seeks to identify and estimate the amount of variance in the dependent variable attributed to one or more independent variables (prediction). Path analysis seeks to identify relationships among a set of variables (explanation). Factor analysis seeks to identify subsets of variables with common shared variance from a much larger set (exploratory factor analysis), or to confirm a measurement model where variables are hypothesized to define a construct (confirmatory factor analysis). Structural equation modeling builds on these methods by incorporating a confirmatory factor analysis approach into the theoretical relationships among the latent variables.

Multiple regression as a general data-analytic technique is widely accepted and used by educational researchers and behavioral scientists. Multiple regression methods basically determine the overall contribution of a set of observed variables to prediction, test full and restricted models for the significant contribution of a variable in a model, or delineate the best subset of multiple independent predictors. Multiple regression equations also permit the use of nominal, ordinal, effect, contrast, or polynomial coded variables (Pedhazur, 1982). The multiple regression approach, however, is not robust to measurement error and model misspecification (Bohrnstedt & Carter, 1971) and forms an additive model rather than a relational model; hence, the emergence of path analysis.

Wright (1921), a biologist, developed path analysis to gain a better understanding of genetic theory. In the early 1960s, the technique became popular in the behavioral and social sciences (Asher, 1976). Path analysis provided the needed methodology for examining theoretical models. It essentially permitted the determination of data fit to a theoretical model, the specifying of a causal relationship from correlated data, and the testing of alternative theoretical models (James, Muliak, & Brett, 1982). Path models are analyzed by simply conducting several multiple regression analyses (Williams & Klimpel, 1974). Path analysis equipped the researcher with a method to specifically relate observed variables on the basis of theory in a manner that was relational (causal) not additive as in multiple regression. For example, Figs. 3.2a, b, and c indicated three different ways a path model could be depicted, depending on whether a correlated causal effect, a mediated causal effect, or an independent causal effect, respectively, is present (Pedhazur, 1982)—that is, for which three different relationships between the two independent variables can be observed in predicting Y (Cohen & Cohen, 1975). The advantage of path analysis over multiple regression analysis is this ability to specify the type of relationship among the independent variables when predicting the dependent variable. The determination of which model is best or correct, however, requires a theoretical perspective and model fit statistics to compare competing theoretical models.

Pedhazur (1982) further cited certain assumptions that must be met in performing path analysis: (a) the relationship among the variables in the model should be linear, additive, and causal; (b) each residual should not be correlated with variable error that precedes it in the model; (c) there is a one-way causal flow in the model; (d) the variables are measured on an interval scale; and (e) the variables are measured without error. These assumptions continue to be cited as necessary for path analysis (Baldwin, 1989; Loehlin, 1992; Tracz, 1992). However, Boyle (1970) and Lyons (1971) previously indicated that nominal or ordinal variables are permissible and that path coefficients can be corrected for measurement error. In addition to these assumptions, certain conditions remain for the appropriate use of path analysis: (a) temporal ordering of the variables in the model; (b) covariation among the variables; and (c) controlling for other causes (Pedhazur, 1982). Tracz (1992) recommended that path analysis be based on sound theory, utilize large samples, meet assumptions, present both standardized and unstandardized path coefficients, and be replicated and/or cross-validated to confirm conclusions.

Path analysis has distinct advantages over multiple regression. It affords the ability to establish a causal relationship among independent variables, specify the specific relationship among the independent variables, and model the complex nature of variable relationships posited by theory. Path analysis also has certain limitations. For example, many path models do not include interaction effects (Newman, Marchant, & Ridenour, 1993), and the observed variables are assumed to be perfectly measured (Bohrnstedt & Carter, 1971). Moreover, the path coefficients are prone to misinterpretation (Tracz, 1992), and the assumption of linear causal relationships precludes testing for apparent nonlinear effects in theoretical models (Pohlmann, 1991).

Structural equation models were developed to resolve the problem of single observed variables and their related measurement error in path analysis. The measurement error of a single variable tends to overstate or understate the impact on the disturbance term of a dependent variable (Frerichs, 1990a, 1990b). Today, it is commonly accepted that multiple observed variables are preferred over a single variable in defining a latent variable (Pedhazur & Schmelkin, 1992). Structural equation models therefore differ from path analysis models in that they use latent variables rather than observed variables and combine a measurement model with a structural model to substantiate theory.

We hope that this background has provided you with the building blocks to bettter understand structural equation modeling.

COMPUTER PROGRAMS

SPSSX Regression Analysis Program

```
TITLE regression with correlation matrix input
COMMENT variable means=0; variances=1; constant=0
MATRIX DATA VARIABLES=Y X1 X2 X3/N=100
BEGIN DATA
1.000
 .507   1.000
 .480    .224   1.000
 .275    .062    .577   1.000
END DATA
REGRESSION MATRIX=IN(*)/
    MISSING=LISTWISE/
    VARIABLES=Y X1 X2 X3/
    DEPENDENT=Y/
    ENTER X1 X2 X3/
FINISH
```

SPSSX Path Analysis Program

```
TITLE path analysis example with correlation matrix input
COMMENT variable means=0; variances=1; constant=0
MATRIX DATA VARIABLES=Y X1 X2 X3/N=100
BEGIN DATA
1.000
 .507   1.000
 .480    .224   1.000
 .275    .062    .577   1.000
END DATA
REGRESSION MATRIX=IN(*)/
    MISSING=LISTWISE/
    VARIABLES=Y X1 X2 X3/
    DEPENDENT=X3/
    ENTER X1 X2/
    DEPENDENT=Y/
    ENTER X1 X2 X3/
FINISH
```

SPSSX Factor Analysis Program

```
TITLE factor analysis example with correlation matrix input
COMMENT variable means=0; variances=1; constant=0
MATRIX DATA VARIABLES=Y X1 X2 X3/N=100
BEGIN DATA
1.000
 .507   1.000
 .480    .224   1.000
 .275    .062    .577   1.000
END DATA
FACTOR VARIABLES=Y X1 X2 X3/
    MATRIX=IN(COR=*)/
    CRITERIA=FACTORS(1)/
    EXTRACTION=ULS/
    ROTATION=NOROTATE/
    PRINT CORRELATION DET INITIAL EXTRACTION ROTATION/
    FORMAT SORT/
    PLOT EIGEN/
FINISH
```

EQS5 Regression Analysis Program

```
/TITLE
regression analysis with correlation matrix input
/SPECIFICATIONS
```

```
CASES=100; VARIABLES = 4; ME = ULS;
/LABELS
V1=Y;V2=X1;V3=X2;V4=X3;
/EQUATIONS
V1 = 1*V2 + 1*V3 + 1*V4 + 1*E1;
/VARIANCES
V2,V3,V4=1*;E1=1*;
/COVARIANCES
V2,V3,V4=1*;
/MATRIX
1.000
 .507   1.000
 .480    .224   1.000
 .275    .062    .577   1.000
/END
```

EQS5 Path Analysis Program

```
/TITLE
path analysis with correlation matrix input
/SPECIFICATIONS
CASES=100; VARIABLES = 4; ME = ULS;
/LABELS
V1=Y;V2=X1;V3=X2;V4=X3;
/EQUATIONS
V4 = 1*V2 + 1*V3 + 1*E4;
V1 = 1*V2 + 1*V3 + 1*V4 + 1*E1;
/VARIANCES
V2,V3=1*;
E4,E1=1*;
/COVARIANCES
V2,V3=1*;
/MATRIX
1.000
 .507   1.000
 .480    .224   1.000
 .275    .062    .577   1.000
/END
```

EQS5 Factor Analysis Program

```
/TITLE
factor analysis with correlation matrix input
/SPECIFICATIONS
CASES=100; VARIABLES = 4; ME = ULS;
/LABELS
V1=Y;V2=X1;V3=X2;V4=X3;
```

```
/EQUATIONS
V1 = 1*F1 + 1*E1;
V2 = 1*F1 + 1*E2;
V3 = 1*F1 + 1*E3;
V4 = 1*F1 + 1*E4;
/VARIANCES
F1 = 1.0;E1 TO E4=1*;
/MATRIX
1.000
 .507   1.000
 .480    .224   1.000
 .275    .062    .577   1.000
/DIAGRAM
E1 E2 E3 E4;
V1 V2 V3 V4;
   F1  ;
/END
```

LISREL8-SIMPLIS Regression Analysis Program[1]

```
Regression of Y
Observed variables: Y X1 X2 X3
Correlation matrix:
1.000
 .507   1.000
 .480    .224   1.000
 .275    .062    .577   1.000
Sample size: 100
Equation: Y = X1 X2 X3
End of Problem
```

LISREL8-SIMPLIS Path Analysis Program

```
Path Analysis of Y
Observed variables: Y X1 X2 X3
Correlation matrix:
1.000
 .507   1.000
 .480    .224   1.000
 .275    .062    .577   1.000
Sample size: 100
Equation: X3 = X1 X2
```

---

[1]Include the Means: statement with each respective variable's mean value to obtain the intercept term. A correlation or covariance matrix can be input. Use Covariance matrix: statement when inputting a covariance matrix.

```
Equation: Y = X1 X2 X3
End of Problem
```

LISREL8-SIMPLIS Factor Analysis Program

```
Factor analysis with correlation matrix input
Observed variables: V1 V2 V3 V4
Correlation matrix:
1.000
 .507   1.000
 .480    .224   1.000
 .275    .062    .577   1.000
Sample size: 100
Latent Variables: Factor1
Relationships:
V1 - V4 = Factor1
Print Residuals
Lisrel Output
End of Problem
```

REFERENCES

Asher, H. B. (1976). *Causal modeling.* Quantitative Applications in the Social Sciences, Vol. 3. Beverly Hills, CA: Sage.

Baldwin, B. (1989). A primer in the use and interpretation of structural equation models. *Measurement and Evaluation in Counseling and Development, 22,* 100–112.

Bashaw, W. L., & Findley, W. G. (1968). *Symposium on general linear model approach to the analysis of experimental data in educational research.* (Project No. 7-8096). Washington, DC: U.S. Department of Health, Education, and Welfare.

Bohrnstedt, G. W., & Carter, T. M. (1971). Robustness in regression analysis. In H. L. Costner (Ed.), *Sociological methodology* (pp. 118–146). San Francisco: Jossey-Bass.

Boyle, R. P. (1970). Path analysis and ordinal data. *American Journal of Sociology, 75,* 461–480.

Cleary, T. A. (1969). Error of measurement and the power of a statistical test. *British Journal of Mathematical and Statistical Psychology, 22,* 49–55.

Cochran, W. G. (1968). Errors of measurement in statistics. *Technometrics, 10,* 637–666.

Cochran, W. G. (1970). Some effects of errors of measurement on multiple correlation. *Journal of the American Statistical Association, 65,* 22–34.

Cohen, J., & Cohen, P. (1975). *Applied multiple regression/correlation analysis for the behavioral sciences.* Hillsdale, NJ: Lawrence Erlbaum Associates.

Cuttance, P. F. (1983). Covariance structure and structural equation modelling in research: A conceptual overview of LISREL modelling. *Multiple Linear Regression Viewpoints, 12,* 1–63.

Darlington, R. B. (1968). Multiple regression in psychological research and practice. *Psychological Bulletin, 69,* 161–182.

Draper, N. R., & Smith, H. (1966). *Applied regression analysis.* New York: Wiley.

Edwards, A. L. (1979). *Multiple regression and the analysis of variance and covariance.* San Francisco: Freeman.

Frerichs, D. K. (1990a). LISREL: Historical Overview. *LISREL Newsletter, 1*(1), 1–4.

Frerichs, D. K. (1990b). Measurement error in single indicator models. *LISREL Newsletter, 1*(2), 1–4.

Fuller, W. A. (1987). *Measurement error models.* New York: Wiley.

Fuller, W. A., & Hidiroglou, M. A. (1978). Regression estimates after correcting for attenuation. *Journal of the American Statistical Association, 73,* 99–104.

Houston, S. R., & Bolding, J. T., Jr. (1974). Part, partial, and multiple correlation in commonality analysis of multiple regression models. *Multiple Linear Regression Viewpoints, 5,* 36–40.

Huberty, C. J. (1989). Problems with stepwise methods—better alternatives. In B. Thompson (Ed.), *Advances in social science methodology, Vol. 1* (pp. 43–70). Greenwich, CT: JAI.

James, L. R., Muliak, S. A., & Brett, J. M. (1982). *Causal analysis: Assumptions, models, and data.* Beverly Hills, CA: Sage.

Jöreskog, K. G., & Sörbom, D. (1986). *LISREL VI user's guide: Analysis of linear structural relationships by maximum likelihood, instrumental variables, and least squares methods.* Mooresville, IN: Scientific Software, Inc.

Kelly, F. J., Beggs, D. L., McNeil, K. A., Eichelberger, T., & Lyon, L. (1969). *Multiple regression approach.* Carbondale: Southern Illinois University Press.

Kim, J., & Mueller, C. W. (1978). *Introduction to factor analysis: What it is and how to do it.* Beverly Hills, CA: Sage.

Lewis, E. L., & Mouw, J. T. (1978). *The use of contrast coefficients.* Carbondale: Southern Illinois University Press.

Loehlin, J. C. (1992). *Latent variable models: An introduction to factor, path, and structural analysis* (2nd ed.). Hillsdale, NJ: Lawrence Erlbaum Associates.

Lomax, R. G. (1992). *Statistical concepts: A second course for education and the behavioral sciences.* White Plains, NY: Longman.

Long, J. S. (1983). *Confirmatory factor analysis.* Beverly Hills, CA: Sage.

Lyons, M. (1971). Techniques for using ordinal measures in regression and path analysis. In H. L. Costner (Ed.), *Sociological methodology* (pp. 147–171). San Francisco: Jossey-Bass.

Mallows, C. L. (1966, March). *Choosing a subset regression.* Paper presented at the Joint Meetings of the American Statistical Association, Los Angeles.

Marascuilo, L. A., & Levin, J. R. (1983). *Multivariate statistics in the social sciences: A researcher's guide.* Monterey, CA: Brooks/Cole.

McNeil, K. A., Kelly, F. J., & McNeil, J. T. (1975). *Testing research hypotheses using multiple linear regression.* Carbondale: Southern Illinois University Press.

Meredith, W. (1964). Canonical correlations with fallible data. *Psychometrika, 29,* 55–65.

Newman, I. (1988). *There is no such thing as multivariate analysis: All analyses are univariate.* President's Address at Mid-Western Educational Research Association, October 15, 1988, Chicago.

Newman, I., Marchant, G. J., & Ridenour, T. (1993, April). *Type VI errors in path analysis: Testing for interactions.* Paper presented at the annual meeting of the American Educational Research Association, Atlanta.

Pedhazur, E. J. (1982). *Multiple regression in behavioral research: Explanation and prediction* (2nd ed.). New York: Holt, Rinehart & Winston.

Pedhazur, E. J., & Schmelkin, L. P. (1992). *Measurement, design, and analysis: An integrated approach.* Hillsdale, NJ: Lawrence Erlbaum Associates.

Pohlmann, J. T. (1991, April). *Issues in path analysis: Strengths and problems.* Paper presented at the annual meeting of the American Educational Research Association, Chicago.

Roscoe, J. T. (1975). *Fundamental research statistics for the behavioral sciences* (2nd ed.). New York: Holt, Rinehart & Winston.

Schumacker, R. E. (1991). Relationship between multiple regression, path, factor, and LISREL analyses. *Multiple Linear Regression Viewpoints, 18*(1), 28–46.

Schumacker, R. E., & Williams, J. D. (1993). Teaching ordinal and criterion scaling in multiple regression. *Multiple Linear Regression Viewpoints, 20*(1), 25–31.

Schumacker, R. E. (1994). A comparison of the Mallows Cp and principal component regression criteria for best model selection. *Multiple Linear Regression Viewpoints, 21*(1), 12–22.

Specht, D. A. (1975). On the evaluation of causal models. *Social Science Research, 4,* 113–133.

SPSSX users' guide (3rd ed.). (1988). New York: McGraw-Hill.

Subkoviak, M. J., & Levin, J. R. (1977). Fallibility of measurement and the power of a statistical test. *Journal of Educational Measurement, 14,* 47–52.

Sutcliffe, J. P. (1958). Error of measurement and the sensitivity of a test of significance. *Psychometrika, 23,* 9–17.

Tatsuoka, M. M., & Lohnes, P. R. (1988). *Multivariate analysis: Techniques for educational and psychological research* (2nd ed.). New York: Macmillan.

Thompson, B., Smith, Q. W., Miller, L. M., & Thomson, W. A. (1991, January). *Stepwise methods lead to bad interpretations: Better alternatives.* Paper presented at the annual meeting of the Southwest Educational Research Association, San Antonio.

Tracz, S. M. (1992). The interpretation of the beta weights in path analysis. *Multiple Linear Regression Viewpoints, 19*(1), 7–15.

Tracz, S. M., Brown, R., & Kopriva, R. (1991). Considerations, issues, and comparisons in variable selection and interpretation in multiple regression. *Multiple Linear Regression Viewpoints, 18,* 55–66.

Werts, C. E., Rock, D. A., Linn, R. L., & Jöreskog, K. G. (1976). Comparison of correlations, variances, covariances, and regression weights with or without measurement error. *Psychological Bulletin, 83*(6), 1007–1013.

Williams, J. D. (1974a). Path analysis and causal models as regression techniques. *Multiple Linear Regression Viewpoints, 5*(3), 1–20.

Williams, J. D. (1974b). *Regression analysis in educational research.* New York: MSS Information Corporation.

Williams, J. D., & Klimpel, R. J. (1974). Path analysis and causal models as regression techniques. *Multiple Linear Regression Viewpoints, 5*(3), 1–20.

Wolfle, L. M. (1977). An introduction to path analysis. *Multiple Linear Regression Viewpoints, 8*(1), 36–61.

Wolfle, L. M. (1979). Unmeasured variables in path analysis. *Multiple Linear Regression Viewpoints, 9*(1), 20–56.

Wolfle, L. M. (1982). Causal models with unmeasured variables: An introduction to LISREL. *Multiple Linear Regression Viewpoints, 11*(2), 9–54.

Wright, S. (1921). Correlation and causation. *Journal of Agricultural Research, 20,* 557–585.

Wright, S. (1934). The method of path coefficients. *Annals of Mathematical Statistics, 5,* 161–215.

Wright, S. (1960). Path coefficients and path regression: Alternative or complementary concepts? *Biometrics, 16,* 189–202.

Zuccaro, C. (1992). Mallows' C_p statistic and model selection in multiple linear regression. *Journal of the Market Research Society, 34,* 163–172.

4

DEVELOPING STRUCTURAL EQUATION MODELS: PART I

Key Concepts:

Model specification
Identification
Estimation
Testing fit
Respecification
Developing measurement models for latent variables
Developing structural equation models

Structural equation models have been developed in a number of academic disciplines to substantiate theory. Structural equation models have further helped to establish the relationship between latent variables or constructs given a theoretical perspective. The structural equation modeling approach involves developing measurement models to define latent variables and then establishing relationships or structural equations among the latent variables. Consequently, the focus of this chapter is on providing researchers with a better understanding of how to develop structural equation models. A deliberate attempt was made to minimize matrix and statistical notation so that the reader could better understand the structural equation modeling approach.

4.1 FIVE STEPS IN STRUCTURAL EQUATION MODELING

The five steps that characterize most structural equation modeling applications were listed in Bollen and Long (1993):

1. Model specification.
2. Identification.
3. Estimation.
4. Testing fit.
5. Respecification.

The first step, *model specification*, refers to the initial theoretical model the researcher formulates. Obviously, you should hypothesize this model on the basis of a review of the research literature in your substantive area or postulate it on the basis of a theory. The second step, *identification*, is to ask whether unique values can be found for the parameters to be estimated in the theoretical model. In some instances, the analysis may not converge or reach a solution (find unique parameter values), even after 100 iterations, because the model is misspecified! The third step, *estimation*, requires knowledge of the various estimation techniques that are used depending on the variable scale and/or distributional property of the variable(s) used in the model—least squares, maximum likelihood, and so forth. The fourth step, *testing fit*, involves interpreting model fit or comparing fit indices for alternative or nested models. The researcher is faced with choosing among numerous fit indices that subjectively indicate whether the data fit the theoretical model. The fifth step, *respecification*, usually occurs when the model fit indices suggest a poor fit. In this instance, the researcher makes a decision regarding how to delete, add, or modify paths in the model, and then subsequently reruns the analysis.

Model modification indices and/or tests of paths from the initial model guide the researcher in this effort. Since these steps form the basis for investigating a theoretical model in structural equation modeling, we further address them here and in subsequent chapters.

4.2 MEASUREMENT MODELS

Confirmatory factor analysis methods reflect measurement models in which observed variables define constructs or latent variables. (The term *covariance structure analysis* is also used to refer to the analysis of measurement models.) Latent variables are not directly measurable (they are factors or constructs—e.g., spatial ability) but must be inferred. The loading of each observed variable on a factor indicates its correlation with the construct of interest, and in its commonality (common variance) with other variables it identifies the latent variable (Kim & Mueller, 1978a, 1978b).

Measurement models are defined for both independent and dependent latent variables. Figure 4.1a presents a measurement model that defines an independent latent variable, and Fig. 4.1b presents a measurement model that defines a dependent latent variable. How well the observed variables measure each latent variable is assessed by h^2, or the sum of the factor loadings squared divided by the number of variables. The fit indices in chapter 7 are also used to determine model fit. The expression $1 - h^2$ indicates the amount of variance not explained, or the degree to which the latent variable is not defined by the observed variables. The measurement model involves specifying which observed variables define a construct (i.e., it is associated with confirmatory factor analysis) and reflects the extent to which the observed variables are assessing the latent variables in terms of reliability and validity. Latent variables are typically diagrammed using ellipses (ovals) or circles, while the observed variables are diagrammed using rectangles or squares.

Two or more independent latent variables can covary, or change together. Figure 4.1c depicts two independent latent variables that covary; each latent variable is defined by two observed variables. A curved arrow drawn from one latent variable to another indicates that they are correlated. Arrows pointing toward the observed variables indicate each variable's measurement error. A curved arrow joining a pair of measurement error terms indicates that they covary or are correlated as depicted in Fig. 4.1d. In Fig. 4.1e, two latent independent variables define a second latent variable. This is referred to as a *second-order confirmatory factor analysis*. For example, job satisfaction and supervisor satisfaction could combine to define a second-order latent variable called career longevity.

Measurement models for independent latent variables can therefore be unidimensional, can be correlated, or can define a higher-order latent variable. These relationships are specified on the /EQUATIONS and/or /COVARIANCES

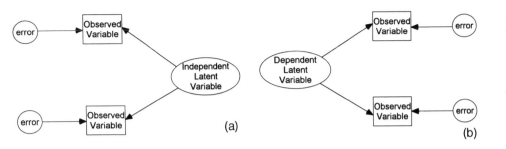

(a)

(b)

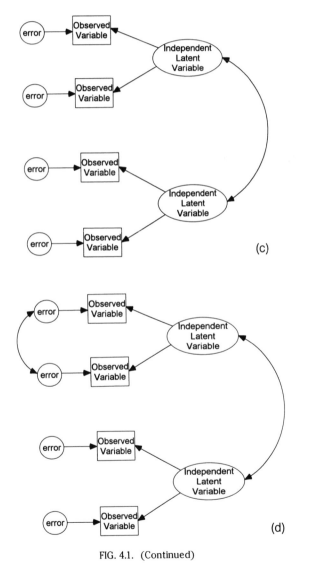

(c)

(d)

FIG. 4.1. (Continued)

65

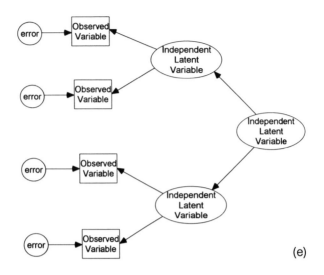

(e)

FIG. 4.1. Measurement model types. (a) Independent latent variable. (b) Dependent latent variable. (c) Correlated independent latent variables. (d) Correlated error terms of independent latent variable. (e) Second-order independent latent variable.

commands in EQS5. For example, the different EQS5 equations needed to specify a unidimensional, a correlated, and a second-order latent variable, respectively, are:

Unidimensional latent variable:

```
/EQUATIONS
    V1 = F1 + E1;
    V2 = F1 + E2;
    V3 = F1 + E3;
```

Correlated latent variables:

```
/EQUATIONS
    V1 = F1 + E1;
    V2 = F1 + E2;
    V3 = F1 + E3;
    V4 = F2 + E4;
    V5 = F2 + E5;
    V6 = F2 + E6;
/COVARIANCES
    F1,F2 = 1*;
```

Second-order latent variable:

```
/EQUATIONS
    V1 = F1 + E1;
    V2 = F1 + E2;
    V3 = F1 + E3;
    V4 = F2 + E4;
    V5 = F2 + E5;
    V6 = F2 + E6;
    F1 = F3 + D1;
    F2 = F3 + D2;
/VARIANCES
    F3 = 1.0;
    D1,D2 = 1*;
    E1 TO E6 = 1*;
/CONSTRAINTS
    (D1,D1) = (D2,D2);
```

The EQS5 program syntax makes the specification of a unidimensional latent variable straightforward. Each observed variable is set equal to the latent variable plus its unique measurement error. The computer output will indicate the factor loadings and corresponding measurement error terms. The correlation between two latent independent variables is also easy to specify using the /COVARIANCES command. The expression F1,F2 = 1*; serves to indicate that a parameter is to be estimated, in this case, the correlation between the two latent independent variables. The EQS5 program provided in the computer program section at the end of the chapter computes the factor loadings, observed variable error, and correlation between the two factors. The /CONSTRAINTS command is needed in the second-order EQS5 program; otherwise the model will be just-identified (see Rindskopf & Rose, 1988, for the rationale). Basically, at least one parameter in a higher-order latent variable model must be fixed. In our example using a single second-order latent variable, the researcher can check the variances on the computer output to ensure that they are approximately equal, thereby justifying the equality constraint.

The LISREL8-SIMPLIS program also easily specifies these types of measurement models. The unidimensional, correlated, and second-order latent variable measurement models are presented here using the Latent Variables: and Relationships: commands.

Unidimensional latent variable:

```
Latent Variables: Factor1
Relationships:
    V1-V3 = Factor1
```

Correlated latent variables:

```
Latent Variables: Factor1 Factor2
Relationships:
  V1-V3 = Factor1
  V4-V6 = Factor2
Let Factor1 and Factor2 correlate
```

Second-order latent variable:

```
Latent Variables: Factor1 Factor2 Factor3
Relationships:
  V1-V3   = Factor1
  V4-V6   = Factor2
  Factor3 = Factor1 Factor2
Set the variance of Factor1 and Factor2 equal
```

The LISREL8-SIMPLIS specification of a single unidimensional latent variable is also straightforward. Notice that no observed variable measurement error needs to be specified. Also, the dash character permits similarly referenced variables to be included on a single line. The LISREL8-SIMPLIS program computer output will indicate the factor loadings and measurement error for each respective observed variable. The correlation between two latent variables is automatically specified when the LISREL8-SIMPLIS command language is used. We have added the LET command here for heuristic purposes only. It is not required, because the variables by default are allowed to covary unless otherwise specified. The LISREL8-SIMPLIS command language for a second-order latent variable model does not require the specification of observed measurement error or latent variable measurement error. The equality constraint, to prevent a just-identified model, can be established using the SET command.

4.3 STRUCTURAL EQUATION MODELS

Structural equation modeling is also referred to as *latent-variable analysis* or *linear structural relationships* (Duncan, 1975; Loehlin, 1992). These terms are used because structural equation models establish the relationship between latent variables. In establishing latent-variable relationships, structural equation models differ from path analysis models, which use only observed variables (Lomax, 1982; Long, 1983). Given the importance of establishing relationships among theoretical constructs, structural equation models have become widely used in the social and behavioral sciences (Anderson, 1987; Bollen & Ting, 1991; Fassinger, 1987; Saris & Stronkhorst, 1984).

In building structural equation models, one must first specify the measurement models, as previously discussed. The confirmatory factor-analytic techniques assess how well the observed variables define the latent variables of interest. In structural equation models, both the independent and dependent latent-variable measurement models are used. The structural equations specify the prediction of the dependent latent variable(s) by the independent latent variable(s).

Structural models can take several different forms. For example, a single independent latent variable can predict a single dependent latent variable (Fig. 4.2a); both latent dependent variables may have a reciprocal relationship (Fig. 4.2b); two independent latent variables can correlate in the prediction of a single dependent latent variable (Fig. 4.2c); or one independent latent variable can predict another latent variable, which in turn predicts a third latent variable (Fig. 4.2d).

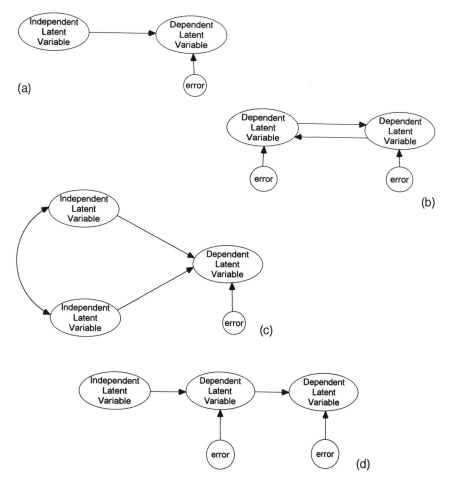

FIG. 4.2. Structural model types. (a) One predictor. (b) Reciprocal prediction. (c) Two predictors that covary. (d) Mediated prediction.

The EQS5 program syntax does not require matrix notation for expressing the measurement and structural equations in a model (Bentler, 1992). The EQS5 program, as noted before, uses four basic prefixes to specify equations: observed variables (V), observed-variable error (E), latent variables (F), and latent-variable error (D). The /EQUATIONS statement identifies which observed variables define which latent variables and their corresponding residual error, as well as the structural equations that relate the latent independent and dependent variables. The equations can be taken directly from the paths of the observed- and latent-variable relationships diagrammed in the model.

A path diagram can be helpful in depicting the specific relationships between the independent and dependent latent variables of interest, given a theoretical perspective. For example, the Bentler–Weeks EQS5 representation of a structural model that combines the latent-variable measurement models into a structural model is depicted in Fig. 4.3.

The use of the EQS5 prefixes permits diagramming the structural model so that both the observed variables and their associated measurement error (in measurement models), and the relationships of independent to dependent latent variables (in the structural model) and their errors of prediction, can be indicated. The path diagram in Fig. 4.3 uses the standard accepted graphing techniques, in which squares or rectangular boxes identify observed variables and circles or ellipses (ovals) identify latent variables. Arrows that lead from a circle or an ellipse to the square boxes identify observed variables that measure the respective latent variables. For example, V1 and V2 are observed variables that define the latent independent variable F1. Likewise, V3 and V4 are observed variables that define the latent dependent variable F2. Each of the observed variables has a corresponding measurement error term prefixed by an E. In the Bentler–Weeks representation, when an arrow leads from one latent variable to another, it defines the independent latent variable, the dependent latent variable, and the error-of-prediction or disturbance term. In Fig. 4.3, F1 is an independent latent variable predicting F2, a dependent latent variable, with error of prediction D2.

The Bentler–Weeks representation, therefore, only uses three matrices to define structural equation models: (1) a variance–covariance matrix of independent latent variables, (2) a regression coefficient matrix of independent and dependent variables, and (3) a regression matrix of only dependent variables.

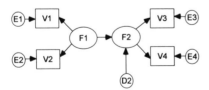

FIG. 4.3. Bentler–Weeks structural equation model.

The /EQUATIONS command to specify the model in Fig. 4.3 would be as follows:

```
/EQUATIONS
  V1 = F1 + E1;
  V2 = F1 + E2;
  V3 = F2 + E3;
  V4 = F2 + E4;
  F2 = F1 + D2;
```

Each observed variable is designated using a V prefix, and is specified to load on a latent variable denoted using the F prefix. Each observed variable has a corresponding measurement error specified by using an E prefix. These represent the measurement model. The structural equation is indicated by a path from the latent independent variable to the latent dependent variable, and indicated as F2 = F1 + D2;. This represents the structural model, and the equation indicates that the latent dependent variable, F2, is predicted by the latent independent variable, F1, with an equation prediction error or disturbance term, D2. The /EQUATIONS command therefore includes both the *measurement* models for the latent variables (independent and dependent) and the *structural* model, which establishes the relationship between the independent and dependent latent variables. The complete EQS5 program for the model depicted in Fig. 4.3 is found in the computer program section at the end of the chapter.

The LISREL8-SIMPLIS command language is just as easy to use to specify the measurement models for the latent independent and dependent variables, as well as the relationships in the structural equation model. For example, the Observed Variables: command specifies the observed variables in the data input. The observed variables can be identified using up to eight characters to name them; names may include generic variable names such as X1, V1, or Y1. In our example, the observed variables were named X1, X2, Y1, and Y2. A Covariance matrix: command is used to specify the variance–covariance matrix among these observed variables, and a Sample size: command is used to indicate the number of subjects. A Latent variable: command is then used to provide names for the latent variables, again using up to eight characters; names include F1, Factor1, etc. In our example the latent variables were named Factor1 and Factor2. The Relationships: command is used to specify the measurement models and structural equations. The LISREL8-SIMPLIS commands to specify the latent variables and their relationships for Fig. 4.3 would be:

```
Latent Variables: Factor1 Factor2
Relationships:
  X1 - X2 = Factor1
  Y1 - Y2 = Factor2
  Factor2 = Factor1
```

The LISREL8-SIMPLIS command language does not require any specification of error terms for the observed variables in the measurement models, or the equation prediction error for the structural equation. Additionally, one does not have to enter an expression, such as 1*, before any of the observed variables to have parameters estimated. The complete LISREL8-SIMPLIS program is given in the computer program section at the end of the chapter.

If you have not already purchased one of these programs or inquired about their availability at your computing center, now is a good time to contact the sources listed in chapter 1. You will soon find out how easy it is to run these confirmatory measurement models and structural equation models on your personal computer in MS Windows!

4.4 TWO-STEP APPROACH

James, Mulaik, and Brett (1982) proposed a two-step modeling approach that emphasized the analysis of two conceptually distinct latent variable models: measurement and structural. Anderson and Gerbing (1988) further described their approach by stating that the measurement model provided an assessment of convergent and discriminant validity and the structural model provided an assessment of predictive validity. Mulaik, James, Alstine, Bennett, Lind, and Stilwell (1989) also expanded the idea of assessing the fit of the structural equation model among latent variables (that is, the structural model) independently of assessing the fit of the observed variables to the latent variables (that is, measurement model). Their rationale was that even with a few latent variables, most parameter estimates define the relationships of the observed variables to the latent variables in the measurement model, rather than the structural equation relationships of the latent variables themselves. Jöreskog and Sörbom (1993, p. 113) summarized these thoughts when they stated:

> The testing of the structural model, i.e., the testing of the initially specified theory, may be meaningless unless it is first established that the measurement model holds. If the chosen indicators for a construct do not measure that construct, the specified theory must be modified before it can be tested. Therefore, the measurement model should be tested before the structural relationships are tested. It may be useful to do this for each construct separately, then for the constructs taken two at a time, and then for all constructs simultaneously. In doing so, one should let the constructs themselves be freely correlated, i.e., the covariance matrix of the constructs should be unconstrained.

We have found it prudent to follow their advice. In the establishment of measurement models for either latent independent or dependent variables, it is best to identify a few good indicators of the latent variable. In our example, we intentionally used only a few indicators to define or measure the latent variables. We have also found that when selecting only a few indicator variables, it is easier to check how well each observed variable defines a latent variable, that is, to examine the factor loadings, reliabilities, and amount of latent-variable variance explained. For example, rather than use the items that constituted a test, use the test scores. In addition, one can calculate the reliability of the test scores and fix that value in the model, thus reducing the need to estimate one parameter. Once latent variables are adequately defined (measured), and only then, does it make sense to examine the latent-variable relationships in a structural model. Hereto, a researcher should establish a theoretical basis for the latent-variable relationships.

4.5 SUMMARY

This chapter has focused on how to develop structural equation models using path diagrams, indicated the relationships using EQS5 and LISREL8-SIMPLIS command language, and noted the basic concepts of measurement and structural equation models. Basically, confirmatory factor analysis yields a measurement model for defining and assessing the latent variables, and structural equations are specified between the independent latent variables and the dependent latent variables to indicate the structural model. The path diagrams using squares or rectangles for observed variables and circles or ellipses (ovals) for latent variables afford a diagramming method to indicate the combined measurement models and structural model.

An important point to emphasize in diagramming structural equation models is that the relationships among the latent variables are subject to substantive theory (model specification and model validity). The use of this methodology is also impacted by the requirement of sufficient sample size, interpretation of model fit indices, missing data, outliers, parameter identification, multivariate normality, and the research hypothesis being tested (Fornell, 1983). Bagozzi and Yi (1988) also cited problems with the evaluation of model fit and concerns related to validity, cross validation, power, and generalizations from structural models. Future efforts by researchers will help to further clarify these issues and bring into focus the five steps of structural equation modeling, especially given the usefulness of structural equation models to theory.

COMPUTER PROGRAMS

EQS5 Program

```
/TITLE
 Measurement Models and Structural Model
/SPECIFICATIONS
  CAS=200; VAR=4; ME=ML;
```

```
/EQUATIONS
  V1 = F1 + E1;
  V2 = F1 + E2;
  V3 = F2 + E3;
  V4 = F2 + E4;
  F2 = F1 + D2;
/VARIANCES
        F1 = 1*;
  E1 TO E4 = 1*;
        D2 = 1*;
/MATRIX
1.024
 .792    1.077
1.027     .919    1.844
 .756     .697    1.244    1.286
/DIAGRAM
  E1   E2   E3   E4;
  V1   V2   V3   V4;
     F1        F2        D2;
/END
```

LISREL8-SIMPLIS Program

```
Measurement models and Structural Model
Observed Variables: X1 X2 X3 X4
Covariance matrix:
1.024
 .792    1.077
1.027     .919    1.844
 .756     .697    1.244    1.286
Sample size: 200
Latent Variables: Factor1 Factor2
Relationships:
  X1-X2 = Factor1
  X3-X4 = Factor2
  Factor2 = Factor1
End of Problem
```

REFERENCES

Anderson, J. G. (1987). Structural equation models in the social and behavioral sciences: Model building. *Child Development, 58*, 49–64.

Anderson, J. C., & Gerbing, D. W. (1988). Structural equation modeling in practice: A review and recommended two-step approach. *Psychological Bulletin, 103*(3), 411–423.

Bagozzi, R. P., & Yi, Y. (1988). On the evaluation of structural equation models. *Journal of the Academy of Marketing Science, 16*(1), 74–94.

Bentler, P. M. (1992). *EQS structural equations program manual*. Los Angeles: BMDP Statistical Software.

Bollen, K. A., & Long, J. S. (Eds.). (1993). *Testing structural equation models*. Newbury Park, CA: Sage.

Bollen, K. A., & Ting, K. (1991). Statistical computing software reviews. *The American Statistician, 45*(1), 68–73.

Duncan, O. D. (1975). *Introduction to structural equation models*. New York: Academic Press.

Fassinger, R. (1987). Use of structural equation modeling in counseling psychology research. *Journal of Counseling Psychology, 34*, 425–440.

Fornell, C. (1983). Issues in the application of covariance structure analysis: A comment. *Journal of Consumer Research, 9*, 443–450.

James, L. R., Mulaik, S. A., & Brett, J. M. (1982). *Causal analysis: Assumptions, models, and data*. Beverly Hills, CA: Sage.

Jöreskog, K. G., & Sörbom, D. (1993). *LISREL8: Structural equation modeling with the SIMPLIS command language*. Hillsdale, NJ: Lawrence Erlbaum Associates.

Kim, J., & Mueller, C. W. (1978a). *Factor analysis: Statistical methods and practical issues*. Beverly Hills, CA: Sage.

Kim, J., & Mueller, C. W. (1978b). *Introduction to factor analysis: What it is and how to do it*. Beverly Hills, CA: Sage.

Loehlin, J. C. (1992). *Latent variable models: An introduction to factor, path, and structural analysis* (2nd ed.). Hillsdale, NJ: Lawrence Erlbaum Associates.

Lomax, R. G. (1982). A guide to LISREL-type structural equation modeling. *Behavior Research Methods and Instrumentation, 14*, 1–8.

Long, J. S. (1983). *Confirmatory factor analysis*. Beverly Hills, CA: Sage.

Mulaik, S. A., James, L. R., Alstine, J. V., Bennett, N., Lind, S., & Stilwell, C. D. (1989). Evaluation of goodness-of-fit indices for structural equation models. *Psychological Bulletin, 105*, 430–445.

Rindskopf, D., & Rose, T. (1988). Some theory and applications of confirmatory second-order factor analysis. *Multivariate Behavioral Research, 23*, 51–67.

Saris, W. E., & Stronkhorst, L. H. (1984). *Causal modelling in nonexperimental research: An introduction to the LISREL approach*. Amsterdam: Sociometric Research Foundation.

5

DEVELOPING STRUCTURAL EQUATION MODELS: PART 2

---◆◆◆---

Chapter Outline:

Key Concepts:

Observed (indicator) variables
Latent variables
Factor loadings and structure coefficients
Equation errors and measurement errors
Total, direct, and indirect "effects"

In the previous chapters, we examined some basic concepts underlying structural equation modeling, some of which you were probably familiar with. These basic concepts serve as building blocks for structural equation modeling. In this chapter we add some new concepts that you may not be as familiar with. We consider the concepts of observed or indicator variables, latent variables, structure coefficients, equation errors, factor loadings, measurement errors, different covariance terms, diagrams of structural equation models, and different types of "effects" (total, direct, and indirect "effects"). Chapter 11 further describes the basic model presented in this chapter, but uses the traditional LISREL8 matrix notation format. We have included the matrix format in chapter 11 because it can be outputted by the SIMPLIS program, and the presentation further aids in understanding how eight different matrices are used to analyze structural equation models in LISREL8.

5.1 OBSERVED (INDICATOR) VARIABLES AND LATENT VARIABLES

For analysis procedures that you are already familiar with, the use of X and Y to denote variables is quite sufficient. We might use X to refer to a set of predictor (independent) variables and Y to refer to one or more criterion (dependent) variables; this is the case in multiple linear regression, analysis of variance, and all general linear models. In structural equation modeling, however, the defining of variables is somewhat more complex.

In structural equation modeling, there are two major types of variables: observed, or indicator variables; and latent variables. Latent variables are variables that are not directly observable or measured; they must be observed or measured indirectly, hence, inferred. For example, intelligence is a latent variable and represents a psychological construct. Intelligence cannot be directly observed (e.g., through visual inspection of an individual), and thus there is no single, agreed-upon definition or measure of intelligence. However, intelligence can be indirectly measured through observed or indicator variables. Observed or indicator variables are variables that are directly observable or measured. For example, the Wechsler Intelligence Scale for Children–Revised (WISC–R) is an instrument commonly used to measure children's intelligence. The instrument itself represents one definition or interpretation of intelligence. Other researchers rely on other definitions or interpretations, and thus other instruments (e.g., the Stanford–Binet Intelligence Scale). To summarize, latent variables (e.g., intelligence) are not directly observable but can be indirectly measured or inferred through observable or indicator variables (e.g., by means of WISC–R).

Let us further examine the concept behind latent variables. Consider a simple model in which we propose that one latent variable influences a second latent variable. For instance, say that intelligence is believed to have an impact on subsequent scholastic achievement, as could be depicted in the following:

Intelligence → achievement.

In this instance, intelligence is an independent or predictor variable of achievement, which is a dependent or criterion variable. Any latent variable that is influenced by some other latent variable in the model is known as a *latent dependent variable*. As was shown, a latent dependent variable has at least one directed line or arrow leading into it from another latent variable. Any latent variable that is not influenced by any other latent variable in the model is known as a *latent independent variable*. As shown, the latent independent variable intelligence does not have any directed lines or arrows leading into it from another latent variable. In our simple model, intelligence is the latent independent variable with no directed lines or arrows leading into it from other latent variables in the model, and achievement is the latent dependent variable, with a directed line or arrow leading into it from intelligence.

Consider adding a third latent variable to our model, such that achievement is measured at two points in time. This model would be depicted as follows:

Intelligence → achievement$_1$ → achievement$_2$.

Intelligence is still a latent independent variable. Achievement$_2$ is clearly a latent dependent variable, because there is a directed line or arrow leading into it from achievement$_1$. However, there is one directed line or arrow leading into achievement$_1$ from intelligence, and another leading from it to achievement$_2$. In other words, achievement$_1$ is influenced by intelligence and subsequently influences achievement$_2$. Thus, achievement$_1$ might be considered both an independent and a dependent latent variable, depending on how you look at it. To simplify matters, we shall define such a latent variable as a dependent latent variable, because there is a directed line or arrow leading into it from another latent variable in the model. The key, then, is to look for the arrows between the latent variables. If no arrows lead into a latent variable from another latent variable in the model, then it is a latent *independent* variable (as was intelligence). If any arrows lead into a latent variable from another latent variable in the model, then it is a latent *dependent* variable (as were achievement$_1$ and achievement$_2$).

Next, let us consider the concept behind the observed or indicator variables. The latent independent variables are measured by observed independent variables, traditionally denoted by the *X*s. The latent dependent variables are measured by observed dependent variables, traditionally denoted by Ys. Following our example, we might choose the WISC–R and the Stanford–Binet as observed independent measures of the latent independent variable intelligence. We can denote these observed variables as X_1 and X_2. For each of the achievement latent dependent variables, we might choose the California Achievement Test and the Metropolitan Achievement Test as our observed dependent measures. If these measures are observed at two points in time, then we can denote the observed variables of achievement$_1$ as Y_1 and Y_2, and those of achievement$_2$ as Y_3 and Y_4, respectively.

In our example, each latent variable is measured by two observed variables. What is the benefit of using more than one observed variable to assess a latent variable? In using a single observed variable to assess a latent variable, we assume that no measurement error is associated with the measurement of that latent variable. In other words, it is assumed that the latent variable is perfectly measured by the single observed variable. We define measurement error quite generally here to include errors due to reliability and validity problems. Reliability is concerned with the ability of a measure to be consistent. That is, would Kristen's score on the WISC–R be about the same if measured today as compared with next week? Evidence of score reliability could be shown when a measure is given to the same individual or group of individuals at two points in time and the scores are roughly equivalent. If only a single measure of a latent variable is used and it is not very reliable, then our latent variable is not assessed very well. If the reliability of a single observed measure of a latent variable is known, then it is prudent to specify or fix the value in the model.

Validity is concerned with the extent to which scores accurately define the construct. Our interest in validity is related to how well we can make an inference from the scores on the latent variable, that is, how well test scores assess what they purport to measure. Does Kristen's score on the WISC–R really measure her intelligence, or something else, such as her height (e.g., in centimeters)? Evidence of validity could be shown when two indicators of the same latent variable are substantially correlated. Thus, if the WISC–R and height were both used as indicators of the latent variable intelligence, we would expect them to be unrelated (or at least not substantially correlated). If only a single measure of a latent variable is used and it is not very valid (e.g., if height is used to measure intelligence), then our latent variable is not assessed very well. However, establishing the reliability of the single observed variable helps in estimating the validity coefficient or factor loading in our measurement model.

If we wanted to select observed measures of intelligence, the selection of both the WISC–R and height would certainly include some measurement error, and the selection of only height would be fraught with measurement error. Thus, in the selection of observed measures to define a given latent variable, we need to consider measures that show evidence of both reliability and validity for the intended purpose of our study. Because of the inherent difficulty involved in obtaining reliable and valid measurement with a single measure, we strongly encourage you to consider multiple measures of each latent variable. There are a few obvious exceptions to this recommendation, such as when there are accepted measuring instruments (which boost validity) and rules for using them (which boost reliability), or when only one observed measure is available. In the latter case you have no choice other than to assume that there is no measurement error (whether this is a correct assumption or not), or you must specify a reliability value for the single measure. Jöreskog and Sörbom (1993, p. 37) provided a rationale and example for setting the reliability of a single observed measure:

> The verbal intelligence test VERBINTM is a fallible measure and it is therefore unreasonable to assume that its error variance is zero. Instead, we assume that the reliability of VERBINTM is 0.85. It is argued that an arbitrary value of 0.85 is a better assumption than an equally arbitrary value of 1.00. The assumed value of the reliability will affect parameter estimates as well as standard errors. A reliability of 0.85 for VERBINTM is equivalent to an error variance of 0.15 times the variance of VERBINTM. Thus, we assume that the error variance of VERBINTM is $0.15 \times 3.65^2 = 1.998$.

If we can specify a reasonable reliability value for an observed variable, then multiplying the observed variable's variance by 1 minus the reliability provides a reasonable estimate of error variance. In the LISREL8-SIMPLIS program, a single observed variable's error variance can be set, and so the reliability of the single observed variable is automatically defined. This is accomplished by using the SET command as follows:

```
SET the error variance of VERTINTM to 1.998
```

Later in this chapter, we further present how measurement error is explicitly a part of structural equation modeling. The basic concept, however, is that multiple observed variables used in defining a particular latent variable permit measurement error to be estimated through structural equation modeling. This provides the researcher with additional information about the measurement characteristics of the observed variables. When there is only a single observed indicator of a latent variable, then measurement error cannot be estimated through structural equation modeling. The EQS5 and LISREL8-SIMPLIS programs, however, permit the specification of reliabilities for single or multiple variables, whether the values are known or require our best guess. In the next two sections of this chapter, we discuss the two models that make up structural equation modeling: the measurement model and the structural model.

5.2 MEASUREMENT MODEL

As previously mentioned, the researcher specifies the measurement model to allow for certain relationships between the latent variables and the observed variables. Using our previous example, suppose that the latent independent variable intelligence was measured by two observed variables, the WISC–R and the Stanford–Binet. Our latent dependent variables achievement$_1$ and achievement$_2$ are each measured by the same two observed variables, the California Achievement Test and the Metropolitan Achievement Test. These observed variables are actually a composite of numerous individual items. It should be pointed out that one could use each item on an instrument as an observed variable, hence confirming the unidimensional construct of the instrument, using traditional factor-analytic techniques. The use of items from an instrument, however, to measure the latent variables in a structural model increases the degrees of freedom in the structural equation model and may cause problems in model fit. Suffice it to say that measurement characteristics at the item level might be more appropriate for exploratory data-reduction methods than they are for structural equation models.

The researcher is typically interested in having the following questions answered about the observed variables: To what extent are the observed variables actually measuring the hypothesized latent variable—that is, how good is the California test as a measure of achievement? Which observed variable is the best measure of a particular latent variable—that is, is the California test a better measure of achievement than the Metropolitan test? To what extent are the observed variables actually measuring something other than the hypothesized latent variable—that is, is the California test measuring something other than achievement, such as quality of education received? These are the types of questions that measurement models address.

In our measurement model, each latent variable is assessed by two indicator variables. The relationships between the observed variables and the latent variables are described by factor loadings. The factor loadings provide us with information about the extent to which a given observed variable is able to measure the latent variable. They serve as a validity coefficient. Measurement error is defined as that portion of an observed variable that is measuring something other than what the latent variable is hypothesized to measure. It serves as a measure of reliability. Measurement error could be the result of (a) an observed variable that is measuring some other latent variable, (b) unreliability, or (c) a second-order factor. For example, the California test may be measuring something besides achievement, or it may not be a very reliable measure. Thus, we would like to know about the amount of measurement error associated with each observed variable.

In our measurement model, there are six measurement equations, one for each observed variable, which can be illustrated as follows:

$$\text{California}_1 = \text{function of achievement}_1 + \text{error}$$
$$\text{Metropolitan}_1 = \text{function of achievement}_1 + \text{error}$$
$$\text{California}_2 = \text{function of achievement}_2 + \text{error}$$
$$\text{Metropolitan}_2 = \text{function of achievement}_2 + \text{error}$$
$$\text{WISC–R} = \text{function of intelligence} + \text{error}$$
$$\text{Stanford–Binet} = \text{function of intelligence} + \text{error}$$

A more explicit definition of the measurement model is possible using either the EQS5 or the LISREL8-SIMPLIS command language for the indicator and latent variables under consideration. Let us begin with the EQS5 program, where the measurement model equations are written in terms of "V" variables for the observed indicator variables, "F" variables for the latent variables or factors, and "E" variables for the measurement errors. The following labels are used in the EQS5 program to better describe these variables: $F1$ = achievement$_1$, $F2$ = achievement$_2$, $F3$ = intelligence, $V1$ = California$_1$, $V2$ = Metropolitan$_1$, $V3$ = California$_2$, $V4$ = Metropolitan$_2$, $V5$ = WISC–R, and $V6$ = Stanford–Binet. The measurement model equations in EQS5 would be specified as:

```
/EQUATIONS
      V1 = F1 + E1;
      V2 = F1 + E2;
      V3 = F2 + E3;
      V4 = F2 + E4;
      V5 = F3 + E5;
      V6 = F3 + E6;
```

Since up to eight characters can be used to describe variables in the LISREL8-SIMPLIS program, one can expand the variable labels in the measurement model equations directly. The measurement model equations are specified using either the `Relationships:` or `Paths:` command (both methods are equivalent). For the `Relationships:` command, both the latent variables and the observed variables can be written as eight-character variable names, or in generic terms as Vs, Fs, and Es. The observed variables are given on the left-hand side of the equation (with spaces between the multiple observed variable names) and the latent variables on the right-hand side of the equation, as in the measurement equations that follow (where Achieve1 refers to achievement$_1$, Intell refers to intelligence, Achieve2 refers to achievement$_2$, Cal1 refers to California$_1$, Metro1 refers to Metropolitan$_1$,

Cal2 refers to California$_2$, Metro2 refers to Metropolitan$_2$, WISCR refers to WISC-R, and Stanford refers to Stanford-Binet):

```
Relationships:
  Call Metro1 = Achieve1
  Cal2 Metro2 = Achieve2
WISCR Stanford = Intell
```

For the Paths : command, the latent variables are depicted to the left of the arrow and the observed variables to the right of the arrow (with spaces between the multiple observed variable names), as in the following measurement equations:

```
Paths:
  Achieve1 -> Call Metro1
  Achieve2 -> Cal2 Metro2
  Intell -> WISCR Stanford
```

In summary, our particular model suggests that there are six factor loadings of interest. Other measurement models of these same latent and observed variables could be developed that contain different configurations of factor loadings (such as allowing the Stanford-Binet to be a measure of both intelligence and achievement$_1$). The assessment of latent variables by observed variables is part of the science of structural equation modeling and involves decisions about specifying and testing measurement models. Thinking about which factor loadings and which observed variables to include in a measurement model is part of that process.

5.3 STRUCTURAL MODEL

The researcher specifies the structural model to allow for certain relationships among the latent variables depicted by directed lines or arrows. In section 5.1, we specified that intelligence and achievement were related in a specific way. That is, it was our belief that intelligence had some influence on later achievement. Thus, one result from the structural model is an indication of the extent to which these a priori hypothesized relationships are supported by our sample data. Are intelligence and achievement related? How strong, exactly, is the influence of intelligence on achievement? Could there be other latent variables that we need to consider to get a better understanding of the influences on achievement? These are the types of questions that structural models address. As discussed in section 5.2, the researcher must first specify a measurement model to indicate that the latent variables are measured well (are valid and reliable) by selected observed variables. Afterwards, we can specify a structural model.

At this point we need to provide a more explicit definition of the structural model, and a specific notational system for the latent variables under consideration. Let us return to our previous example:

$$\text{Intelligence} \rightarrow \text{achievement}_1 \rightarrow \text{achievement}_2.$$

Since there are two latent dependent variables, there will be two structural equations. The first equation should indicate that achievement$_1$ is some function of intelligence. The second equation should indicate that achievement$_2$ is some function of achievement$_1$. It is these equations that compute the structure coefficients, which are of interest to us, because they indicate the strength (i.e., weak or strong) and direction (i.e., positive or negative) of the relationships among the latent variables. Each structural equation also contains an equation prediction error or disturbance term that indicates the portion of the latent dependent variable that is not explained or predicted by the latent independent variables in that equation. These two equations can be illustrated as follows:

$$\text{Achievement}_1 = \text{function of intelligence} + \text{error}$$
$$\text{Achievement}_2 = \text{function of achievement}_1 + \text{error}.$$

In this example, there are two structure coefficients. The first is for the influence of intelligence on achievement$_1$, and the second is for the influence of achievement$_1$ on achievement$_2$. Since there are two equations, there will also be two equation prediction error or disturbance terms.

The EQS5 and LISREL8-SIMPLIS command language permit an easy way to specify structural relationships among latent variables. First, in the EQS5 program (Bentler, 1993), the structural equations are written in terms of "F" variables for the latent variables or factors, and "D" variables for the equation errors or disturbances. The /LABEL command allows us to further describe these variables: F1 = achievement$_1$, F2 = achievement$_2$, and F3 = intelligence. The EQS5 structural equations would be specified as:

```
/EQUATIONS
      F1 = F3 + D1;
      F2 = F1 + D2;
```

Notice that F3 (intelligence) is predicting F1 (achievement$_1$) and F1 is predicting F2 (achievement$_2$). The dependent latent variables therefore appear on the left side of the equation, while the independent latent variables are indicated on the right side of the structural equations along with the prediction error terms.

In the LISREL8-SIMPLIS program, the structural model can be denoted in terms of either Relationships: or Paths: commands (both methods are equivalent). For the `Relationships:` command, the latent variables can be written using either eight-character variable names or generic values (F1, F2, etc.) with the latent dependent variable on the left side of the equality (=) sign, as in the structural equations that follow (where Achieve1 refers to achievement$_1$, Intell refers to intelligence, and Achieve2 refers to achievement$_2$):

```
Relationships:
  Achieve1 = Intell
  Achieve2 = Achieve1
```

For the `Paths:` command, the latent variables can also be written using either variable names or generic names, with the latent dependent variable to the right of the arrow, as in the following structural equations:

```
Paths:
  Intell -> Achieve1
  Achieve1 -> Achieve2
```

Notice that no specification of equation prediction error is required for using either the `Relationships:` or `Paths:` commands.

In summary, our model suggests that there are two structure coefficients of interest. Other structural models, using these same latent variables, could be specified that contain different structure coefficients (such as allowing intelligence to influence achievement$_2$). Thus, part of the science of structural equation modeling involves the researcher's decision about which structural model(s) to explicitly specify and test. Thinking about which structure coefficients and which latent variables to include in a structural model is part of that process.

5.4 COVARIANCES

As we noted earlier, in chapter 3, structural equation modeling involves the decomposition of covariances; thus, a synonym for this type of modeling is *covariance structure analysis*, or *covariance structure modeling*. In this section, we further explore how covariances are analyzed. There are three different covariance terms that we need to define and understand. From the structural model, there are two covariance terms to consider. First, there is a covariance matrix of the latent independent variables. This consists of the variances for each latent independent variable, as well as covariances among them. While we are interested in the variances (e.g., the amount of variance associated with the latent independent variable intelligence), the covariances may or may not be part of our theoretical model. In our model, there is only one latent independent variable, and so there is only one variance term and no covariance term.

If we specified two latent independent variables in a different model—for example, intelligence and home background—we could include a covariance term for them. We would then be hypothesizing that intelligence and home background are correlated or covary because we believe that some common unmeasured latent variable is influencing both of them. We could also hypothesize that a latent variable not included in the model, such as parenting ability, influences both intelligence and home background. In other words, intelligence and home background covary, or are correlated because of their mutual influence from parenting ability, which has not explicitly been included in the model (but which perhaps could be included).

In the EQS5 program, variances and covariances are specified using the /VARIANCES and /COVARIANCES commands, respectively. For our example, the /VARIANCES would be automatically given in the output for F3 (the latent independent variable intelligence). A covariance term, if one existed, would be given in the output under /COVARIANCES for F3, F4, the covariance between F3 and F4. In the LISREL8-SIMPLIS program, the variance term would automatically be given or implied for the latent independent variable intelligence. A covariance term, if one existed, would also automatically be given or implied in the program. If one desired the two latent independent variables intelligence and home background to be uncorrelated or to have a covariance of 0 (zero), then one would specify the following in the LISREL8-SIMPLIS program:

```
Set the Covariance between Intell and HomeBack to 0
```

The second set of covariance terms that we need to define and understand is in the covariance matrix of the equation prediction errors. This consists of the variances for each equation prediction error (i.e., the amount of unexplained variance for each structural equation), as well as the covariances among them. While we are interested in the variances, the covariances may or may not be part of our model. We could specify that two equation prediction errors are correlated or covary, perhaps because some unmeasured latent variable is leading to error in both equations. An example of this might be where parental occupational status (i.e., parental income) is not included as a latent variable in a model where children's education (in years) and children's occupational status (e.g., income at age 30) are latent dependent variables. The structural equations for children's education and children's occupational status would then both contain equation prediction error due to the omission of parental occupational status. Because the same latent variable was not included in both equations, we expect that the equation prediction errors for these two equations would covary or be correlated. Please note that our model does not contain any such covariance terms.

In the EQS5 program, these terms are specified using the /VARIANCES and /COVARIANCES commands, respectively. In our example, the variances are specified in the program under the /VARIANCES command for D1 and D2 (D1 TO D2 = 1*;), and their covariance would be specified in the program under the /COVARIANCES command (D1, D2 = 1*;), although not part of our model and program. In the LISREL8-SIMPLIS program, the variance and covariance terms are automatically included in the computer program for each structural equation. Since the covariance terms are assumed by the program to be set to zero, one must specify in the program any covariance terms one wants estimated. A covariance term, if one existed between achievement$_1$ and achievement$_2$, would be specified using the following command:

```
Set the Error Covariance between Achieve1 and Achieve2 free
```

The third set of covariance terms in the measurement model we need to define and understand is concerned with the variances and covariances of the measurement errors. While we are interested in the variances (i.e., the amount of measurement error variance associated with each observed variable), the covariances may or may not be part of our model. We could hypothesize that the measurement errors for two observed variables are correlated or covary (the hypothesis is known as *correlated measurement error*). This might be expected in our model where the indicators of the latent variables achievement$_1$ and achievement$_2$ are the same (e.g., the California Achievement Test). We might believe that the measurement error associated with the California Achievement Test at Time 1 is related to the measurement error for the California Achievement Test at Time 2.

In the EQS5 program, these variances and covariances are specified using the /VARIANCES and /COVARIANCES commands, respectively. In our example, the variances are specified in the program under the /VARIANCES command for E1 through E9 (E1 to E9 = 1*;), and the covariances are specified in the program under the /COVARIANCES command (E6, E7 = 1*;). In the LISREL8-SIMPLIS program, the variance and covariance terms are automatically specified in the program for each observed variable. Once again, the covariance terms are assumed by the program to be set to zero, and so one must specify any covariance term of interest and allow it to become free (estimated). A covariance term, if one existed between the measurement errors for the California Achievement Test at Times 1 and 2, would be specified using the following command:

```
Set the Error Covariance between Cal1 and Cal2 free
```

There is one final covariance term that we need to mention, and it really represents the ultimate covariance term. From the parameters we estimate in the structural model, the measurement model, and the covariances, we can generate an ultimate matrix of covariances for the overall model. This matrix is implied by the overall model and is denoted by Σ (see chap. 11 for further explanation). As we shall discuss in chapter 6, one of the purposes of the statistical analysis is to estimate the parameters of the model and then to test the overall fit of the data to our model. In short, the parameters in Σ are estimated from the sample matrix S, which is composed of the sample variances and covariances among our observed variables. As we discuss later, the closeness of the values in the covariance matrix, Σ, as implied by our model, and the sample covariance matrix, S, as implied by our sample data, gives us one indication of the fit of our model. More information about fit indices is found in chapter 7.

5.5 DIAGRAMMING STRUCTURAL EQUATION MODELS

At this point you are probably thinking, enough with the equations. Can we make some connections to reality? Consequently, in this section, we consider how to depict the structural equation model graphically, and in section 5.7 we provide a detailed example of all of the concepts described in this and the previous chapter.

We previously described in this chapter our rationale for the measurement model and structural model, but did not diagram them. Only a few years ago models had to be diagrammed by hand with templates and straightedges. Today, individual programs are available to diagram models (e.g., LISPATH uses LISREL matrix notation—Marcoulides, 1994; or one can use Harvard Graphics, CorelDraw, etc.), and the newer Windows-based personal computer programs provide a diagram of the model (e.g., LISREL8-SIMPLIS, after the program runs; EQS5, uses the /DIAGRAM command or DRAW option; and AMOSDraw, uses models for analysis and has a separate graphics user interface with an icon toolbox to draw diagrams). Thus, the time of having to use CorelDraw, PCPaint, Harvard Graphics, and similar standalone graphics programs has passed (although these skills still come in handy). In the future, we suspect that the structural equation modeling programs will be even more capable of providing model diagrams for export into word-processing packages. You can accomplish model exporting now by using AMOSDraw for Windows and putting the image on the clipboard. Then, while in your word-processing package for Windows (e.g., WordPerfect), simply paste the diagram into the document. You can also print directly from AMOSDraw. EQS5 also has these capabilities, as do some of the other graphics packages.

When using the structural equation modeling programs or standalone graphics packages, please keep in mind the following graphing conventions that have come to be adopted over the years. Observed variables are enclosed by *rectangles* or *squares*, latent variables are enclosed by *ellipses* (*ovals*) or *circles*, and error terms (i.e., measurement errors and equation errors) are not enclosed, or in our case have been included in smaller circles. The following relationships are depicted by *straight lines* (i.e., with an arrow at only one end): (a) the structure coefficients that relate the latent variables to one another, (b) the factor loadings that relate the latent variables to the observed variables, (c) the relationships between the measurement errors and their observed variable, and (d) the relationships between the equation prediction errors and their respective latent dependent variables. The following relationships are depicted by *curved lines* with arrows at both ends, because they represent covariances: (a) covariances among the latent independent variables, (b) covariances among the equation prediction errors, and (c) covariances among the measurement errors.

In the LISREL8-SIMPLIS program, the `Path Diagram` command may be used to generate the following five different path diagrams: (a) S for structural relationships (i.e., the structural model), (b) X for independent measurement relationships (i.e., the measurement model for the Xs), (c) Y for dependent measurement relationships (i.e., the measurement model for the Ys); (d) R for error covariances (i.e., the covariances among the measurement errors), and (e) B for basic model (i.e., both the structural and measurement models). The B diagram, or basic model, for our example is shown in Fig. 5.1.

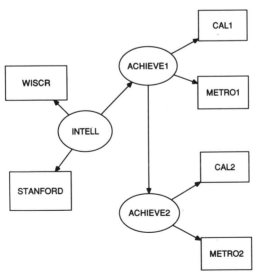

FIG. 5.1. Basic model in LISREL8 (B diagram).

The latent independent variable, intelligence, is defined by two observed variables, WISC–R and Stanford. We have chosen not to indicate their respective measurement error terms here. Similarly, $achievement_1$ and $achievement_2$ are defined by the California and Metropolitan tests, with their respective measurement errors also not indicated. Our interest is in the prediction of $achievement_1$ by intelligence, and then the subsequent prediction of $achievement_2$ by $achievement_1$.

5.6 TOTAL, DIRECT, AND INDIRECT "EFFECTS"

To this point, we have not used the terms *cause* and *effect* to refer to the latent independent and dependent variables, respectively. The reason is that structural equation models can at best only provide evidence of weak causal inference. Strong cause–effect inferences can be made only from experimental studies. Unfortunately, researchers have used these terms to describe structural equation modeling to the present. We often see the terms *cause*, *effect*, and *causal modeling* used in the research literature. We do not endorse this practice and therefore do not use these terms here. However, one term related to "effects" remains in common practice, and thus we use it. The term has to do with total, direct, and indirect "effects." Although we would prefer the use of something like *influences* rather than "*effects*," we realize a need to be consistent in our meaning. Please realize this caveat here, as we use the term in quotation marks ("effect" or "effects").

In order to fully illustrate this concept, we need to modify our model slightly to include a structural relationship between intelligence and $achievement_2$, which can be illustrated as:

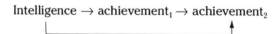

We define a direct "effect" between two latent variables when a single directed line or arrow connects them. A direct "effect" is measured by a structure coefficient. For instance, intelligence has a direct "effect" on $achievement_1$, intelligence has a direct "effect" on $achievement_2$ (which we now must add to the model depicted in Fig. 5.1), and $achievement_1$ has a direct "effect" on $achievement_2$.

We define an indirect "effect" between two latent variables when no single straight line or arrow directly connects them but when the first latent variable may be reached from the second latent variable through one or more other latent variables via their paths. An indirect "effect" is measured by the product of the structure coefficients involved. For instance, in our original model in Fig. 5.1, intelligence has an indirect "effect" on $achievement_2$ through achievement$_1$, measured by the product of the structure coefficients of the two direct "effects."

Finally, we define a total "effect" between two latent variables as the sum of any direct "effects" and/or indirect "effects" that connect them. For instance, the total "effect" of intelligence on achievement$_1$ is simply its direct "effect." The total "effect" of achievement$_1$ on achievement$_2$ is also simply its direct "effect." The total "effect" of intelligence on achievement$_2$ is the sum of (a) its direct "effect" and (b) the product of its two direct "effects" (i.e., the indirect "effect"). We describe another example of these "effects" in the next section.

5.7 EXAMPLE OF A COMPLETE STRUCTURAL EQUATION MODEL

We now specify a new model to further discuss how to diagram a model, specify the equations related to the model, and discuss the "effects" apparent in the model. This serves both as a second illustration of the concepts contained in this chapter and as a summary. The example we use is a model of educational achievement and aspirations. As shown in Fig. 5.2, there are four latent variables in the model depicted by ellipses: two latent independent variables, home background (abbreviated Home), and ability; and two latent dependent variables, aspirations (Aspire) and achievement (Achieve). Three of these latent variables are assessed by two indicator variables; and one latent variable, home background, is assessed by three indicator variables. The indicator variables are depicted in the rectangles

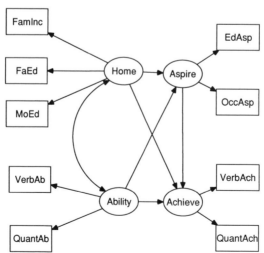

FIG. 5.2. Structural equation model (B diagram in LISREL8).

as follows: (a) for home background, family income (FamInc), father's education (FaEd), and mother's education (MoEd); (b) for ability, verbal ability (VerbAb) and quantitative ability (QuantAb); (c) for aspirations, educational aspiration (EdAsp) and occupational aspiration (OccAsp); and (d) for achievement, verbal achievement (VerbAch) and Quantitative Achievement (QuantAch). In the structural model, both latent independent variables are hypothesized to influence both latent dependent variables by using straight lines, resulting in four structure coefficients. Additionally, one latent dependent variable, Aspire, influences another latent dependent variable, Achieve, which specifies one additional structure coefficient in the model. We have also indicated by a curved arrow that the two latent independent variables Home and Ability covary.

In the measurement model, there are nine equations, one for each observed variable, which can be illustrated as follows:

Educational aspiration	=	function of aspirations + error
Occupational aspiration	=	function of aspirations + error
Verbal achievement	=	function of achievement + error
Quantitative achievement	=	function of achievement + error
Family income	=	function of home background + error
Father's education	=	function of home background + error
Mother's education	=	function of home background + error
Verbal ability	=	function of ability + error
Quantitative ability	=	function of ability + error

In the EQS5 program, the measurement model equations are written in terms of "V" variables for the observed indicator variables, "F" variables for the latent variables or factors, and "E" variables for the measurement errors of the observed variables. Once again, we can further describe these variables using a /LABEL command as F1 = Aspire, for aspirations; F2 = Achieve, for achievement; F3 = Home, for home background; F4 = Ability, for ability; V1 = EdAsp, for educational aspiration; V2 = OccAsp, for occupational aspiration; V3 = VerbAch, for verbal achievement; V4 = QuantAch, for quantitative achievement; V5 = FamInc, for family income; V6 = FaEd, for father's education; V7 = MoEd, for mother's education; V8 = VerbAb, for verbal ability; and V9 = QuantAb, for quantitative ability. This results in the following EQS5 measurement model equations:

```
/EQUATIONS
    V1 = F1 + E1;
    V2 = F1 + E2;
    V3 = F2 + E3;
    V4 = F2 + E4;
    V5 = F3 + E5;
```

```
V6 = F3 + E6;
V7 = F3 + E7;
V8 = F4 + E8;
V9 = F4 + E9;
```

In the LISREL8-SIMPLIS command language, the measurement model equations are written using variable names or generic terms: V1, X1, F1, etc. In the `Relationships:` command, the observed variables are specified on the left-hand side of the equation (with spaces between the multiple observed variable names) and the latent variables on the right-hand side. The LISREL8-SIMPLIS measurement equations are specified using variable names as:

```
Relationships:
  EdAsp OccAsp      = Aspire
  VerbAch QuantAch = Achieve
  FamInc FaEd MoEd  = Home
  VerbAb QuantAb    = Ability
```

For the `Paths:` command, the latent variables are specified to the left of the arrow and the observed variables to the right of the arrow (with spaces between the multiple observed variable names). These measurement equations are indicated as:

```
Paths:
  Aspire   -> EdAsp OccAsp
  Achieve -> VerbAch QuantAch
  Home     -> FamInc FaEd MoEd
  Ability -> VerbAb QuantAb
```

The structural equations for the model can be illustrated as:

Aspirations = home background + ability + error
Achievement = aspirations + home background + ability + error

In EQS5 (Bentler, 1993), the structural equations are written in terms of "F" variables for the latent variables or factors and "D" variables for the equation prediction errors or disturbances. The `/LABEL` command allows us to further describe these variables: F1 = Aspire, for aspirations; F2 = Achieve, for achievement; F3 = Home, for home background; and F4 = Ability, for ability. The EQS5 structural equations are specified as:

```
/EQUATIONS
  F1 = F3 + F4 + D1;
  F2 = F1 + F3 + F4 + D2;
```

In LISREL8-SIMPLIS (Jöreskog & Sörbom, 1993), the structural model can be specified using either a `Relationships:` or a `Paths:` command. Using a `Relationships:` command, the latent variables can be written as variable names (notice that either spaces or plus signs can be used between the latent independent variables) in the structural equations as:

```
Relationships:
  Aspire = Home Ability
  Achieve = Aspire Home Ability
```

For the `Paths:` command, the latent variables are specified to either the left or the right of the arrow (with spaces between the latent variables) as:

```
Paths:
  Home Ability -> Aspire
  Aspire Home Ability -> Achieve
```

Next, we must consider the three different types of covariances. First, we check for variances and covariances among the latent independent variables. For our model, there would be separate variance terms for home background and ability, and a term for the covariance between home background and ability. All of these terms would be automatically specified in the programs for both EQS5 and LISREL8-SIMPLIS. Second, we check for variances and covariances among the equation prediction errors. In the model, there would be separate variance terms for each of the two structural equations (i.e., aspirations and achievement) and no covariance term. These terms are also automatically specified in the programs for both EQS5 and LISREL8-SIMPLIS. Finally, we need to check for variance and covariance terms among the measurement errors of the observed variables. For the model depicted in Fig. 5.2, there are nine variance terms for the indicator variables and no covariance terms. These are also automatically specified in both software packages. If you would prefer to see the parameter estimates in the matrices used for the model, simply add the command LISREL OUTPUT before the END OF PROBLEM command in the LISREL8-SIMPLIS program.

Finally, the "effects" for this model need to be considered. The direct "effects" for aspirations are home background and ability. The direct "effects" for achievement are home background, ability, and aspirations. The indirect "effects" for achievement are ability through aspirations, and home background through aspirations. Thus, the total "effects" can be computed, and are illustrated as:

Home → Aspire   = direct effect
Ability → Aspire = direct effect
Home → Achieve = direct effect + indirect effect through Aspire

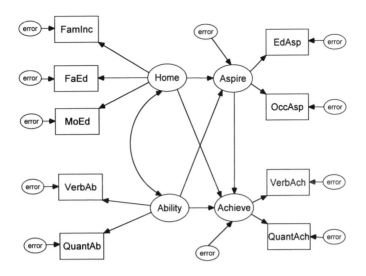

FIG. 5.3. Complete structural equation model.

Ability → Achieve = direct effect + indirect effect through Aspire
Aspire → Achieve = direct effect

The direct, indirect, and total "effects" are printed when using the LISREL OUTPUT command in the LISREL8-SIMPLIS program. These values are the parameter estimates for the paths in the model.

The complete structural model including the associated errors for the observed variables and the prediction errors of the two latent dependent variables is diagrammed in Fig. 5.3. The structure coefficients of interest are indicated by the paths from home background and ability to aspirations, home background and ability to achievement, and, finally, aspirations to achievement. Home background and ability, as indicated by a curved arrow, covary in their prediction of the two latent dependent variables. Both the complete EQS5 and LISREL8-SIMPLIS computer programs are included at the end of this chapter.

5.8 SUMMARY

In this chapter we have further considered the basic elements of structural equation modeling. We began the chapter with a look at observed and latent variables. Next, a discussion of the measurement and structural models was included. Here we extended some of the basic concepts found in confirmatory factor analysis (measurement model) and linear regression (structural model). In addition, several new concepts were introduced, such as structure coefficients, equation errors, factor loadings, measurement errors, various covariance terms, and direct, indirect, and total "effects." Afterward, we examined how structural equation models are diagrammed. The EQS5 and LISREL8-SIMPLIS syntax for the measurement and structural equations were included to illustrate and summarize these concepts.

You can review chapter 11 if you are interested in the LISREL8 matrix notation and output for the structural equation model postulated in this chapter. It is easier to run this basic model, however, using the LISREL8-SIMPLIS command language, and then simply adding the LISREL OUTPUT command to obtain the matrix output. We have chosen to include the matrix notation and concepts at the end of the book in chapter 11 so that you can further explore the matrix algebra involved in structural equation modeling.

In chapter 6, we begin a formal discussion of methods of estimation, assumptions, types of models, model identification, and model specification or respecification. This continues our discussion of the five steps involved in structural equation modeling listed in chapter 4.

COMPUTER PROGRAMS

EQS5 Program

```
/TITLE
 STRUCTURAL EQUATION MODEL EXAMPLE
/SPECIFICATIONS
 CAS=200; VAR=9; ME=ML;
/LABELS
 V1=EDASP;V2=OCCASP;V3=VERBACH;V4=QUANTACH;V5=FAMINC;V6=FAED;
 V7=MOED;V8=VERBAB;V9=QUANTAB;F1=ASPIRE;F2=ACHIEVE;F3=HOME;
 F4=ABILITY;
/EQUATIONS
 V1= F1 + E1;
 V2=1*F1 + E2;
 V3= F2 + E3;
 V4=1*F2 + E4;
 V5= F3 + E5;
 V6=1*F3 + E6;
 V7=1*F3 + E7;
 V8= F4 + E8;
 V9=1*F4 + E9;
 F1=1*F3 + 1*F4 + D1;
 F2=1*F1 + 1*F3 + 1*F4 + D2;
/VARIANCES
 E1 TO E9 = 1*;
 D1 TO D2 = 1*;
```

```
/COVARIANCES
 F3,F4=1*;
/MATRIX
1.024
 .792 1.077
1.027  .919 1.844
 .756  .697 1.244 1.286
 .567  .537  .876  .632  .852
 .445  .424  .677  .526  .518  .670
 .434  .389  .635  .498  .475  .545  .716
 .580  .564  .893  .716  .546  .422  .373  .851
 .491  .499  .888  .646  .508  .389  .339  .629  .871
/END
```

LISREL8-SIMPLIS Program

```
Structural Equation Model Example
Observed Variables: EDASP OCCASP VERBACH QUANTACH FAMINC FAED
                    MOED VERBAB QUANTAB
Covariance matrix:
1.024
 .792 1.077
1.027  .919 1.844
 .756  .697 1.244 1.286
 .567  .537  .876  .632  .852
 .445  .424  .677  .526  .518  .670
 .434  .389  .635  .498  .475  .545 .716
 .580  .564  .893  .716  .546  .422 .373 .851
 .491  .499  .888  .646  .508  .389 .339 .629 .871
Sample size: 200
Latent Variables: ASPIRE ACHIEVE HOME ABILITY
Relationships:
 EDASP OCCASP = ASPIRE
 VERBACH QUANTACH = ACHIEVE
 VERBAB QUANTAB = ABILITY
 FAMINC FAED MOED = HOME
 ASPIRE = ABILITY HOME
 ACHIEVE = ASPIRE ABILITY HOME
End of Problem
```

REFERENCES

Bentler, P. M. (1993). *EQS/Windows user's guide, version 4.0.* Los Angeles: BMDP Statistical Software, Inc.

Jöreskog, K. G., & Sörbom, D. (1993). *LISREL8: Structural equation modeling with the SIMPLIS command language.* Hillsdale, NJ: Lawrence Erlbaum Associates.

Marcoulides, G. A. (1994). Generating structural equation path diagrams using LISPATH. *Educational and Psychological Measurement, 53,* 675–678.

CHAPTER

6

ESTIMATION

Chapter Outline:

6.1 Identification

6.2 Estimation Procedures and Assumptions

6.3 Model Specification or Respecification

6.4 Example Structural Equation Model

6.5 Summary

Computer Programs
    EQS5
    LISREL8-SIMPLIS

References

Key Concepts:

Fixed, free, and constrained parameters
Under-, just-, and overidentified models
Recursive versus nonrecursive models
Methods of estimation
Model specification, misspecification, and respecification
Misspecification search

In chapter 3, we examined the basic building blocks of structural equation modeling. In chapters 4 and 5, we considered the concepts of observed or indicator variables, latent variables (both latent independent and latent dependent variables), structure coefficients, equation prediction errors, factor loadings, measurement errors, several covariance terms, diagrams of structural equation models, and different types of "effects" (total, direct, and indirect "effects"). In this chapter, we build upon those concepts by examining how to estimate the coefficients in a structural equation model. We therefore consider the identification problem, recursive versus nonrecursive structural models, estimation procedures and their assumptions, and model specification or respecification.

6.1 IDENTIFICATION

In structural equation modeling, it is crucial that the researcher resolve the identification "problem" prior to the estimation of parameters. In the identification problem, we ask the following question: On the basis of the sample data contained in the sample covariance matrix, S, and the theoretical model implied by the population covariance matrix, Σ, can a unique set of parameter estimates be found? For example, the theoretical model might suggest that $X + Y =$ some value, the data might indicate that $X + Y = 10$, and yet it may be that no unique solution for X and Y exists. One solution is that $X = 5$ and $Y = 5$; another, that $X = 2$ and $Y = 8$; and so on, because there are an infinite number of solutions for this problem. The problem is that there are not enough constraints on the model and the data to obtain unique estimates of X and Y. Therefore, if we wish to solve this problem, we need to impose some constraints. One such constraint might be to fix the value of X to 1; then, Y would have to be 9. We have solved the identification problem in this instance by imposing one constraint. However, except for simplistic models, the solution to the identification problem in structural equation modeling is not so easy (although algebraically one can usually solve the problem).

Each potential parameter in a model must be specified to be either a *free* parameter, a *fixed* parameter, or a *constrained* parameter. A free parameter is a parameter that is unknown and therefore one that you want to estimate. A fixed parameter is a parameter that is not free but rather fixed to a specified value, typically either 0 or 1. A constrained parameter is a parameter that is unknown but is constrained to equal one or more other parameters.

For further illustration, recall the model depicted in Fig. 5.3. In the measurement model, the observed variables, educational aspiration and occupational aspiration, load on the latent variable, aspirations. On the basis of substantive reasoning, we did not allow these observed variables to load on any other latent variable (e.g., achievement). Thus, the observed variable *loadings* on the latent variable *aspirations* represent free parameters to be estimated, and any other loadings using these observed variables are constrained or not allowed and represent fixed parameters (i.e., fixed to 0). Thus, in order to solve the identification problem for the measurement model, some constraints are necessary (i.e., some parameters have to be fixed or not allowed). For example, in our model, we allowed only educational aspiration and occupational aspiration to load on one latent variable (aspirations). The other observed variables were similarly constrained to load on only a single latent variable.

Additional constraints in the measurement model are also necessary for identification purposes. Either one indicator for each latent variable must have a factor loading fixed to 1, or the variance of each latent variable must be fixed to 1. In the case of the former, these indicators are defined as *reference* indicators, and this is the preferred method for constraints in the measurement models containing X and Y variables. The reason for imposing these constraints is to set the measurement scale for each latent variable, primarily because of an indeterminacy between the variance of the latent variable and the loadings of the observed variables on that factor. Utilizing either of these methods will eliminate the scale indeterminacy problem, but not necessarily the identification problem, and so additional constraints may be necessary.

Model identification, therefore, depends on the specification of parameters as fixed, free, or constrained. Once the model is specified and the parameter specifications are indicated, the parameters are combined to form one and only one Σ (model-implied variance–covariance matrix). A problem still exists, however, in that there may be several sets of parameter values in these matrices that can form the same Σ. If two or more sets of parameter values generate the same Σ, then they are equivalent. If a parameter has the same value in all equivalent sets, the parameter is identified. If all of the parameters of a model are identified, the entire model is identified. If one or more of the parameters are not identified, then the entire model is not identified.

Traditionally, there have been three levels of model identification. They depend on the amount of information in the matrix, S, necessary for uniquely estimating the parameters of the model. First, a model is said to be *underidentified* (or not identified) if one or more parameters may not be uniquely determined because there is not enough information in the matrix S. Second, a model is said to be *just-identified* if all of the parameters may be uniquely determined because there is just enough information in the matrix S. Third, a model is said to be *overidentified* when there is more than one way of estimating a parameter (or parameters) because there is more than enough information in the matrix S. If a model is either just- or overidentified, then the model is said to be identified. If a model is underidentified, the parameter estimates are not to be trusted. However, such a model may become identified if additional constraints are imposed.

There are several conditions for establishing the identification of a model. A necessary, but insufficient, condition for identification is the *order condition*, under which the number of free (or independent) parameters to be estimated must be less than or equal to the number of distinct values in the matrix S. That is, only the diagonal variances and one set of off-diagonal covariances, either above or below the diagonal, are counted. For example, since $s_{12} = s_{21}$, only one of these covariances is counted. The number of distinct values in the matrix S is equal to $\frac{1}{2}(p + q)(p + q + 1)$, where p is the number of observed dependent variables and q is the number of observed independent variables. However, this is only a necessary condition; it does not mean that the model is identified.

While the order condition is easy to assess, other sufficient conditions are not (e.g., the rank condition). The sufficient conditions require us to algebraically determine whether each parameter in the model can be estimated from the covariance matrix S. Unfortunately, proof of these conditions is often problematic in practice, particularly for the applied researcher. But there are some procedures that the applied researcher can use. For a more detailed discussion of these conditions, refer to Bollen (1989) or Jöreskog and Sörbom (1988). The basic concepts behind these procedures are discussed next.

One set of procedures involves methods for avoiding identification problems. Three methods are described here. First, we have already described fixing the scales of the latent variables. As mentioned, this is necessary for model identification. Second, reciprocal or nonrecursive structural models are sometimes a source of the identification problem. A structural model is recursive when all of the structural relationships are unidirectional, as no two latent variables are reciprocally related—that is, so that no feedback loops may exist whereby a latent variable feeds back upon itself. Nonrecursive structural models include a reciprocal or bidirectional relationship, so that there is feedback (e.g., models that allow achievement$_1$ and achievement$_2$ to influence each other). For a nonrecursive model, ordinary least squares (OLS; see section 6.2) is not an appropriate method of estimation. Third, it is good advice to begin with as parsimonious (simple) a model as possible, and with a minimum number of parameters. Include only those parameters that you consider to be absolutely crucial. If this model is identified, then you can consider including other parameters in subsequent models.

A second set of procedures involves methods for checking on the identification of a model. One method is Wald's (1950) rank test, provided in the EQS5 computer program. A second, related method is described by Wiley (1973),

Keesling (1972), and Jöreskog and Sörbom (1988), among others. This test has to do with the inverse of the information matrix and is computed by programs such as LISREL8 and EQS5. Unfortunately, these methods are not 100% reliable, and there is no general necessary-and-sufficient test available for the applied researcher. At present, consider the following advice. Use whatever methods are available for identification. If you still suspect that there is an identification problem, we suggest you follow the recommendation of Jöreskog and Sörbom (1988). The first step is to analyze the sample covariance matrix S and save the estimated population matrix Σ. The second step is to analyze the estimated population matrix Σ. If the model is identified, then the estimates from both analyses should be identical. Another option, often recommended, is to use different starting values in separate analyses. If the model is identified, then the estimates should be identical.

6.2 ESTIMATION PROCEDURES AND ASSUMPTIONS

Recall from chapters 4 and 5 the various coefficients that form the basis of structural equation modeling. The structural model made use of the structure coefficients, the covariance matrix of the latent independent variables, and the covariance matrix of the structural equation prediction errors. The measurement model used the factor loadings for both X and Y variables and the covariance matrices of their measurement errors. In this section, we examine different methods for estimating these parameters (i.e., estimates of the population parameters).

We want to obtain estimates for each of the parameters specified in the model that produce the matrix Σ, such that the parameter values are as close as possible to those in S, our sample covariance matrix of the observed or indicator variables. This estimation process involves the use of a particular *fitting function* to minimize the difference between Σ and S. Several fitting functions or estimation procedures are currently available. Some of the earlier methods included unweighted or ordinary least squares (ULS or OLS), generalized least squares (GLS), and maximum likelihood (ML).

The ULS estimates are consistent, have no distributional assumptions or associated statistical tests, and are scale-dependent (i.e., changes in variable scale yield different solutions or sets of estimates). In fact, of all the estimators described here, only the ULS estimation method is scale-dependent. The GLS and ML methods are scale-free, which means that if we transform the scale of one or more of our observed variables, the untransformed and transformed variables will yield estimates that are properly related, i.e., that differ by the transformation. The GLS procedure involves a weight matrix W, such as S^{-1}, the inverse of the sample covariance matrix. Both GLS and

ML estimation methods have desirable asymptotic properties (i.e., large sample properties), such as minimum variance and unbiasedness. Also, both GLS and ML estimation methods assume multivariate normality of the observed variables (the sufficient conditions are that the observations are independent and identically distributed and that kurtosis is zero). The WLS, or weighted least-squares, estimation method generally requires a large sample size and as a result is considered an asymptotically distribution-free (ADF) estimator that does not depend upon the normality assumption (see Raykov & Widaman, 1995, for a further discussion concerning the use of ADF estimators).

If standardization of the latent variables is desired, one may obtain a standardized solution (and thereby standardized estimates) when the variances of the latent variables are fixed at 1. A separate but related issue is standardization of the observed variables. When the unit of measurement for the indicator variables is of no particular interest to the researcher (i.e., arbitrary or irrelevant), then only an analysis of the correlation matrix is typically of interest. The analysis of correlations usually gives correct chi-square values, but sometimes estimates standard errors incorrectly. There are ways to specify a model, analyze a correlation matrix, and obtain correct standard errors, as seen in chapter 3. The SEPATH structural equation modeling program by Steiger (1995) does permit correlation matrix input and computes the correct standard errors. Since the correlation matrix implies a standardized scaling among the observed variables, the parameters estimated for the measurement model (in particular, the factor loadings) will be of the same order of magnitude (i.e., on the same scale). When the same indicator variables are measured either over time (i.e., in longitudinal analysis), for multiple samples, or when equality constraints are imposed on two or more parameters, an analysis of the covariance matrix is appropriate and recommended so as to capitalize on the metric similarities of the variables (Lomax, 1982).

More recently, other estimation procedures have been developed for the analysis of covariance structure models. Beginning with LISREL V, automatic starting values have been provided for all parameter estimates. These are referred to as *initial estimates* and involve a fast, noniterative procedure (unlike other methods such as ML, which is iterative). The initial estimates involve the instrumental variables and least-squares methods (ULS and the two-stage least-squares method, or TSLS) developed by Hagglund (1982). Often, the user may wish to obtain only the initial estimates (for cost efficiency), or to use them as starting values in subsequent analyses. The initial estimates are consistent and rather efficient relative to the ML estimator and have been shown, as in the case of the centroid method, to be considerably faster, especially in large-scale measurement models (Gerbing & Hamilton, 1994).

If one can assume multivariate normality of the observed variables, then moments beyond the second (i.e., skewness and kurtosis) can be ignored. When the normality assumption is violated, parameter estimates and standard errors are suspect. One alternative is the previously mentioned method of GLS, which assumes multivariate normality and stipulates that kurtosis be zero (Browne, 1974). Browne (1982, 1984) later recognized that the weight matrix of GLS may be modified to yield asymptotically distribution-free (ADF) or WLS estimates, standard errors, and test statistics. Others (Bentler, 1983; Shapiro, 1983) have developed more general classes of ADF estimators. All of these methods are based on using the GLS method and specifying that the weight matrix is to be of a certain form; for Bentler, they include both distribution-specific and distribution-free estimates, although none of these methods take multivariate kurtosis into account. Research by Browne (1984) suggests that goodness-of-fit indices and standard errors of parameter estimates derived under the assumption of multivariate normality should not be employed if the distribution of the observed variables has a nonzero value for kurtosis. Here, one of the methods mentioned in this paragraph should be utilized.

An implicit assumption of ML estimators is that information contained in the first- and second-order moments (i.e., location and dispersion, respectively) of the observed variables is sufficient that information contained in higher-order moments (i.e., skewness and kurtosis) can be ignored. If the observed variables are interval-scaled and multivariate normal, then the ML estimates, standard errors, and chi-square test are appropriate. However, if the observed variables are ordinal-scaled and/or extremely skewed or peaked (and thus non-normally distributed), then the ML estimates, standard errors, and chi-square test may not be appropriate.

The application of categorical response variables to structural equation modeling was pioneered by Muthén (1982, 1984). Muthén proposed a three-stage limited-information GLS estimator that provided a large-sample chi-square test of the model and large-sample standard errors. The Muthén CVM (categorical variable methodology) approach is believed to produce more suitable coefficients of association than the ordinary Pearson product–moment correlations and covariances applied to ordered categorical variables (Muthén, 1983). This is particularly so with markedly skewed categorical variables, where correlations must be "stretched" to assume values throughout the -1, $+1$ range, as is done in the PRELIS2 computer program. The CVM approach is implemented in Muthén's LISCOMP computer program.

The PRELIS2 computer program handles ordinal variables by computing a polychoric correlation for two ordinal variables (Olsson, 1979) and a polyserial correlation for an ordinal and an interval variable (Olsson, Drasgow, & Dorans, 1982), where the ordinal variables are assumed to have an underlying bivariate normal distribution (which is not necessary with the Muthén approach). All correlations (i.e., the Pearson, polychoric, and polyserial) are then used by PRELIS2 to create an asymptotic covariance matrix for input into LISREL8. The reader is cautioned to *not directly* use mixed types of correlation matrices or covariance matrices in EQS5 or LISREL8-SIMPLIS programs (instead, use an asymptotic covariance matrix produced by PRELIS2 as input in a LISREL8-SIMPLIS or LISREL8 matrix program).

During the last decade or so, we have seen considerable research on the behavior of methods of estimation under various conditions. The most crucial conditions were characterized by a lack of multivariate normality and interval-level variables. When the data are generated from non-normally distributed populations and/or represent discrete variables, the normal theory estimators—and, in particular, standard errors and the model fit indices, discussed in chapter 7—are suspect. According to theoretical and simulation research dealing with non-normality, one of the distribution-free or weighted procedures (e.g., ADF, WLS, GLS) should be used (Lomax, 1989). In dealing with noninterval variables, the research indicates that only when categorical data show small skewness and kurtosis (in the range of −1 to +1) should normal theory be used. When these conditions are not met, several options already mentioned are recommended. These include the use of tetrachoric, polyserial, and polychoric correlations rather than Pearson product–moment correlations, or the use of one of the distribution-free or weighted procedures (e.g., some or all of these are available in computer programs such as PRELIS2, a LISREL8 preprocessor; LISCOMP; or EQS5). Considerable research remains to be conducted to determine what the optimal estimation procedure is for a given set of conditions.

6.3 MODEL SPECIFICATION OR RESPECIFICATION

A given model is said to be properly specified when the true model, the one that generated the data, is deemed consistent with the model tested. The ultimate goal of the applied researcher is to determine which model generated the sample covariance matrix. Thus, the question of interest is, to what extent does the true model deviate from the model tested? If the true model is not consistent with the model tested, then the model is said to be misspecified. The difference between the true model and the model tested may be due to errors of omission and/or inclusion of any variable or parameter. For example, an important structure coefficient may have been omitted from the model tested. A misspecified model may result in biased parameter estimates; this bias is known as *specification error*. In the presence of specification error, it is likely that one's theoretical model may not be deemed statistically acceptable (see chap. 7). There are a number of procedures available for the detection of specification errors so that more properly specified subsequent models may be evaluated (during respecification). In general, these procedures are used for performing what is called a *specification search* (Leamer, 1978). The purpose of a specification search is to alter the original model in the search for a model that is "best fitting" in some sense and yields parameters having practical significance and substantive meaning. If a parameter has no substantive meaning to the applied researcher, then it should never be included in a model. Substantive interest must be the guiding force in a specification search; otherwise, the resultant model will not have practical value or importance. There are procedures designed to detect and correct for specification errors. Typically, applications of structural equation modeling include some type of specification search, informal or formal, although the search process may not always be explicitly stated in a research report.

An obvious intuitive method is to consider the statistical significance of each parameter estimated in the model. Once parameter estimates are obtained, standard errors for each estimate are also of interest. A ratio of the parameter estimate to the estimated standard error can be formed as a "t value," although it is actually normally distributed (use the z or unit normal distribution). All parameters should be (a) in the expected direction and (b) statistically different from zero. A specification strategy would be to fix parameters that are not statistically significant (i.e., having small t values) to 0 in a subsequent model. Care should be taken, however, because statistical significance is related to sample size; parameters may be not significant with small samples but significant with larger samples. Also, substantive theoretical interests must be considered. If a parameter is not significant but is of sufficient substantive interest, then the parameter should probably remain in the model. The guiding rule should be that the parameter estimates make sense to you. Parameters should be in the expected direction and sufficient in number to be substantively meaningful (Fraas & Newman, 1994). Variance parameters, for example, should not have negative values. If an estimate makes no sense to you, how are you going to explain it—how is it going to be of substantive value, that is, meaningful?

Another intuitive method of examining misspecification is to examine the residual matrix (i.e., the differences between the observed covariance matrix S and the model implied covariance matrix Σ; referred to as fitted residuals in the LISREL8 program output). These values should be small in magnitude and should not be larger for one variable than another. Large values overall indicate serious general model misspecification, while large values for a single variable indicate misspecification for that variable only, probably in the structural model (Bentler, 1989). Standardized or "normalized" residuals can also be examined. Theoretically, these can be treated like standardized z scores, and hence problems can be more easily detected from the standardized residual matrix than from the unstandardized residual matrix. Large standardized residuals (larger than, say, 1.96 or 2.58) indicate that a particular covariance is not well explained by the model. The model should be examined to determine ways in which this particular covariance could be explained (e.g., by freeing some parameters).

Sörbom (1975) considered misspecification of correlated measurement error terms in the analysis of longitudinal data. He proposed considering the first-order partial derivatives, which have values of zero for free parameters and nonzero values for fixed parameters. The largest value, in absolute terms, indicated the fixed parameter most likely to improve model fit. A second model, with this parameter now free, is then estimated and goodness of fit assessed. Sörbom defines an acceptable fit as occurring when the difference between two models successive chi-square values is not significant. The derivatives of the second model are examined and the process continues until an acceptable fit is achieved. Sörbom's procedure, however, is restricted to the derivatives of the observed variables and provides indications of misspecification only in terms of correlated measurement error.

More recently, other procedures have been developed to examine model specification. In the LISREL8-SIMPLIS program, modification indices are reported for all nonfree parameters. These indices were developed by Sörbom (1986) and represent an improvement over the first-order partial derivatives already described. A modification index for a particular nonfree parameter indicates that if this parameter were allowed to become free in a subsequent model, then the chi-square goodness-of-fit value would be predicted to decrease by at least the value of the index. In other words, if the value of the modification index for a nonfree parameter is 50, then when this parameter is allowed to be free in a subsequent model, the value of chi-square will decrease by at least 50. Thus, large modification indices would suggest ways in which the model might be altered by allowing the corresponding parameters to become free and in which the researcher might thus arrive at a better-fitting model. As reported in an earlier LISREL manual (Jöreskog & Sörbom, 1988, p. 44), "(t)his procedure seems to work well in practice," although there is little research on these indices.

The LISREL8 program includes an automatic model modification option. Here, the nonfree parameter with the largest modification index will automatically become free in a second model. The procedure continues as long as a user-invoked significance level is met. While the user may specify that certain parameters always remain fixed for substantive reasons, extreme caution must be taken to maintain a theoretical approach to model testing, which means perhaps not even using this option!

The LISREL8 program also provides squared multiple correlations for each observed variable separately and coefficients of determination for all of the observed variables jointly. These values indicate how well the observed variables serve as measures of the latent variables and are scaled from 0 to 1. Squared multiple correlations are also given for each structural equation separately and coefficients of determination for the structural equations jointly. These values serve as an indication of the strength of the structural relationships and are also scaled from 0 to 1.

Some relatively new indices are the *expected parameter change, Lagrange multiplier*, and *Wald statistics*. The expected parameter change statistic in the LISREL8 and EQS5 programs indicates the estimated change in the magnitude and direction of each nonfree parameter if it were to become free (rather than the predicted change in the goodness-of-fit test as with the modification indices). This could be useful, for example, if the sign of the potential free parameter is not in the expected direction—say, positive instead of negative. This would suggest that such a parameter should remain fixed. The Lagrange multiplier and Wald statistics are provided in the EQS5 program. The Lagrange multiplier statistic allows one to evaluate the effect of freeing a set of fixed parameters in a subsequent model (referred to by Bentler, 1986, as a *forward search*). Since the Lagrange multiplier statistic can consider a set of parameters, it is considered the multivariate analogue of the modification index. The Wald statistic is used to evaluate whether the free parameters in a model are necessary in a statistical sense. It indicates which parameters should be dropped from a model and is referred to by Bentler (1986) as a *backward search*. Since the Wald statistic can consider a set of parameters, it is considered the multivariate analogue of the *t* values.

Empirical research suggests that specification searches are most successful when the model tested is very similar to the model that generated the data. More specifically, researchers would begin with a known true model from which sample data were generated. The true model was then misspecified. The goal of the specification search was to begin with the misspecified model and determine whether the true model could be located. If the misspecified model was more than two or three parameters different from the true model, then the true model could not be located. Unfortunately, in these studies the true model was almost never located through the specification search, regardless of the search procedure or combination of procedures that were used (e.g., see Baldwin & Lomax, 1990; Gallini, 1983; Gallini & Mandeville, 1984; MacCallum, 1986; Saris & Stronkhorst, 1984; Tippets, 1992).

What is clear to date is that there is no single existing procedure sufficient for finding a properly specified model. As a result, there has been a flurry of research in recent years to determine what combination of procedures is most likely to yield a properly specified model (e.g., Chou & Bentler, 1990; Herbing & Costner, 1985; Kaplan, 1988, 1989, 1990; MacCallum, 1986; Saris & Satorra, 1988; Saris, Satorra, & Sörbom, 1987; Silvia & MacCallum, 1988). No optimal strategy has been found yet! Interestingly, though, a computer program known as TETRAD was developed by Glymour, Scheines, Spirtes, and Kelly (1987) and the new version, TETRAD II, thoughtfully reviewed by Wood

(1995) offers new search procedures. More research is needed to determine which methods are successful for conducting a specification search. Given our lengthy discussion about specification search procedures, some practical advice is warranted for the applied researcher. The following is our own suggested eight-step procedure for a specification search:

1. Let substantive theory and prior research be your guide.

2. See Rule 1. When you are sufficiently satisfied that Rule 1 has been met, move to Rule 3.

3. Conduct a specification search, first on the measurement model, and then on the structural model.

4. For each model tested, look to see if the parameters are of the expected magnitude and direction, and examine several appropriate goodness-of-fit indices.

Steps 5 through 7 can be followed in an iterative fashion. For example, you might go from Step 5 to Step 6, and successively on to Steps 7, 6, 5, and so on.

5. Examine the statistical significance of the nonfixed parameters, and possibly the Wald statistic. Look to see if any nonfixed parameters should be fixed in a subsequent model.

6. Examine the modification indices, expected parameter change statistics, and possibly the Lagrange multiplier statistic. Look to see if any fixed parameters should be freed in a subsequent model.

7. Consider examining the normalized residual matrix to see if anything suspicious is occurring (e.g., values larger for a particular observed variable).

8. Once a final acceptable model is tested, cross-validate it with a new sample, or use half of the sample to find a properly specified model using the other half to check it (cross validation index, or CVI), or report a single sample cross validation index (ECVI) for alternative models (Cudeck & Browne, 1983; Kroonenberg & Lewis, 1982).

6.4 EXAMPLE STRUCTURAL EQUATION MODEL

In this section, we refer back to the structural equation model example and program described in chapter 5, for further consideration of *identification*, *estimation*, and *model specification or respecification*, which are part of the five steps discussed in chapter 4. As previously shown in Fig. 5.3, there are four latent variables in the model: two latent independent variables (home background and ability) and two latent dependent variables (aspirations and achievement). In the structural model, each latent independent variable is hypothesized to influence each latent dependent variable, resulting in four structure coefficients, and the model contains one additional structure coefficient for the influence of aspirations on achievement. Also, we specified in the model and program that the latent independent variables covary. We can also see that there are no reciprocal paths in the model. Thus, the model is recursive. The model would be nonrecursive or reciprocal if we specified paths from aspirations to achievement, and back again from achievement to aspirations, so that they would influence each other. The equations for the measurement model were illustrated as:

Educational aspiration	= function of aspirations(*)	+ error
Occupational aspiration	= function of aspirations	+ error
Verbal achievement	= function of achievement(*)	+ error
Quantitative achievement	= function of achievement	+ error
Family income	= function of home background(*)	+ error
Father's education	= function of home background	+ error
Mother's education	= function of home background	+ error
Verbal ability	= function of ability(*)	+ error
Quantitative ability	= function of ability	+ error

The structural equations for the example were illustrated as:

Aspirations   = home background + ability + error
Achievement = aspirations + home background + ability + error

The asterisk signifies that a factor loading was fixed to 1. Thus, for each latent variable, one factor loading has been fixed to 1 to identify the model, and the program uses that variable's scale for the latent variable.

The covariance terms were specified next. The covariance matrix for the latent independent variables consisted of variances for home background and ability, and a covariance between home background and ability. The covariance matrix for the structural equation prediction errors consists of two error variances, one for each structural equation. The covariance matrix of measurement errors for the observed variables (indicators) of the latent independent variables consists of five error variances on the diagonal (one for each observed variable). The covariance matrix of measurement errors for the observed variables (indicators) of the latent dependent variables consists of four error variances on the diagonal (one for each observed variable).

The sample covariance matrix for the modeled data is shown in Table 6.1. The number of unique variances and covariances in the sample covariance matrix, S, is equal to $\frac{1}{2}(p+q)(p+q+1) = \frac{1}{2}(4+5)(4+5+1) = 45$.

TABLE 6.1
Sample Covariance Matrix for Example Data

Variable	1	2	3	4	5	6	7	8	9
1. EdAsp	1.024								
2. OccAsp	.792	1.077							
3. VerbAch	1.027	.919	1.844						
4. QuantAch	.756	.697	1.244	1.286					
5. FamInc	.567	.537	.876	.632	.852				
6. FaEd	.445	.424	.677	.526	.518	.670			
7. MoEd	.434	.389	.635	.498	.475	.545	.716		
8. VerbAb	.580	.564	.893	.716	.546	.422	.373	.851	
9. QuantAb	.491	.499	.888	.646	.508	.389	.339	.629	.871

The number of parameters to be estimated (i.e., free parameters) is equal to 25. Thus, the model is *overidentified*, because the number of unique variances and covariances is greater than the number of parameters to be estimated.

Although several different methods of estimation have been described in this chapter, for this example we have chosen the maximum-likelihood estimation method (feel free to examine and compare the results using the other methods of estimation). Our intention is to look at the results for the model specified in Fig. 5.3 (Model 1), in hopes of finding information that would lead us to a properly specified model, Model 2. The results for the ML estimation are shown in Table 6.2. All of the parameter estimates are of the expected magnitude and direction (based on previous research; Lomax, 1985). All of the parameter estimates are significantly different from zero ($p < .05$), with one exception. Since this parameter was nonsignificant, but was of substantive interest, we did not remove it from the model.

The various fit indices shown in Table 6.2 indicate that the fit of Model 1 could be improved (see chap. 7 for further explanation). The modification indices and expected parameter change statistics for Model 1 (see Table 6.3) indicate that the largest modification index is for an omitted parameter (MoEd,FaEd = 40.072), with the corresponding expected parameter change statistic equal to .205. The normalized residuals for Model 1 are shown in Table 6.4, where the largest covariance is for mother's education with father's education. When the misspecified parameter is allowed to become free (estimated) in Model 2, the fit of the model dramatically improves (see Table 6.2), and the modification indices, expected parameter change statistics, and normalized residuals are generally satisfactory (these are not shown here).

The specification of Model 1 (Fig. 5.3), our initial model, required a substantive relationship grounded in theory (Step 1, model specification—see chap. 4). We next resolved the problem of identification and determined

TABLE 6.2
Maximum-Likelihood (ML) Estimates for Models 1 and 2

Estimates	Model 1	Model 2
OccAsp loading	.916	.917
QuantAch loading	.759	.753
FaEd loading	1.006	.782
MoEd loading	.963	.720
QuantAb loading	.949	.949
Aspire → achieve	.548	.527
Home → aspire	.411	.506
Home → achieve	.242[a]	.300[a]
Ability → aspire	.589	.446
Ability → achieve	.751	.686
Home variance	.533	.662
Ability variance	.663	.662
Home, ability covariance	.432	.538
Aspire equation error variance	.335	.319
Achieve equation error variance	.224	.227
EdAsp error variance	.160	.160
OccAsp error variance	.352	.351
VerbAch error variance	.205	.193
QuantAch error variance	.342	.349
FamInc error variance	.319	.190
FaEd error variance	.130	.265
MoEd error variance	.222	.373
VerbAb error variance	.188	.189
QuantAb error variance	.275	.274
FaEd,MoEd error covariance	−	.172
Goodness-of-fit indices:		
χ^2	57.10	19.21
df	21	20
p value	.000	.508
GFI	.938	.980
AGFI	.868	.954
RMSR	.047	.015

[a]Estimates not significantly different from zero ($p < .05$); all other estimates are significantly different from zero. The χ^2 values for Model 1 and Model 2 can be checked for significance using Table A.2 in the Appendix.

that our model had unique parameters that could be estimated (Step 2, identification—see chap. 4). We chose the maximum-likelihood estimation method, which met the distributional and scaling assumptions of our variables (Step 3, estimation—see chap. 4). We then ran the sample covariance matrix with the specified model to obtain parameter estimates and fit statistics (Step 4, testing fit—see chap. 4). We determined from the parameter estimate and fit information that the model needed to be respecified. We

TABLE 6.3
Modification Indices and Expected Parameter Change Statistics for Model 1

Parameter Estimates	Modification Indices	Expected Parameter Change
EdAsp loading on aspire	.103	.187
OccAsp loading on aspire	.103	−.172
VerbAch loading on ach	.665	.175
QuantAch loading on ach	.665	−.133
FamInc loading on home	35.413	.621
FaEd loading on home	5.720	−.228
MoEd loading on home	9.899	−.229
VerbAb loading on ability	.389	.090
Quantab loading on ability	.389	−.086
OccAsp, EdAsp covariance	.000	.000
VerbAch, EdAsp covariance	2.817	.055
VerbAch, OccAsp covariance	1.615	−.043
QuantAch, EdAsp covariance	.404	−.018
QuantAch, OccAsp covariance	.000	.000
QuantAch, VerbAch covariance	.000	.000
FaEd, FamInc covariance	7.920	−.091
MoEd, FamInc covariance	10.438	−.098
MoEd, FaEd covariance	**40.072**[a]	**.205**
VerbAb, FamInc covariance	2.248	.037
VerbAb, FaEd covariance	.007	−.002
VerbAb, MoEd covariance	.988	−.021
QuantAb, FamInc covariance	1.135	.028
QuantAb, FaEd covariance	.015	−.002
QuantAb, MoEd covariance	1.234	−.025
QuantAb, VerbAb covariance	.000	.000

Note. The modification indices and parameter change values are for relationships not specified in Model 1.

[a]The highest modification index indicates that including this relationship in a subsequent test of the model would improve the fit between Σ and S.

TABLE 6.4
Normalized Residual Matrix for Model 1

	1	2	3	4	5	6	7	8	9
1. EdAsp	.000								
2. OccAsp	.000	.000							
3. VerbAch	1.442	−.802	.000						
4. QuantAch	−.799	−.362	.000	.000					
5. FamInc	3.537	3.090	5.341	2.788	.000				
6. FaEd	−2.258	−.564	−2.632	−.848	−2.814	.000			
7. MoEd	−1.028	−1.030	−2.146	−.855	−3.231	**6.330**	.000		
8. VerbAb	.864	1.968	−2.279	1.331	4.586	−.912	−2.142	.000	
9. QuantAb	−2.546	.185	1.797	−.563	3.467	−1.271	−2.387	.000	.000

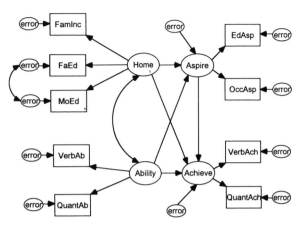

FIG. 6.1. Model 2: respecified model with error covariance.

subsequently selected to change a single relationship in the model—to estimate the covariance term between mother's and father's education (Step 5, respecification—chap. 4). Upon running the analysis with this covariance term specified, the model fit was determined to be acceptable. Figure 6.1 depicts Model 2 with the covariance between mother's and father's education level indicated by a curved arrow between their respective error terms. The computer programs for EQS5 and LISREL8-SIMPLIS with this covariance term added are found in the computer program section at the end of the chapter.

6.5 SUMMARY

In this chapter, we considered the estimation of parameters in structural equation modeling. The chapter began with a look at model identification (under, just-, and overidentified models), the different types of parameters (fixed, free, and constrained), and recursive versus nonrecursive models. Next, we discussed the various types of estimation procedures, their underlying assumptions, and some general guidelines to when each is appropriate. We then described the specification search process in which information is used to arrive at a more properly specified model. Finally, we further discussed the previous model in chapter 5 to illustrate all of these concepts. This chapter therefore further illustrated the five steps in structural equation modeling. In chapter 7, we discuss the several model fit indices available in EQS5 and LISREL8-SIMPLIS that are used to determine whether a model is parsimonious, suggest which competing or alternative models are better, or examine submodels (nested models).

COMPUTER PROGRAMS

EQS5 Program

```
/TITLE
 STRUCTURAL EQUATION MODEL EXAMPLE
/SPECIFICATIONS
 CAS=200; VAR=9; ME=ML;
/LABELS
 V1=EDASP;V2=OCCASP;V3=VERBACH;V4=QUANTACH;V5=FAMINC;V6=FAED;
 V7=MOED;V8=VERBAB;V9=QUANTAB;F1=ASPIRE;F2=ACHIEVE;F3=HOME;
 F4=ABILITY;
/EQUATIONS
 V1=   F1 + E1;
 V2=1*F1 + E2;
 V3=   F2 + E3;
 V4=1*F2 + E4;
 V5=   F3 + E5;
 V6=1*F3 + E6;
 V7=1*F3 + E7;
 V8=   F4 + E8;
 V9=1*F4 + E9;
 F1=1*F3 + 1*F4 + D1;
 F2=1*F1 + 1*F3 + 1*F4 + D2;
/VARIANCES
 E1 TO E9 = 1*;
 D1 TO D2 = 1*;
/COVARIANCES
 E6,E7 = 1*;
 F3,F4 = 1*;
/MATRIX
1.024
 .792 1.077
1.027   .919 1.844
 .756   .697 1.244 1.286
 .567   .537  .876  .632 .852
 .445   .424  .677  .526 .518 .670
 .434   .389  .635  .498 .475 .545 .716
 .580   .564  .893  .716 .546 .422 .373 .851
 .491   .499  .888  .646 .508 .389 .339 .629 .871
/END
```

LISREL8-SIMPLIS Program

```
Structural Equation Model Example
Observed Variables: EDASP OCCASP VERBACH QUANTACH FAMINC FAED MOED VERBAB
```

```
QUANTAB
Covariance matrix:
1.024
 .792 1.077
1.027  .919 1.844
 .756  .697 1.244 1.286
 .567  .537  .876  .632  .852
 .445  .424  .677  .526  .518  .670
 .434  .389  .635  .498  .475  .545  .716
 .580  .564  .893  .716  .546  .422  .373  .851
 .491  .499  .888  .646  .508  .389  .339  .629  .871
Sample Size: 200
Latent Variables: ASPIRE ACHIEVE HOME ABILITY
Relationships:
EDASP OCCASP      = ASPIRE
VERBACH QUANTACH = ACHIEVE
VERBAB QUANTAB   = ABILITY
FAMINC FAED MOED = HOME
ASPIRE           = ABILITY HOME
ACHIEVE          = ASPIRE ABILITY HOME
```
Let the error covariances of MOED and FAED correlate
```
End of Problem
```

REFERENCES

Baldwin, B., & Lomax, R. G. (1990). *Measurement model specification error in LISREL structural equation models.* Paper presented at the annual meeting of the American Educational Research Association, Boston.

Bentler, P. M. (1983). Some contributions to efficient statistics in structural models: Specification and estimation of moment structures. *Psychometrika, 48,* 493–517.

Bentler, P. M. (1986). *Lagrange multiplier and Wald tests for EQS and EQS/PC.* Unpublished manuscript. Los Angeles: BMDP Statistical Software, Inc.

Bentler, P. M. (1989). *Theory and implementation of EQS: A structural equations program.* Los Angeles: BMDP Statistical Software.

Bollen, K. A. (1989). *Structural equations with latent variables.* New York: Wiley.

Browne, M. W. (1974). Generalized least-squares estimators in the analysis of covariance structures. *South African Statistical Journal, 8,* 1–24.

Browne, M. W. (1982). *Covariance structures.* In D. M. Hawkins (Ed.), *Topics in applied multivariate analysis.* Cambridge, England: Cambridge University Press.

Browne, M. W. (1984). Asymptotically distribution-free methods for the analysis of covariance structures. *British Journal of Mathematical and Statistical Psychology, 37,* 62–83.

Chou, C.-P., & Bentler, P. M. (1990, April). *Power of the likelihood ratio, Lagrange multiplier, and Wald tests for model modification in covariance structure analysis.* Paper presented at the annual meeting of the American Educational Research Association, Boston.

Cudeck, R., & Browne, M. W. (1983). Cross-validation of covariance structures. *Multivariate Behavioral Research, 18,* 147–167.

Fraas, J. W., & Newman, I. (1994). A binomial test of model fit. *Structural Equation Modeling: A Multidisciplinary Journal, 1,* 268–273.

Gallini, J. K. (1983). Misspecifications that can result in path analysis structures. *Applied Psychological Measurement, 7*, 125–137.

Gallini, J. K., & Mandeville, G. K. (1984). An investigation of the effect of sample size and specification error on the fit of structural equation models. *Journal of Experimental Education, 53*, 9–19.

Gerbing, D. W., & Hamilton, J. G. (1994). The surprising viability of a simple alternate estimation procedure for construction of large-scale structural equation measurement models. *Structural Equation Modeling: A Multidisciplinary Journal, 1*, 103–115.

Glymour, C. R., Scheines, R., Spirtes, P., & Kelly, K. (1987). *Discovering causal structure*. Orlando, FL: Academic Press.

Hagglund, G. (1982). Factor analysis by instrumental variable methods. *Psychometrika, 47*, 209–222.

Herbing, J. R., & Costner, H. L. (1985). Respecification in multiple indicator models. In H. M. Blalock, Jr. (Ed.), *Causal models in the social sciences* (2nd ed.). New York: Aldine.

Jöreskog, K. G., & Sörbom, D. (1988). *LISREL 7: A guide to the program and applications*. Chicago: SPSS.

Kaplan, D. (1988). The impact of specification error on the estimation, testing, and improvement of structural equation models. *Multivariate Behavioral Research, 23*, 69–86.

Kaplan, D. (1989). Model modification in covariance structure analysis: Application of the parameter change statistic. *Multivariate Behavioral Research, 24*, 285–305.

Kaplan, D. (1990). Evaluating and modifying covariance structure models: A review and recommendation. *Multivariate Behavioral Research, 25*, 137–155.

Keesling, J. W. (1972). *Maximum likelihood approaches to causal flow analysis*. Unpublished dissertation, University of Chicago, Department of Education.

Kroonenberg, P. M., & Lewis, C. (1982). Methodological issues in the search for a factor model: Exploration through confirmation. *Journal of Educational Statistics, 7*, 69–89.

Leamer, E. E. (1978). *Specification searches*. New York: Wiley.

Lomax, R. G. (1982). A guide to LISREL-type structural equation modeling. *Behavioral Research Methods & Instrumentation, 14*, 1–8.

Lomax, R. G. (1985). A structural model of public and private schools. *Journal of Experimental Education, 53*, 216–226.

Lomax, R. G. (1989). Covariance structure analysis: Extensions and developments. In B. Thompson (Ed.), *Advances in social science methodology: Vol. 1*. Greenwich, CT: JAI.

MacCallum, R. (1986). Specification searches in covariance structure modeling. *Psychological Bulletin, 100*, 107–120.

Muthén, B. (1982). *Some categorical response models with continuous latent variables*. In K. G. Jöreskog & H. Wold (Eds.), *Systems under indirect observation: Causality, structure, prediction*. Amsterdam: North-Holland.

Muthén, B. (1983). Latent variable structural equation modeling with categorical data. *Journal of Econometrics, 22*, 43–65.

Muthén, B. (1984). A general structural equation model with dichotomous, ordered categorical, and continuous latent variable indicators. *Psychometrika, 49*, 115–132.

Olsson, U. (1979). Maximum likelihood estimation of the polychoric correlation coefficient. *Psychometrika, 44*, 443–460.

Olsson, U., Drasgow, F., & Dorans, N. J. (1982). The polyserial correlation coefficient. *Psychometrika, 47*, 337–347.

Raykov, T., & Widaman, K. F. (1995). Issues in applied structural equation modeling research. *Structural Equation Modeling, 2*(4), 289–318.

Saris, W. E., & Satorra, A. (1988). Characteristics of structural equation models which affect the power of the likelihood ratio test. In W. E. Saris & I. N. Gallhofer (Eds.), *Sociometric research: Vol. 2. Data analysis*. New York: St. Martin's Press.

Saris, W. E., Satorra, A., & Sörbom, D. (1987). The detection and correction of specification errors in structural equation models. In C. C. Clogg (Ed.), *Sociological methodology*. Washington, DC: American Sociological Association.

Saris, W. E., & Stronkhorst, L. H. (1984). *Causal modelling in nonexperimental research: An introduction to the LISREL approach*. Amsterdam: Sociometric Research Foundation.

Shapiro, A. (1983). Asymptotic distribution theory in the analysis of covariance structures (a unified approach). *South African Statistical Journal, 17*, 33–81.

Silvia, E. S. M., & MacCallum, R. (1988). Some factors affecting the success of specification searches in covariance structure modeling. *Multivariate Behavioral Research, 23*, 297–326.

Sörbom, D. (1975). Detection of correlated errors in longitudinal data. *British Journal of Mathematical and Statistical Psychology, 27*, 229–239.

Sörbom, D. (1986). *Model modification*. (Research Report 86-3). Uppsala, Sweden: University of Uppsala, Department of Statistics.

Steiger, J. H. (1995). SEPATH. In *STATISTICA 5.0*. Tulsa, OK: StatSoft.

Tippets, E. (1992, April). *A comparison of methods for evaluating and modifying covariance structure models*. Paper presented at the annual meeting of the American Educational Research Association, San Francisco.

Wald, A. (1950). A note on the identification of economic relations. In T. C. Koopmans (Ed.), *Statistical inference in dynamic economic models*. New York: Wiley.

Wiley, D. E. (1973). The identification problem for structural equation models with unmeasured variables. In A. S. Goldberger & O. D. Duncan (Eds.), *Structural equation models in the social sciences*. New York: Seminar Press.

Wood, P. K. (1995). TETRAD II: Tools for causal modeling. *Structural Equation Modeling: A Multidisciplinary Journal, 2*, 277–287.

7

GOODNESS-OF-FIT CRITERIA

Chapter Outline:

Exercises

References

Key Concepts:

Model Fit, Model Parsimony, Model Comparison Fit Indices
Measurement Model versus Structural Model interpretation
Parameter and model significance tests

In previous chapters, we considered various types of relationships in measurement and structural models, provided an example model and diagram, explained how the parameters of such a model could be estimated, and showed how the model could be improved by using the modification indices. In this chapter, we further examine the numerous criteria for assessing model fit, and we offer suggestions of how and when these criteria might be used. What complicates matters is that several goodness-of-fit (GOF) criteria have been developed to assist the researcher in interpreting structural equation models under differing model-building assumptions. The fit indices available in EQS5 and LISREL8-SIMPLIS are discussed in this chapter.

7.I TYPES OF GOODNESS-OF-FIT CRITERIA IN EQS5 AND LISREL8-SIMPLIS

The determination of model fit in structural equation modeling is not as straightforward as it is in other statistical approaches in multivariable procedures such as the analysis of variance, multiple regression, path analysis, discriminant analysis, and canonical analysis. These multivariable methods use observed variables that are assumed to be measured without error, and they have statistical tests with known distributions. Structural equation modeling fit indices have *no single* statistical test of significance that identifies a correct model given the sample data. In fact, none of the GOF criteria, except χ^2, have an associated statistical test of significance (see Table 7.1 for fit indices and their interpretation).

Many of the GOF criteria have been formulated to range in value from 0 (no fit) to 1 (perfect fit) and are subjectively assessed as to what is an acceptable model fit. Some researchers have suggested that a structural equation model with a GOF value of .90 or higher is acceptable (Baldwin, 1989; Bentler & Bonett, 1980). Although the various structural equation modeling programs report a variety of GOF criteria, only those outputted by EQS5 and LISREL8-SIMPLIS are discussed here (see Table 7.2). Since other structural equation modeling software programs may have differing GOF

TABLE 7.1
GOF Criteria and Acceptable Fit Interpretation

GOF Criterion	Acceptable Level	Interpretation
Chi-square	Tabled χ^2 value	Compares obtained χ^2 value with tabled value for given *df*.
Goodness-of-fit (GFI)	0 (no fit) to 1 (perfect fit)	Value close to .90 reflects a good fit.
Adjusted GFI (AGFI)	0 (no fit) to 1 (perfect fit)	Value adjusted for *df*, with .90 a good model fit.
Root-mean-square residual (RMR)	Researcher defines level	Indicates the closeness of Σ to S matrix.
Root-mean-square error of approximation (RMSEA)	< .05	Value less than .05 indicates a good model fit.
Tucker–Lewis index	0 (no fit) to 1 (perfect fit)	Value close to .90 reflects a good model fit.
Normed fit index	0 (no fit) to 1 (perfect fit)	Value close to .90 reflects a good model fit.
Normed chi-square	1.0 to 5.0	Less than 1.0 is a poor model fit. Higher than 5.0 reflects a need for improvement.
Parsimonious fit index	0 (no fit) to 1 (perfect fit)	Compares values in alternative models.
Akaike information criterion	0 (perfect fit) to negative value (poor fit)	Compares values in alternative models.

indices, it would be prudent to check the other software programs for any additional GOF indices they output. In any case, for practical research applications, it is recommended that various GOF criteria be used in combination to assess *model fit*, *model comparison*, and *model parsimony*; assessing them could ultimately involve running the sample data in more than one statistical package (Hair, Anderson, Tatham, & Black, 1992) to obtain the set of preferred GOF criteria.

Some fit indices can be computed given knowledge of the null model (independence, where the covariances are assumed to be zero in the model) χ^2, null model *df*, hypothesized model χ^2, hypothesized model *df*, number of observed variables in the model, and sample size. The formulas for the normed fit index (NFI), normed fit index 2 (NFI2), Tucker–Lewis index (TLI), parsimonious fit index (PFI), parsimonious fit index 2 (PFI2), relative noncentrality index (RNI), and centrality index (CI) using these values are:

$$NFI = \frac{\chi^2_{null} - \chi^2_{model}}{\chi^2_{null}}$$

$$NFI2 = \frac{\chi^2_{null} - \chi^2_{model}}{\chi^2_{null} - df_{model}}$$

$$TLI = \frac{(\chi^2_{null}/df_{null}) - (\chi^2_{model}/df_{model})}{(\chi^2_{null}/df_{null}) - 1}$$

$$PFI = \frac{df_{model}}{df_{null}} \times NFI$$

$$PFI2 = \frac{2 \times df_{model}}{n \text{ of variables} \times (n \text{ of variables} - 1)} \times NFI2$$

$$RNI = \frac{(\chi^2_{null} - df_{null}) - (\chi^2_{model} - df_{model})}{\chi^2_{null} - df_{null}}$$

$$CI = e^D, \text{ where } D = -.5 \times \frac{\chi^2_{model} - df_{model}}{\text{sample size}}.$$

TABLE 7.2
Goodness-of-Fit Criteria in EQS5 and LISREL8-SIMPLIS[a]

Program	GOF Criteria
EQS5	Chi-square
	Satorra–Bentler scaled chi-square
	Akaike information criterion (AIC)
	Bozdogan consistent AIC (CAIC)
	Normal-theory RLS chi-square (reweighted LS)
	Bentler and Bonett normed fit index
	Bentler and Bonett non-normed fit index
	Bentler comparative fit index
LISREL8-SIMPLIS	Chi-square
	Noncentrality parameter
	Minimum fit function
	Root-mean-square error (RMSEA)
	Expected cross validation index (ECVI)
	Akaike information criterion (AIC)
	Bozdogan consistent AIC (CAIC)
	Root-mean-square residual (RMR)
	Goodness-of-fit index (GFI)
	Adjusted goodness-of-fit index (AGFI)
	Parsimonious goodness-of-fit index (PGFI)
	Normed fit index (NFI)
	Non-normed fit index (NNFI)
	Parsimonious normed fit index (PNFI)
	Comparative fit index (CFI)
	Incremental fit index (IFI)
	Relative fit index (RFI)
	Critical N (CN)

aEQS5 software also computes basic statistics from raw data files—for example, descriptive statistics—while PRELIS2 accomplishes this for LISREL8.

The model fit indices produced by both the LISREL8-SIMPLIS and EQS5 programs in chapter 6 for Model 2 are presented next. The model chi-square value was 19.17, df = 20, p = .51, compared with the null model (independence) chi-square = 1407.10, df = 36, p = .00. Since the chi-square value is nonsignificant, the data fit the hypothesized model. Other fit indices, such as GFI and RMSEA, are also within acceptable limits, further suggesting an appropriate model fit.

LISREL8-SIMPLIS Goodness-of-Fit Summary Output

```
CHI-SQUARE WITH 20 DEGREES OF FREEDOM = 19.17 (P = 0.51)
ESTIMATED NON-CENTRALITY PARAMETER (NCP) = 0.0
90 PERCENT CONFIDENCE INTERVAL FOR NCP = (0.0 ; 13.53)

MINIMUM FIT FUNCTION VALUE = 0.096
POPULATION DISCREPANCY FUNCTION VALUE (F0) = 0.0
90 PERCENT CONFIDENCE INTERVAL FOR F0 = (0.0 ; 0.068)
ROOT MEAN SQUARE ERROR OF APPROXIMATION (RMSEA) = 0.0
90 PERCENT CONFIDENCE INTERVAL FOR RMSEA = (0.0 ; 0.058)
P-VALUE FOR TEST OF CLOSE FIT (RMSEA < 0.05) = 0.90

EXPECTED CROSS-VALIDATION INDEX (ECVI) = 0.35
90 PERCENT CONFIDENCE INTERVAL FOR ECVI = (0.35 ; 0.42)
ECVI FOR SATURATED MODEL = 0.45
ECVI FOR INDEPENDENCE MODEL = 7.16

CHI-SQUARE FOR INDEPENDENCE MODEL
  WITH 36 DEGREES OF FREEDOM = 1407.10
INDEPENDENCE AIC = 1425.10
MODEL AIC = 69.17
SATURATED AIC = 90.00

INDEPENDENCE CAIC = 1463.78
MODEL CAIC = 176.63
SATURATED CAIC = 283.42

ROOT MEAN SQUARE RESIDUAL (RMR) = 0.015
STANDARDIZED RMR = 0.015

GOODNESS OF FIT INDEX (GFI) = 0.98
ADJUSTED GOODNESS OF FIT INDEX (AGFI) = 0.95
PARSIMONY GOODNESS OF FIT INDEX (PGFI) = 0.44

NORMED FIT INDEX (NFI) = 0.99
NON-NORMED FIT INDEX (NNFI) = 1.00
PARSIMONY NORMED FIT INDEX (PNFI) = 0.55
COMPARATIVE FIT INDEX (CFI) = 1.00
```

```
INCREMENTAL FIT INDEX (IFI) = 1.00
RELATIVE FIT INDEX (RFI) = 0.98

CRITICAL N (CN) = 391.00
```

EQS5 Goodness-of-Fit Summary Output

```
INDEPENDENCE MODEL CHI-SQUARE = 1407.099 ON 36 DEGREES OF FREEDOM

INDEPENDENCE AIC = 1335.09857
INDEPENDENCE CAIC = 1180.35915
MODEL AIC = -20.83138
MODEL CAIC = -106.79773

CHI-SQUARE = 19.169 BASED ON 20 DEGREES OF FREEDOM
PROBABILITY VALUE FOR THE CHI-SQUARE STATISTIC IS 0.51089

THE NORMAL THEORY RLS CHI-SQUARE FOR THIS ML SOLUTION IS 18.594.

BENTLER-BONETT NORMED FIT INDEX= 0.986
BENTLER-BONETT NONNORMED FIT INDEX= 1.001
COMPARATIVE FIT INDEX = 1.000
```

The fit indices we chose to interpret in our example were the chi-square, goodness of fit, and root-mean-square error of approximation values. Several of the other fit indices also indicated a good model fit. Overall, the fit indices fall into the category of either *model fit, model comparison,* or *model parsimony* fit indices. Consequently, we discuss the fit indices in these three categories next to understand their development and recommended applications. Extensive comparisons and discussions of many of these fit indices can be found in recent issues of the journals *Psychological Bulletin, Structural Equation Modeling: A Multidisciplinary Journal,* and *Multivariate Behavioral Research.*

7.2 MODEL FIT

Model fit determines the degree to which the structural equation model fits the sample data. Model fit criteria commonly used are chi-square (χ^2), goodness-of-fit index (GFI), adjusted goodness-of-fit index (AGFI), and root-mean-square residual (RMR) (Jöreskog & Sörbom, 1989). These criteria are based on differences between the observed (original, S) and model-implied (reproduced, Σ) correlation or covariance matrix.

Chi-Square (χ^2)

A significant χ^2 value relative to the degrees of freedom indicates that the observed and estimated matrices differ. Statistical significance indicates the probability that this difference is due to sampling variation. A nonsignificant

χ^2 value indicates that the two matrices are not statistically different. The researcher is interested in obtaining a nonsignificant χ^2 value with associated degrees of freedom. A nonsignificant χ^2 test indicates that the data fit the model but that an uncertainty will always persist because other models are possible that may fit the data. Although the χ^2 GOF criterion is the only statistical test procedure, it is sensitive to sample size, because as sample size increases (generally above 200), the χ^2 test has a tendency to indicate a significant probability level. In contrast, as sample size decreases (generally below 100), the χ^2 test indicates nonsignificant probability levels. The χ^2 test is also sensitive to departures from multivariate normality of the observed variables.

Three approaches are commonly used to calculate χ^2 in latent-variable models (Loehlin, 1987): maximum likelihood (ML), generalized least squares (GLS), and unweighted least squares (ULS). Each approach estimates a best-fitting solution and evaluates the model fit. The ML estimates are consistent, unbiased, efficient, scale-invariant, scale-free, and normally distributed if the observed variables meet the multivariate normality assumption. The GLS estimates have the same properties of the ML approach under a less stringent multivariate normality assumption and provide an approximate chi-square test of model fit to the data. The ULS estimates do not depend on a normality distribution assumption; however, the estimates are not as efficient, nor are they scale-invariant or scale-free. The ML χ^2 statistic is $\chi^2 = (n - 1)F_{ML}$, the GLS χ^2 statistic is $\chi^2 = (n - 1)F_{GLS}$, and the ULS χ^2 statistic is $\chi^2 = (n - 1)F_{ULS}$, where:

$$F_{ML} = \text{tr } (S\Sigma^{-1}) - (p + q) + \ln |\Sigma| - \ln |S|$$
$$F_{GLS} = .5 \text{ tr } [(S - \Sigma)S^{-1}]^2$$
$$F_{ULS} = .5 \text{ tr } [(S - \Sigma)^2]$$
$$df = .5 (p + q)(p + q + 1) - t$$

t = total number of independent parameters estimated
n = number of observations
$(p + q)$ = number of observed variables analyzed

and where tr indicates the trace.

Goodness-of-Fit (GFI) and Adjusted Goodness-of-Fit (AGFI) Indices

The GFI is based on a ratio of the sum of the squared differences between the observed and reproduced matrices to the observed variances, thus allowing for scale. The GFI measures the amount of variance and covariance in S that is predicted by the reproduced matrix Σ. The GFI index can be computed for ML, GLS, or ULS estimates (Bollen, 1989). For example, the original correlation matrix, S, in chapter 3 was:

$$S = \begin{bmatrix} .507 & & \\ .481 & .244 & \\ .276 & .062 & .577 \end{bmatrix},$$

and the reproduced (estimated) correlation matrix, Σ, was:

$$\Sigma = \begin{bmatrix} .272 & & \\ .542 & .321 & \\ .362 & .215 & .427 \end{bmatrix}.$$

The goodness-of-fit index (GFI) using the unweighted least squares approach (ULS) would be computed as:

$$\begin{aligned} \text{GFI} &= 1 - \tfrac{1}{2} \operatorname{tr} (S - \Sigma)^2 \\ &= 1 - \tfrac{1}{2} (1.308 - 1.02)^2 \\ &= 1 - .041 \\ &= .959. \end{aligned}$$

The values 1.308 and 1.02 are the sums of the diagonal values in the respective correlation matrices and represent the trace of the matrix.

The AGFI adjusts the GFI index for the degrees of freedom of a model relative to the number of variables. The AGFI index is computed as $1 - [(k/df)(1 - \text{GFI})]$, where k = the number of unique values in S, or $(p + q)(p + q + 1)/2$, and df = the number of degrees of freedom in the model. The GFI and AGFI indices can be used to compare the fit of two different models with the same data or compare the fit of models with different data, such as male and female data sets.

Root-Mean-Square Residual (RMR)

The RMR index uses the square root of the mean squared differences between matrix elements in S and Σ. It is used to compare the fit of two different models with the same data. The RMR index is computed as $\text{RMR} = [(1/k) \Sigma_{ij} (s_{ij} - \sigma_{ij})^2]^{1/2}$. The EQS5 computer program outputs the residual covariance matrix, which is used to compute RMR. This can be requested in LISREL8-SIMPLIS by use of the `PRINT RESIDUALS` command.

7.3 MODEL COMPARISON

Given the role chi-square has in model fit of latent-variable models, two other indices have emerged as variants for model comparison: the Tucker–Lewis index (TLI) and the normed fit index (NFI) (Bentler & Bonett, 1980, 1982; Loehlin, 1987). These criteria typically compare a proposed model with a null model. In the EQS5 and LISREL8-SIMPLIS programs, the null model is indicated by the independence-model chi-square value. The null model could also be any model that establishes a base for expecting other models to be different.

Tucker–Lewis Index (TLI)

Tucker and Lewis (1973) initially developed the TLI for factor analysis but later extended it to structural equation modeling. The measure can be used to compare alternative models or a proposed model against a null model. The TLI is computed using the χ^2 statistic as follows: $[(\chi^2_{null}/df_{null}) - (\chi^2_{proposed}/df_{proposed})]/[(\chi^2_{null}/df_{null}) - 1]$; it is scaled from 0 (no fit) to 1 (perfect fit).

Normed Fit Index (NFI), Comparative Fit Index (CFI), Relative Noncentrality Index (RNI)

The NFI is a measure that rescales chi-square into a 0 (no fit) to 1.0 (perfect fit) range (Bentler & Bonett, 1980). It is used to compare a restricted model with a full model using a baseline null model as follows: $(\chi^2_{null} - \chi^2_{model})/\chi^2_{null}$. Bentler (1990) developed a new coefficient of comparative fit within the context of specifying a population parameter and distribution, such as a population comparative fit index, to overcome the deficiencies in NFI for nested models. The rationale for assessment of comparative fit in the nested-model approach involved a series of models that ranged from least restrictive (M_i) to saturated (M_s). Corresponding to this sequence of nested models was a sequence of GOF test statistics with associated degrees of freedom. The new comparative fit index (CFI) measures the improvement in noncentrality in going from model M_i to M_k and uses the noncentral χ^2 (d_k) distribution with noncentrality parameter λ_k to define comparative fit as $[\lambda_i - \lambda_k]/\lambda_i$.

McDonald and Marsh (1990) further explored the noncentrality and GOF issue by examining nine GOF indices as functions of noncentrality and sample size. They concluded that only the Tucker–Lewis index and their relative noncentrality index (RNI) were unbiased in finite samples and recommended them for testing null or alternative models. For absolute measures of fit that do not test null or alternative models, they recommended d_k (Steiger & Lind, 1980), because it is a linear function of χ^2, or a normed measure of centrality m_k (McDonald, 1989), because neither of these vary systematically with sample size. The GOF measures of centrality are useful when selecting among a few competing models based upon theoretical considerations.

7.4 MODEL PARSIMONY

Parsimony refers to the number of estimated coefficients required to achieve a specific level of fit. Basically, an overidentified model is compared with a restricted model. The AGFI measure discussed previously will also provide an index of model parsimony. Other indices that indicate model parsimony are normed chi-square (NC), parsimonious fit index (PFI), and Akaike information criterion (AIC). Parsimony-based fit indices for multiple indicator models were reviewed by Williams and Holahan (1994). They indicated that the AIC performed the best (see their article for more detail on additional current indices and related references). The model-parsimony goodness-of-fit indices take into account the number of parameters required to achieve a given value for chi-square.

Normed Chi-Square (NC)

Jöreskog (1969) proposed that χ^2 be adjusted by the degrees of freedom to assess model fit. The NC measure can identify two kinds of inappropriate models: (a) a model that is overidentified and capitalizes on chance, or (b) models that do not fit the observed data and need improvement. The NC measure, like many others, is affected by sample size. It is calculated as NC $= \chi^2/df$.

Parsimonious Fit Index (PFI)

The PFI measure is a modification of the NFI measure (James, Mulaik, & Brett, 1982). The PFI, however, takes into account the number of degrees of freedom used to obtain a given level of fit. Parsimony is achieved with a high degree of fit for fewer degrees of freedom in specifying coefficients to be estimated. The PFI is used to compare models with different degrees of freedom and is calculated as PFI $= (df_{proposed}/df_{null})$ NFI.

Akaike Information Criterion (AIC)

The AIC measure is used to compare models with differing numbers of latent variables, much as the PFI is used (Akaike, 1987). The AIC measure will always be negative, but values close to zero indicate a more parsimonious model. The AIC indicates both model fit (S and Σ elements similar) and a model not overidentified (parsimony). The AIC measure is calculated as $\chi^2 - 2df$, where df = degrees of freedom in the model.

Mulaik, James, Alstine, Bennett, Lind, and Stilwell (1989) evaluated the χ^2, NFI, GFI, AGFI, and AIC goodness-of-fit indices. They concluded that these indices fail to assess parsimony and are insensitive to misspecification of structural relationships. The reader is referred to their definitive work for additional information. This outcome should not be surprising, because it has been suggested that a "good" fit index is one that is independent of sample size, accurately reflects differences in fit, imposes a penalty for inclusion of additional parameters (Marsh, Balla, & McDonald, 1988), and supports the choice of the true model when it is known (McDonald & Marsh, 1990). That is, no GFI can actually meet all of these criteria.

In summary, we have presented a few of the available fit indices to assess model fit, model comparison, or model parsimony. We recommend that once you feel comfortable using these fit indices for your specific model application, you check the references cited for additional information on their usefulness and/or limitations. Much controversy and discussion has ensued following their initial description about their subjective interpretation and appropriateness under specific modeling conditions (see Marsh, Balla, & Hau, 1996, for further discussion). Further research and discussion will surely follow.

7.5 TWO-STEP APPROACH TO MODELING

Anderson and Gerbing (1988) proposed a two-step model-building approach that emphasized the analysis of two conceptually distinct models: measurement and structural. The "confirmatory" measurement, or factor analysis, model specified relationships among measured (observed) variables underlying the latent variables. The "confirmatory" structural model specified relationships among the latent variables as posited by theory. The measurement model provided an assessment of convergent and discriminant validity, and the structural model provided an assessment of nomological validity.

Mulaik et al. (1989) expanded the idea of model fit by assessing relative fit of the structural equation model among latent variables independently of assessing the fit of the indicator variables to the latent variables (measurement model). They proposed a relative normed fit index (RNFI) that makes the following adjustment to separately estimate the effects of the structural model from the measurement model: $\text{RNFI}_j = (F_u - F_j)/[F_u - F_m - (df_j - df_m)]$, where $F_u = \chi^2$ of the full model, $F_j = \chi^2$ of the structural equation model, $F_m = \chi^2$ of the measurement model, $df_j = $ degrees of freedom for the structural equation model, and $df_m = $ degrees of freedom for the measurement model. A corresponding relative parsimony ratio (RP) was also given by $\text{RP}_j = (df_j - df_m)/(df_u - df_m)$, where $df_j = $ degrees of freedom for the structural equation model, $df_m = $ degrees of freedom for the measurement model, and $df_u = $ degrees of freedom for the null model. In comparing different models for fit, Mulaik and coworkers multiplied RP_j by RNFI_j to obtain a relative parsimonious fit index appropriate for assessing how well and to what degree the models explained both relationships in the measurement of latent variables and the structural relationship among the latent variables by themselves. McDonald and Marsh (1990), however, doubted whether model parsimony and goodness of fit could be captured by this multiplicative form, because it is not a monotonic increasing function of model complexity.

Obviously, further research will be needed to clarify these issues. We recommend that the measurement models of your latent variables be established first, and then structural models establishing relationships among the latent independent and dependent variables be formed. It is even plausible when running this structural model to fix the factor loadings and error terms from the measurement model and/or to examine to what extent they change as a result of the structural model relationships.

7.6 PARAMETER FIT DETERMINATION

Individual parameter estimates in a model can be meaningless even though GOF criteria indicate an acceptable model. Therefore, interpretation of parameter estimates in a model is essential. Modification indices aid in this effort, but a first step in examining parameter estimates is whether they have the correct sign (either plus or minus) and are within an expected reasonable range of values. Given a specified model with standardized coefficients, for example, relative comparisons among the parameter estimates and variable effects are possible. An examination of parameter estimates can also help in initially identifying a faulty or misspecified model. In some cases, as previously mentioned, initial parameter estimates can also serve as start values, that is, TSLS (two-stage least-squares) estimates in LISREL8.

Sometimes parameter estimates take on impossible values, as in the case of a correlation between two variables that exceeds 1, or in the case where a negative variance is encountered (known as a Heywood case). Also, if the error variance for a variable is near zero, the indicator variable implies an almost perfect measure of the latent variable, which may not be the case. Outliers can also influence parameter estimates. Sufficient sample size ($n >$ 150) and several indicators per latent variable (three or more) have also been recommended to produce reasonable and stable parameter estimates (Anderson & Gerbing, 1984).

Once these issues have been taken into consideration, the interpretation of modification indices and subsequent changes in model fit indices can begin, but there is still a need for guidance provided by a theoretical model and the researcher's expertise. Researchers should use the indices as "potential indicators" of misfit rather than "givens" for respecifying or modifying a model. Cross validation or replication using another independent sample, once an acceptable model is achieved, is always recommended to ensure stability of parameter estimates and validity of the model (Cliff, 1983). Bootstrap procedures also afford a resampling method, given a single sample, to determine the efficiency and precision of sample estimates (Lunneborg, 1987). These topics are discussed further in chapter 10.

Significance tests of parameter estimates for nested models include the likelihood ratio (LR), Lagrange multiplier (LM), and Wald (W) tests. Each will be briefly explained, but first, a clarification of nested models. Nested models imply that a sample variance–covariance matrix with an initial model is being compared with a restricted model in which a parameter estimate has been set equal to zero. This is analogous to testing full and restricted models in multiple regression. In structural equation modeling, the intent is to determine the significance of the decrease in the χ^2 value for the full model. For GLS, ML, and WLS estimation methods, this involves determining the significance of the χ^2 with one degree of freedom ($\chi^2 > 3.84$, $df = 1$) for a single parameter estimate to determine the significance of the reduction in χ^2 that should equal or exceed the modification index value for the parameter estimate set equal to zero.

The likelihood ratio (LR) examines the difference in χ^2 values between the initial (full) model and the restricted (modified) model where a parameter estimate has been set equal to zero. The LR test is calculated as χ^2_{Full} – $\chi^2_{Restricted}$, with degrees of freedom equal to $df_{Full} - df_{Restricted}$. For example, if the initial model yielded a $\chi^2 = 46$, $df = 20$, and the restricted model yielded a $\chi^2 = 26$, $df = 19$, then LR = 20 with $df = 1$, which is statistically significant ($\chi^2 > 3.84$, $df = 1$, $\alpha = .05$).

The Lagrange multiplier (LM) test compares the fit of the restricted model with lesser restricted models given the same sample variance–covariance matrix. It has the benefit of requiring only estimation of the restricted model. The LM distribution is a chi-square variate with df equal to the difference in degrees of freedom between the restricted models that are compared.

The Wald (W) test establishes an $r \times 1$ vector, $r(\theta)$, of constraints (parameters chosen by the researcher to be set to zero). If an examination of this vector yields values greater than zero, then the restricted model is not valid, and the researcher must go back to interpretation of the initial model. The W statistic is also a chi-square distribution with df equal to the number of constraints in $r(\theta)$. Both LM and W do not require separate estimations of initial (full) and modified (restricted) models as in the case of LR. The LM statistic, however, tests whether restrictions can be deleted. The W statistic tests whether restrictions imposed on a model are valid.

As a practical approach, the researcher using EQS5 will most likely examine LM or W statistics. The LM test indicates parameters that need to be *included* in the model. The LM test therefore indicates potential missing parameters in a model. A researcher would free the restriction on a parameter estimate that leads to the largest reduction in the chi-square estimate, thereby including it in the model. This process would be repeated again in subsequent models until an acceptable model fit was achieved. EQS5 permits the testing of *all* significant parameters in a subsequent model by using the following command:

```
/PRINT
  RETEST = 'MODEL2.EQS'; LMTEST=YES;
```

The RETEST subcommand specifies the file 'MODEL2.EQS' that will contain the revised model setup for a subsequent model analysis. This model setup will include all the parameters that were found to be statistically significant in the multivariate LM test for the initial model. The newly added parameters will not have start values indicated for them, but all other parameter estimates will have their initial model estimates indicated as start values. The researcher should understand that this method may cause meaningless parameters to be included in a subsequent model. We therefore recommend that the 'MODEL2.EQS' file be examined and any parameters that are not meaningful be deleted. In some models, it may be prudent to select only one significant parameter to add to a subsequent model analysis. Afterwards, if warranted, add another, and retest the new model. This process of adding one significant parameter at a time and retesting the newer model has its own rewards—the testing of nested models. A researcher would obviously not use the RETEST subcommand in this instance.

The W test indicates parameters that might need to be *deleted* in a model. The W test therefore indicates parameters that are nonsignificant in a model and therefore if deleted in a subsequent model might improve model fit. The deletion of *all* nonsignificant parameters in the initial model is accomplished by the following command:

```
/PRINT
    RETEST='MODEL2.EQS'; WTEST=YES;
```

The deletion of all nonsignificant parameter estimates is indicated in the new model setup contained in the file 'MODEL2.EQS'. All parameter estimates in the file with a zero (0) in front of them will not be included in a subsequent model analysis. Obviously, they could be edited out of the file, but this is not necessary. Once again, we caution the researcher that such automatic model respecification can cause problems. For example, residual variances may be nonsignificant, causing parameters to be dropped. We suggest editing the file and including a start value followed by an asterisk for any meaningful parameters; for example, in our previous model we left a nonsignificant parameter in the model because it was theoretically meaningful.

In LISREL8-SIMPLIS, the researcher will most likely be guided by the modification indices with their associated change (decrease) in chi-square when respecifying a model. For Model 1, the modification indices were given as:

```
THE MODIFICATION INDICES SUGGEST TO ADD THE
PATH TO   FROM      DECREASE IN CHI-SQUARE   NEW ESTIMATE

FAMINC   ABILITY      35.5                    0.51
MOED     ABILITY       9.8                   -0.24
```

THE MODIFICATION INDICES SUGGEST TO ADD AN ERROR COVARIANCE
BETWEEN   AND DECREASE IN CHI-SQUARE NEW ESTIMATE

FAED	FAMINC	7.9	-0.09
MOED	FAMINC	10.5	-0.10
MOED	**FAED**	**40.2**	**0.21**

On the basis of these modification indices, we chose to include an error covariance for MoEd,FaEd (mother's education, father's education) in our subsequent model analysis, Model 2, because it gave us the largest decrease in our model chi-square value. The resultant model fit was acceptable, and the chi-square value was nonsignificant. It should be noted that in our subsequent Model 2 analysis, one modification to Model 2 was suggested, namely, adding an error covariance term between VerbAb and VerbAch. We, however, deemed the suggestion to be nonmeaningful in the theoretical model.

7.7 HYPOTHESIS TESTING AND POWER

Once a valid model has been established, structural hypotheses can be tested. For example, certain structural coefficients can be tested against specific values, or one can test whether two coefficients are equal. This hypothesis-testing method ultimately leads to models with fewer parameters. Therefore, the initial (full) model represents the null hypothesis (H_0) while the alternative model with fewer parameters is denoted H_a. Each model would generate a χ^2 goodness-of-fit measure, and the difference between the models for significance testing would be computed as $D^2 = \chi_0^2 - \chi_a^2$, with $df_d = df_0 - df_a$. The D^2 statistic is tested for significance at a specified alpha level (probability of Type I error) where H_0 is rejected if D^2 exceeds the critical tabled χ^2 value with df_d degrees of freedom. The approach is used with GLS, ML, and WLS estimation methods.

Other approaches, not requiring two separate models to yield separate χ^2 values, would be either to (a) generate a two-sided t value for the parameter estimate, or (b) interpret the modification index directly for the parameter estimate as a χ^2 with 1 degree of freedom. The relationship is simply $t^2 = D^2 = MI$ (modification index) for large sample sizes.

The power of this test, or the probability of rejecting H_0 when H_a is true, depends on the "true" model, significance level, degrees of freedom, and sample size. These factors also affect power in other parametric statistical tests (Cohen, 1988). Methods for generating D^2 and power, using LISPOWER, are outlined in the *LISREL 7 User's Reference Guide* (Jöreskog & Sörbom, 1989). Unfortunately, the other GOF criteria have no test of statistical significance, and therefore do not apply.

7.8 SAMPLE SIZE AND SIGNIFICANCE INTERPRETATION

Research suggests that certain GOF indices are less susceptible to sample size. Marsh et al. (1988, 1996) examined the influence of sample size on 30 different GOF indices and found that the Tucker–Lewis index (Tucker & Lewis, 1973), and four new indices based on the Tucker–Lewis were the only ones relatively independent of sample size. Bollen (1990) argued that the claims regarding which GOF indices were affected by sample size needed further clarification. There are actually two sample size effects that are confounded: (a) whether sample size enters into the calculation of the GOF index, and (b) whether the means of the sampling distribution of the GOF index are associated with sample size. Sample size was shown not to affect the calculation of NFI, TL, GFI, AGFI, and CN, but the means of the sampling distribution of these GOF indices were associated with sample size. Bollen concluded that, given a lack of consensus on the best measure of fit, it is prudent to report multiple measures rather than to rely on a single choice. Finally, beware of claims of sample size influence on fit measures that do not distinguish the type of sample size effect. Cudeck and Henly (1991) also argued that a uniformly negative view of the effects of sample size in model selection is unwarranted. They focused instead on the predictive validity of models in the sense of cross validation in future samples while acknowledging that sample size issues are a problem in other statistical decisions and unavoidable in structural equation modeling. One way to determine an appropriate sample size is to compute the critical N (CN) statistic (Hoelter, 1983), which is CN = (χ^2/F) + 1. CN gives the sample size at which the F value would lead to a rejection of H_0: $S = \Sigma$ at a specified alpha level. The CN statistic is outputted by the LISREL8-SIMPLIS program. For a further discussion of this statistic, refer to Bollen and Liang (1988) or Bollen (1989).

Breckler (1990) reviewed the personality and social psychology research literature and found several shortcomings of structural equation modeling, namely, that GOF can be identical for a potentially large number of models, that assumptions of multivariate normality are required, that sample size affects results, and that cross validation of models was infrequently addressed or mentioned. Many of the studies reported only a single GOF index. Breckler concluded that there was cause for concern in the reporting of structural equation modeling findings. Model fit is by itself a subjective approach, because there is no single "correct" model (other models may be equally plausible given the sample data).

What, then, is the solution? The researcher is advised to base structural equation models on *sound theory*, utilize the *two-step approach* discussed previously, employ *model testing* of the latent variables to examine the effectiveness and functionality of the latent variable relationships, and *cross-*

validate or *replicate* the model to determine the stability of the parameter estimates. Model testing takes the researcher to the next step beyond determining whether the model "fits" the sample data. (We do not advocate finding the particular model that fits the data you have obtained; rather, we suggest determining a theoretical basis for a model and then collecting data and assessing the data fit to the model.) We also advocate replication as a means of testing a theoretical structural model!

7.9 SUMMARY

In this chapter, we considered the assessment of goodness of fit for structural equation models. Specifically, we examined different criteria for model fit, model comparison, and model parsimony. Different fit indices have been developed for these three approaches to modeling, and so we briefly described each. However, *no one* index serves as a definite criterion for testing a hypothesized structural model. An "ideal" fit index just does not exist. This should not be surprising, because it has been suggested that an "ideal" fit index is one that is independent of sample size, accurately reflects differences in fit, imposes a penalty for inclusion of additional parameters (Marsh et al., 1988), and supports the choice of a true model when it is known (McDonald & Marsh, 1990).

In this chapter, we also discussed the two-step approach to modeling, the assessing of fit of individual parameters, model respecification, and sample size. This approach involves first establishing valid and reliable indicators of latent variables in a measurement model, and then specifying relationships among the latent variables in a structural model. In chapter 8, we present a more detailed look at the LISREL8-SIMPLIS and EQS5 computer program syntax and output for our model.

EXERCISES

1. Identify the GOF indices that are used to subjectively evaluate model fit, evaluate model parsimony, or compare models.

2. In EQS5, the LM test indicates what about the parameters in an initial model?

3. In EQS5, the W test indicates what about the parameters in an initial model?

4. How are the modification indices in LISREL8-SIMPLIS used?

5. What approach should a researcher take in testing parameter estimates for significance?

6. How does a researcher test for the difference between two models?
7. How are structural equation models affected by power considerations?
8. What is the two-step approach?
9. What do the authors recommend to replace "model fit"?

REFERENCES

Akaike, H. (1987). Factor analysis and AIC. *Psychometrika, 52*, 317–332.

Anderson, J. C., & Gerbing, D. W. (1984). The effects of sampling error on convergence, improper solutions and goodness-of-fit indices for maximum likelihood confirmatory factor analysis. *Psychometrika, 49*, 155–173.

Anderson, J. C., & Gerbing, D. W. (1988). Structural equation modeling in practice: A review and recommended two-step approach. *Psychological Bulletin, 103*, 411–423.

Baldwin, B. (1989). A primer in the use and interpretation of structural equation models. *Measurement and Evaluation in Counseling and Development, 22*, 100–112.

Bentler, P. M. (1990). Comparative fit indexes in structural models. *Psychological Bulletin, 107*, 238–246.

Bentler, P. M., & Bonett, D. G. (1980). Significance tests and goodness-of-fit in the analysis of covariance structures. *Psychological Bulletin, 88*, 588–606.

Bentler, P. M., & Bonett, D. G. (1982). Significance tests and goodness-of-fit in analysis of covariance structures. In C. Fornell (Ed.), *A second generation of multivariate analysis: Measurement and evaluation: Vol. 2*. New York: Praeger.

Bollen, K. A. (1989). *Structural equations with latent variables*. New York: Wiley.

Bollen, K. A. (1990). Overall fit in covariance structure models: Two types of sample size effects. *Psychological Bulletin, 107*, 256–259.

Bollen, K. A., & Liang, J. (1988). Some properties of Hoelter's CN. *Sociological Methods and Research, 16*, 492–503.

Breckler, S. J. (1990). Applications of covariance structure modeling in psychology: Cause for concern? *Psychological Bulletin, 107*, 260–273.

Cliff, N. (1983). Some cautions concerning the application of causal modeling methods. *Multivariate Behavioral Research, 18*, 115–126.

Cohen, J. (1988). *Statistical power analysis for the behavioral sciences* (2nd ed.). Hillsdale, NJ: Lawrence Erlbaum Associates.

Cudeck, R., & Henly, S. J. (1991). Model selection in covariance structures analysis and the "problem" of sample size: A clarification. *Psychological Bulletin, 109*, 512–519.

Hair, J. F., Jr., Anderson, R. E., Tatham, R. L., & Black, W. C. (1992). *Multivariate data analysis with readings* (3rd ed.). New York: Macmillan.

Hoelter, J. W. (1983). The analysis of covariance structures: Goodness-of-fit indices. *Sociological Methods and Research, 11*, 325–344.

James, L. R., Mulaik, S. A., & Brett, J. M. (1982). *Causal analysis: Assumptions, models, and data*. Beverly Hills, CA: Sage.

Jöreskog, K. G. (1969). A general approach to confirmatory maximum likelihood factor analysis. *Psychometrika, 34*, 183–202.

Jöreskog, K. G., & Sörbom, D. (1989). *LISREL 7 user's reference guide*. Mooresville, IN: Scientific Software, Inc.

Loehlin, J. C. (1987). *Latent variable models: An introduction to factor, path, and structural analysis*. Hillsdale, NJ: Lawrence Erlbaum Associates.

Lunneborg, C. E. (1987). *Bootstrap applications for the behavioral sciences: Vol. 1.* Psychology Department, University of Washington, Seattle.

Marsh, H. W., Balla, J. R., & Hau, K.-T. (1996). An evaluation of incremental fit indices: A clarification of mathematical and empirical properties. In G. A. Marcoulides & R. E. Schumacker (Eds.), *Advanced structural equation modeling: Issues and techniques.* Mahwah, NJ: Lawrence Erlbaum Associates.

Marsh, H. W., Balla, J. R., & McDonald, R. P. (1988). Goodness-of-fit indexes in confirmatory factor analysis: The effect of sample size. *Psychological Bulletin, 103,* 391–410.

McDonald, R. P. (1989). An index of goodness-of-fit based on noncentrality. *Journal of Classification, 6,* 97–103.

McDonald, R. P., & Marsh, H. W. (1990). Choosing a multivariate model: Noncentrality and goodness of fit. *Psychological Bulletin, 107,* 247–255.

Mulaik, S. A., James, L. R., Alstine, J. V., Bennett, N., Lind, S., & Stilwell, C. D. (1989). Evaluation of goodness-of-fit indices for structural equation models. *Psychological Bulletin, 105,* 430–445.

Steiger, J. H., & Lind, J. M. (1980, May). *Statistically-based tests for the number of common factors.* Paper presented at Psychometric Society Meeting, Iowa City, IA.

Tucker, L. R., & Lewis, C. (1973). The reliability coefficient for maximum likelihood factor analysis. *Psychometrika, 38,* 1–10.

Williams, L. J., & Holahan, P. J. (1994). Parsimony-based fit indices of multiple indicator models: Do they work? *Structural Equation Modeling: A Multidisciplinary Journal, 1,* 161–189.

8

COMPUTER PROGRAM
EXAMPLES

—————————◆◆◆—————————

Chapter Outline:

Key Concepts:

Computer program syntax
Computer program options
Computer program output
Special features of computer programs

In this chapter, the model presented in Fig. 5.3 (chap. 5) and subsequently respecified as Model 2 in Fig. 6.1 with mother's education and father's education error covariance indicated (chap. 6) is used to further present EQS5 and LISREL8-SIMPLIS computer output. The model included two latent independent variables (home background, ability) and two latent dependent variables (aspirations, achievement). These latent variables were defined using a set of indicator variables identified in the sample variance–covariance matrix in chapter 6 (Table 6.1). The complete program output presented in this chapter uses this sample variance–covariance matrix to analyze model fit using both the EQS5 and LISREL8-SIMPLIS computer programs. A comparison of their program syntax, options, output, and special features is therefore made in the chapter.

If you are using a mainframe computer, check with your computing center to determine whether it has purchased these programs and how or where you can access them. In some cases, these programs are run on the mainframe computer (IBM, VAX, etc.) using standard operating language (CMS, MUSIC), either interactively or without the use of job control language (JCL). The EQS5 and LISREL8-SIMPLIS software programs presented here were personal-computer versions run on an IBM 486 DX/2 66 MHz in MS Windows 3.11. They will also run on an IBM-compatible computer (386 or 486, math coprocessor, 8 Mb of memory), and EQS5 is now also available for the Apple Macintosh.

8.1 SUGGESTED APPROACH TO STRUCTURAL EQUATION MODELING

It might be helpful at this point to present our suggested approach, which expands the five recommended steps for structural equation modeling. The five steps, you may recall, were listed at the beginning of chapter 4; they can serve as a checklist or starting point for most researchers. Our expanded approach is therefore discussed next.

1. Review the relevant research literature to specify a model.

A comprehensive effort to identify relevant variables and their relationships is highly recommended. This will help determine valid and reliable indicator variables of latent variables, provide a theoretical perspective for your model, and help you to establish latent-variable relationships grounded in prior research studies.

2. Identify a model; indicate measurement methods.

In chapter 9, several different types of models are identified. Inherent in each model description is a particular method of handling measurement error. For example, a model could use a single indicator with or without adjustment of measurement error; for example, a reliability value may or may not be specified for a single indicator variable. In multiple-indicator models, consideration must be given to the independent- and dependent-latent-variable errors and the impact they have on the model coefficients. For example, Rigdon (1994) indicated that if the two dependent-latent-variable errors in a reciprocal model were not correlated, the model parameters would be affected. The determination of a measurement model can take several forms: an uncorrelated versus a correlated covariance structure analysis, a first- versus a second-order confirmatory factor analysis, or even a multitrait multimethod analysis, to name just a few. The structural models can also take several forms: nonreciprocal versus reciprocal latent-variable relationships, single or multiple independent latent variables predicting single or multiple dependent latent variables, or even a longitudinal analysis using the same latent variables at different times (Collins & Horn, 1992). Each of these structural models requires understanding and specifying a measurement model with its associated error terms.

3. Conduct preliminary descriptive statistical analyses.

We recommend that a researcher consider all of the basic rules of data collection and analysis prior to forming measurement and/or structural equation models. As we have previously mentioned, these rules pertain to scaling issues, random sampling (representativeness and homogeneity of sample), handling of missing data, collinearity issues, and outlier detection, to name just a few. Issues of multivariate normality, factors that cause non-positive definite matrices, and Heywood cases (negative variance) must also be considered in structural equation models.

4. Estimate parameters in measurement and/or structural models.

The review of the literature should primarily drive the model specification and identification which, for both measurement and structural models, involves diagramming. The researcher should be cognizant of the total, direct, and indirect "effects" specified in the structural model (see chap. 5) and what parameters are to be estimated. Different models (see chap. 9) require varying types of parameter estimates and/or constraints.

We also recommend a two-step approach to structural modeling: conduct a confirmatory factor analysis first, and then formulate the structural relationships among the latent variables. We feel that it is important to validly and reliably measure the latent variables before establishing relationships among them. If the distributional properties of variables and scaling of variables are understood, then selection of a correct estimation technique is possible.

5. Reexamine model identification and estimation.

If you are analyzing a multiple regression model using structural equation modeling software, the model by definition is identified. However, when conducting path analyses, some models will be better at reproducing the sample correlation matrix (variance–covariance matrix) than others. Obviously, the choice of a model to best reproduce the sample matrix must be grounded in theory.

In confirmatory factor analysis, we found that a good rule to try to follow is to have at least three indicators (observed variables) for each latent variable. The amount of variance explained in the latent variables, by the sets of indicator variables, is also prudent to determine. This has been conceptually and practically explained before as a distinction between variance accounted for and unexplained variance in the latent variable.

Depending upon the type of structural model specified, several nested models could be tested, an initial model and an alternative model could be tested, or the parsimony of a model could be assessed. Model identification should therefore be carefully considered. The dynamics related to under-, just-, and overidentified models were previously discussed in chapter 6. Basically, parameters should be free or fixed depending on the theory behind the model.

6. Assess model fit, parsimony, or comparison of models, and respecify model if meaningful.

Several goodness-of-fit indices were presented in chapter 7 for assessing whether data fit the theoretical hypothesized model, deciding whether the addition or deletion of paths in a model would lead to a more parsimonious model, or comparing a model with an alternative model. We have found it helpful in our own research models to add or drop only a single parameter at a time to assess the impact on the model. LISREL8-SIMPLIS provides modification indices to identify the addition or deletion of parameters that would improve the model, and EQS5 provides the LM and Wald tests. As previously mentioned, these indices are useful guides and do not provide a "statistical test" of significance. Recognizing reasonable values for the parameter estimates and knowing the appropriate direction and sign are even more valuable to interpreting the relationships specified in your model.

7. Present and interpret model.

We recommend that the sample size, means, and standard deviations be presented along with the correlation matrix or variance–covariance matrix. Additionally, any original model and final model should be diagrammed. The parameter estimates, standard errors, and model fit indices should also be indicated. Any replication, cross validation, or bootstrapping estimates could further be presented to validate the model (see chap. 10). In the end, the model should ultimately be related back to theory. In some instances, model invariance across samples and/or across time is the true test of substantive meaningfulness.

8.2 EQS5 PROGRAM EXAMPLE

The recursive model in chapter 6 (Fig. 6.1) provides the basis for the EQS5 program output presented in this chapter. The measurement and structural models were also previously explained in chapter 5, and the computer programs were given in the chapter.

The EQS5 Windows program has several features that make the analysis of data and the writing of structural equation programs easy. First, the BUILD EQS feature using EASY BUILD displays a series of questions, after which the software creates the computer program file with the extension .EQS for later editing and analysis. Other standard features that make EQS5 especially appealing include statistical analysis (descriptive statistics, *t* tests, crosstabs, analysis of variance, correlation, regression, and factor analysis), the input and export of matrices or raw data files, multisample analyses, outlier detection, simulation (replication, bootstrap, jackknife), and path diagramming of models. More expanded statistical analysis and functions are possible with the newer EQS5 version running under Windows 3.11 (Bentler & Wu, 1993).

The simplicity of EQS5 programs is quickly noted by the use of only four labeling prefix conventions: V = variable (observed variable), F = factor (latent variable), E = error (residual of observed variable), and D = disturbance (residual of latent variable). The variables V1 to V9 and their associated error terms, sequentially numbered in the measurement model, were related to the latent variables F1 to F4 according to the model in Fig. 6.1. The latent variables in the structural model were then related with sequentially numbered error terms using the prefixes D1 and D2. The use of a TO convention makes specifying a list of these error terms easier in the program (that is, to specify a range of error terms). The Bentler–Weeks representation, which treats variables as either independent or dependent, also serves to simplify the equations and to make them clearer to understand.

The basic program input in EQS5 consists of /SPECIFICATIONS, /EQUATIONS, /VARIANCES, and /END program statements. The other program statements are optional: /TITLE, /LABELS, /COVARIANCES,

/CONSTRAINTS, /INEQUALITIES, /MATRIX, /STANDARD DEVIATIONS, /MEANS, /LMTEST, /WTEST, /TECHNICAL, /DIAGRAM, /PRINT, /SIMU-LATION, and /OUTPUT. The /SPECIFICATIONS statement permits the identification of the number of subjects (cas=200), the number of variables in the variance-covariance matrix (var=9), and the method of estimation one wishes to conduct, in this case maximum likelihood (ME=ML). The /LABELS statement (optional) permits up to eight characters to identify the variables for analysis. EQS5 will automatically use the model specification to select the subset of input variables needed to perform the model analysis. The /EQUATIONS statement reflects the relationships diagrammed in Fig. 6.1. It would be prudent to examine each of these equations yourself to verify that all relationships have been expressed. The /VARI-ANCE statement permits fixed- and free-parameter designations for variance terms. The /COVARIANCE statement, although optional, permits the specification of covariance terms. The /MATRIX statement is not needed if data are in an external computer file; instead, use the /SPECIFICATIONS statement with associated subcommands MA (MA=COV;, MA=RAW;, or MA=COR;) and DA (DA='INPUT.FIL';).

The EQS5 Windows software comes with several example data sets that are explained in the *User's Guide*. These data sets provide the basic introduction necessary to begin using the features available in the software. We have found the software to be very easy to use, especially to generate EQS5 programs using the EASY BUILD option, and have kept the programs manageable by using the data input file options on the /SPECIFICATIONS command.

The EQS5 program for the model in Fig. 6.1 used the /TITLE, /SPECI-FICATION, /LABELS, /EQUATIONS, /VARIANCES, /COVARIANCES, /MATRIX, /DIAGRAM, and /END commands. The /TITLE command permitted us to describe each program run separately. Notice that the text in the /TITLE command does not end in a semicolon! Since the data are in a variance-covariance matrix format and form a part of the program, we did not specify any input data matrix on the /SPECIFICATIONS command. Here we indicated only the sample size, number of indicator variables, and estimation method. The /LABELS command allowed us to expand the generic prefixes used by EQS5 to better describe our observed and latent variables. The /EQUATIONS command was the most critical, because it directly reflected the paths diagrammed in the model and thereby indicated the parameters to be estimated. Care should be taken to properly specify these equations and to include permissible start values if possible. The /VARIANCES command specified the observed variable error terms in our measurement model, as well as the latent dependent error terms (disturbance terms or equation prediction errors) in our structural model. The

/COVARIANCE command specified the two latent independent variables that covary, as well as the error covariances of the two observed variables. The /MATRIX command was used to input the variance–covariance matrix, because it was not read from an external file specified on the /SPECIFI-CATIONS command. The /DIAGRAM command outputted the model as indicated by the positioning of the variable names used in the /EQUATIONS command. The EQS5 program was stopped with the use of an /END command.

The EQS5 program is presented here again for ease of reference:

```
/TITLE
 STRUCTURAL EQUATION MODEL EXAMPLE Figure 6.1
/SPECIFICATIONS
 CAS=200; VAR=9; ME=ML;
/LABELS
V1=EDASP;V2=OCCASP;V3=VERBACH;V4=QUANTACH;V5=FAMINC;V6=FAED;
V7=MOED;V8=VERBAB;V9=QUANTAB;F1=ASPIRE;F2=ACHIEVE; F3=HOME; F4=ABILITY;
/EQUATIONS
        V1=    F1 + E1;
        V2= 1*F1 + E2;
        V3=    F2 + E3;
        V4= 1*F2 + E4;
        V5=    F3 + E5;
        V6= 1*F3 + E6;
        V7= 1*F3 + E7;
        V8=    F4 + E8;
        V9= 1*F4 + E9;
F1=1*F3 + 1*F4 + D1;
F2=1*F1 + 1*F3 + 1*F4 + D2;
/VARIANCES
        E1 TO E9=1*;
        D1 TO D2=1*;
/COVARIANCES
        E6,E7=1*;
        F3,F4=1*;
/MATRIX
1.024
 .792 1.077
1.027   .919 1.844
 .756   .697 1.244 1.286
 .567   .537   .876   .632  .852
 .445   .424   .677   .526  .518  .670
 .434   .389   .635   .498  .475  .545  .716
 .580   .564   .893   .716  .546  .422  .373  .851
 .491   .499   .888   .646  .508  .389  .339  .629  .871
/END
```

8.3 LISREL8-SIMPLIS PROGRAM EXAMPLE

The LISREL8-SIMPLIS command language for Model 2 in Fig. 6.1 was as follows:

```
Model 2 in Figure 6.1
Observed variables: EDASP OCCASP VERBACH QUANTACH FAMINC
                    FAED MOED VERBAB QUANTAB
Covariance matrix:
1.024
 .792 1.077
1.027  .919 1.844
 .756  .697 1.244 1.286
 .567  .537  .876  .632 .852
 .445  .424  .677  .526 .518 .670
 .434  .389  .635  .498 .475 .545 .716
 .580  .564  .893  .716 .546 .422 .373 .851
 .491  .499  .888  .646 .508 .389 .339 .629 .871
Sample size: 200
Latent variables: ASPIRE ACHIEVE HOME ABILITY
Relationships:
    EDASP  OCCASP            = ASPIRE
    VERBACH QUANTACH         = ACHIEVE
    FAMINC  FAED  MOED       = HOME
    VERBAB  QUANTAB          = ABILITY
    ASPIRE                   = HOME ABILITY
    ACHIEVE                  = ASPIRE HOME ABILITY
Let the error covariances of MOED and FAED be correlated
End of Problem
```

In the SIMPLIS program, the Relationships: command specified the parameters to be estimated, or paths in the measurement and structural models. Notice that no error terms needed to be specified for the observed variables in the measurement model, nor equation prediction errors (disturbance terms) in the structural model. Also, the error covariances for MOED and FAED were correlated, on the basis of the modification indices outputted from Model 1, with the command Let the error covariances of MOED and FAED be correlated. Other commands are just as easy to specify in a LISREL8-SIMPLIS program.

Matrix output can be obtained from the LISREL8-SIMPLIS program by simply adding the following command before the end of the program: LISREL OUTPUT RS MI SS SC EF. The output will now be displayed in matrix format (see chap. 11). The options specified on the LISREL OUTPUT command request the following: RS, print residuals; MI, print modification indices; SS, print standardized solution (latent-variable variances are scaled to 1.0); SC, standardize completely (observed and latent variables are standardized); and

EF, print total and indirect "effects" with standard errors. The reader will undoubtedly find the LISREL8-SIMPLIS command language easier to use, and also find the output options available using the LISREL OUTPUT command useful, especially if a former matrix program user.

8.4 COMPUTER OUTPUT COMPARISONS

The computer output from the EQS5 and LISREL8-SIMPLIS programs is presented here to afford a comparison of similarities and differences in style. The parameter estimates in Table 6.2 (chap. 6) will be boldfaced in the computer output for easy identification (note: the computer output has been edited and shortened). The parameter values are comparative within rounding error to three decimal places.

EQS5 Computer Output

```
BENTLER-WEEKS STRUCTURAL REPRESENTATION:

NUMBER OF DEPENDENT VARIABLES = 11
DEPENDENT V'S :  1 2 3 4 5 6 7 8 9
DEPENDENT F'S :  1 2

NUMBER OF INDEPENDENT VARIABLES = 13
INDEPENDENT F'S :  3 4
INDEPENDENT E'S :  1 2 3 4 5 6 7 8 9
INDEPENDENT D'S :  1 2

DETERMINANT OF INPUT MATRIX IS 0.67308D-03

MAXIMUM LIKELIHOOD SOLUTION
PARAMETER ESTIMATES APPEAR IN ORDER.
NO SPECIAL PROBLEMS WERE ENCOUNTERED DURING OPTIMIZATION.

RESIDUAL COVARIANCE MATRIX (S-SIGMA)
```

		V1	V2	V3	V4	V5	V6	V7	V8	V9
EDASP	V1	0.000								
OCCASP	V2	0.000	0.000							
VERBACH	V3	0.011	-0.014	0.000						
QUANTACH	V4	-0.010	-0.006	0.000	0.000					
FAMINC	V5	-0.008	0.009	0.006	-0.024	0.000				
FAED	V6	-0.005	0.011	-0.004	0.013	0.000	0.000			
MOED	V7	0.020	0.009	0.009	0.026	-0.001	0.000	0.000		
VERBAB	V8	0.012	0.043	-0.022	0.027	0.008	0.002	-0.014	0.000	
QUANTAB	V9	-0.048	0.004	0.020	-0.008	-0.002	-0.010	-0.028	0.000	0.000

```
AVERAGE ABSOLUTE COVARIANCE RESIDUALS = 0.0096
AVERAGE OFF-DIAGONAL ABSOLUTE COVARIANCE RESIDUALS = 0.0120
```

LARGEST STANDARDIZED RESIDUALS

V9,V1	V8,V2	V9,V7	V7,V4	V8,V4	V7,V1	V5,V4	V8,V7	V8,V3	V9,V3
0.051	0.045	0.036	0.027	0.026	0.024	-0.022	-0.018	-0.017	0.016

V6,V4	V6,V2	V9,V6	V8,V1	V7,V2	V8,V5	V5,V2	V3,V2	V5,V1	V4,V1
0.014	0.013	-0.013	0.013	0.011	0.010	0.010	-0.010	-0.008	-0.008

GOODNESS OF FIT SUMMARY

INDEPENDENCE MODEL CHI-SQUARE = 1407.098, BASED ON 36 DEGREES OF FREEDOM

INDEPENDENCE AIC = 1335.09823   INDEPENDENCE CAIC = 1180.35882

MODEL AIC = -20.83179   MODEL CAIC = -106.79813

CHI-SQUARE = **19.168** BASED ON 20 DEGREES OF FREEDOM

PROBABILITY VALUE FOR THE CHI-SQUARE STATISTIC IS **0.51092**

THE NORMAL THEORY RLS CHI-SQUARE FOR THIS ML SOLUTION IS 18.596.

BENTLER-BONETT NORMED FIT INDEX = 0.986

BENTLER-BONETT NONNORMED FIT INDEX = 1.001

COMPARATIVE FIT INDEX = 1.000

MEASUREMENT EQUATIONS WITH STANDARD ERRORS AND TEST STATISTICS

```
EDASP     = V1 =    1.000 F1  + 1.000 E1

OCASP     = V2 =     .918*F1  + 1.000 E2
                     .064
                   14.342

VERBACH   = V3 =    1.000 F2  + 1.000 E3

QUANTACH  = V4 =     .753*F2  + 1.000 E4
                     .042
                   18.134

FAMINC    = V5 =    1.000 F3  + 1.000 E5

FAED      = V6 =     .782*F3  + 1.000 E6
                     .064
                   12.185

MOED      = V7 =     .720*F3  + 1.000 E7
                     .069
                   10.372

VERBAB    = V8 =    1.000 F4  + 1.000 E8

QUANTAB   = V9 =     .949*F4  + 1.000 E9
                     .067
                   14.100
```

CONSTRUCT EQUATIONS WITH STANDARD ERRORS AND TEST STATISTICS

```
ASPIRE    = F1 =     .505*F3  +    .447*F4  + 1.000 D1
                     .154          .151
                    3.288         2.963

ACHIEVE   = F2 =     .526*F1  +    .302*F3  +   .685*F3   + 1.000 D2
                     .115          .161         .161
                    4.553         1.876        4.264
```

VARIANCES OF INDEPENDENT VARIABLES

V	F		E		D	
	F3-HOME	**.662**	E1-EDASP	**.161**	D1-ASPIRE	**.318**
		.090		.041		.057
		7.319		3.888		5.606
	F4-ABILITY	**.663**	E2-OCASP	**.350**	D2-ACHIEVE	**.228**
		.088		.048		.057
		7.515		7.356		3.976
			E3-VERBACH	**.193**		
				.051		
				3.808		
			E4-QUANTACH	**.349**		
				.044		
				7.945		
			E5-FAMINC	**.190**		
				.040		
				4.744		
			E6-FAED	**.265**		
				.035		
				7.661		
			E7-MOED	**.373**		
				.044		
				8.497		
			E8-VERBAB	**.188**		
				.035		
				5.402		
			E9-QUANTAB	**.274**		
				.038		
				7.198		

COVARIANCES AMONG INDEPENDENT VARIABLES

V	F		E		D
	F4-ABILITY	**.538**	E7-MOED	**.173**	
	F3-HOME	.070	E6-FAED	.033	
		7.638		5.277	

END OF PROGRAM

LISREL8-SIMPLIS Computer Output

Model 2

LISREL ESTIMATES (MAXIMUM LIKELIHOOD)

     EDASP = 1.00*ASPIRE, Errorvar.= 0.16, R^2 = 0.84
                                       (0.041)
                                       3.88

$$OCCASP = 0.92*ASPIRE, \quad Errorvar.= \quad 0.35, \quad R^2 = 0.67$$
$$(0.064) \qquad\qquad\qquad (0.048)$$
$$14.34 \qquad\qquad\qquad 7.36$$

$$VERBACH = 1.00*ACHIEVE, \quad Errorvar.= \quad 0.19, \quad R^2 = 0.90$$
$$(0.051)$$
$$3.81$$

$$QUANTACH = 0.75*ACHIEVE, \quad Errorvar.= \quad 0.35, \quad R^2 = 0.73$$
$$(0.042) \qquad\qquad\qquad (0.044)$$
$$18.13 \qquad\qquad\qquad 7.95$$

$$FAMINC = 1.00*HOME, \quad Errorvar.= \quad 0.19, \quad R^2 = 0.78$$
$$(0.040)$$
$$4.74$$

$$FAED = 0.78*HOME, \quad Errorvar.= \quad 0.27, \quad R^2 = 0.60$$
$$(0.064) \qquad\qquad\qquad (0.035)$$
$$12.18 \qquad\qquad\qquad 7.66$$

$$MOED = 0.72*HOME, \quad Errorvar.= \quad 0.37, \quad R^2 = 0.48$$
$$(0.069) \qquad\qquad\qquad (0.044)$$
$$10.37 \qquad\qquad\qquad 8.50$$

$$VERBAB = 1.00*ABILITY, \quad Errorvar.= \quad 0.19, \quad R^2 = 0.78$$
$$(0.035)$$
$$5.41$$

$$QUANTAB = 0.95*ABILITY, \quad Errorvar.= \quad 0.27, \quad R^2 = 0.69$$
$$(0.067) \qquad\qquad\qquad (0.038)$$
$$14.10 \qquad\qquad\qquad 7.20$$

Error Covariance for MOED and FAED = **0.17**

$$(0.033)$$
$$5.28$$

$$ASPIRE = 0.51*HOME + 0.45*ABILITY, \quad Errorvar.= 0.32, \quad R^2 = 0.63$$
$$(0.15) \qquad\quad (0.15) \qquad\qquad\qquad\qquad (0.057)$$
$$3.29 \qquad\quad 2.96 \qquad\qquad\qquad\qquad 5.61$$

$$ACHIEVE = 0.53*ASPIRE + 0.30*HOME + 0.69*ABILITY, \quad Error=.23 \quad R^2=.86$$
$$(0.12) \qquad\quad (0.16) \qquad\quad (0.16) \qquad\qquad\qquad (.057)$$
$$4.56 \qquad\quad 1.87 \qquad\quad 4.27 \qquad\qquad\qquad 3.97$$

COVARIANCE MATRIX OF INDEPENDENT VARIABLES

	HOME	ABILITY
HOME	**0.66**	
	(0.09)	
	7.32	
ABILITY	**0.54**	**0.66**
	(0.07)	(0.09)
	7.64	7.51

COVARIANCE MATRIX OF LATENT VARIABLES

	ASPIRE	ACHIEVE	HOME	ABILITY
ASPIRE	0.86			
ACHIEVE	1.02	1.65		
HOME	0.57	0.87	0.66	
ABILITY	0.57	0.91	0.54	0.66

GOODNESS OF FIT STATISTICS

       CHI-SQUARE WITH 20 DEGREES OF FREEDOM = 19.17 (P = 0.51)
          ESTIMATED NON-CENTRALITY PARAMETER (NCP) = 0.0
       90 PERCENT CONFIDENCE INTERVAL FOR NCP = (0.0 ; 13.53)

             MINIMUM FIT FUNCTION VALUE = 0.096
          POPULATION DISCREPANCY FUNCTION VALUE (F0) = 0.0
       90 PERCENT CONFIDENCE INTERVAL FOR F0 = (0.0 ; 0.068)
       ROOT MEAN SQUARE ERROR OF APPROXIMATION (RMSEA) = 0.0
       90 PERCENT CONFIDENCE INTERVAL FOR RMSEA = (0.0 ; 0.058)
       P-VALUE FOR TEST OF CLOSE FIT (RMSEA < 0.05) = 0.90

             EXPECTED CROSS-VALIDATION INDEX (ECVI) = 0.35
       90 PERCENT CONFIDENCE INTERVAL FOR ECVI = (0.35 ; 0.42)
                 ECVI FOR SATURATED MODEL = 0.45
                 ECVI FOR INDEPENDENCE MODEL = 7.16

CHI-SQUARE FOR INDEPENDENCE MODEL WITH 36 DEGREES OF FREEDOM = 1407.10
                 INDEPENDENCE AIC = 1425.10
                        MODEL AIC = 69.17
                    SATURATED AIC = 90.00
                 INDEPENDENCE CAIC = 1463.78
                        MODEL CAIC = 176.63
                    SATURATED CAIC = 283.42

             ROOT MEAN SQUARE RESIDUAL (RMR) = 0.015
                    STANDARDIZED RMR = 0.015
                 GOODNESS OF FIT INDEX (GFI) = 0.98
       ADJUSTED GOODNESS OF FIT INDEX (AGFI) = 0.95
       PARSIMONY GOODNESS OF FIT INDEX (PGFI) = 0.44

                 NORMED FIT INDEX (NFI) = 0.99
             NON-NORMED FIT INDEX (NNFI) = 1.00
       PARSIMONY NORMED FIT INDEX (PNFI) = 0.55
             COMPARATIVE FIT INDEX (CFI) = 1.00
             INCREMENTAL FIT INDEX (IFI) = 1.00
                RELATIVE FIT INDEX (RFI) = 0.98

                 CRITICAL N (CN) = 391.00

8.5 COMPUTER OUTPUT INTERPRETATION

EQS5 Computer Output

The EQS5 computer output initially indicates the covariance matrix to be analyzed. This covariance matrix is different from the variance–covariance matrix inputted into the program when you select fewer observed variables than originally indicated in the covariance matrix for the /EQUATIONS command. In our EQS5 program, we used all the observed variables in the covariance matrix; therefore, the covariance matrix to be analyzed was identical to the one in our program.

Next, the numbers of independent and dependent variables indicated in the /EQUATIONS command are identified according to the Bentler–Weeks structural representation. In our example, there were 13 independent variables: 2 independent *F*s (latent variables); 9 observed-variable measurement errors, or *E*s; and 2 prediction-equation errors, or *D*s. There were 11 dependent variables: nine observed variables, or *V*s; and two dependent latent variables, or *F*s. These are easily identified by examining the equations in the EQS5 program. Any variable indicated on the right-hand side of the equal sign (=) is an independent variable. Variables on the left-hand side of the equation are dependent variables. Notice that in some cases, a variable may appear first on the right-hand side of an equation but later appear on the left-hand side. When this happens, the variables are considered dependent variables.

A residual covariance matrix and a standardized residual covariance matrix are also printed as part of the computer output in EQS5. This residual covariance matrix indicates the difference between the elements in S and Σ. Although the procedure is not recommended today, earlier researchers examined the standardized residual covariance matrix to determine discrepancies in model-implied parameter estimates. You may recall our similar discussion in chapter 3 about the decomposition of a correlation matrix in path analysis. Similar logic is applied here in the examination of the residual covariance matrix. Suffice it to say that if all of the values in the residual covariance matrix were zero (0), then S and Σ would be identical and χ^2 would be equal to 0, indicating a perfect model fit. The EQS5 program further indicates which variables have the largest standardized residuals and provides a distribution of the standardized residuals following the output of the two residual covariance matrices. This distribution of residuals is expected to be normally distributed in large samples.

The goodness-of-fit summary indicates the independence-model chi-square and corresponding model chi-square values. In our example, we constrained the number of paths (parameters) from 36 degrees of freedom to 20, getting a chi-square drop from 1407.10 to 19.17. Certain other fit indices were above the suggested .90 level, further supporting the data fitting the model.

The measurement equations, standard errors, and test statistics are used to determine whether the observed variables assess the latent variables of interest. Then the associated standard errors and test statistics are considered for each construct equation. These equations indicate how well the latent dependent variable can be predicted. As mentioned before, dividing the parameter estimate by its respective standard error (which is indicated directly beneath the parameter estimate) yields the test statistic (within rounding error). The variances of the independent variables and covariances among the independent variables are outputted next. A standardized solution is finally printed, which indicates all the parameter estimates, including the prediction-equation error estimates, which are not indicated in the LISREL8-SIMPLIS output. Similarly, the amount of variance predicted in the structural equations is indicated in the LISREL8-SIMPLIS computer output, but not in the EQS5 computer output. Finally, the correlations are indicated among the independent variables, among the latent variables, among the measurement errors, and/or among the equation errors (not shown).

LISREL8-SIMPLIS Computer Output

The LISREL8-SIMPLIS computer output first identifies the file where the program syntax was read and then prints the lines of program syntax in the file. Then the covariance matrix to be analyzed is printed. Once again, if we do not use all of the observed variables listed on the `Observed Vari-ables:` command in the `Relationships:` command, then this covariance matrix will be different from the one in the program. In other words, it will select only the variances and covariances of the observed variables used in the model.

The parameter estimates are then indicated for all equations included in the `Relationships:` command. Variables do not necessarily have to be listed individually in the equations; for example:

```
Relationships:
   X1-X4 = Factor1
```

is preferred over:

```
Relationships:
        X1 = Factor1
        X2 = Factor1
        X3 = Factor1
        X4 = Factor1
```

for the single-latent-variable measurement model.

Also, the latent variable or factor is standardized by default, unless some other unit of measurement is specified by the user. Using the LISREL OUTPUT command and specifying standardized output further provides standardized factor loadings for X1 through X4. The associated standard error and test statistic for each appear directly below these validity coefficients, permitting a test of their significance.

LISREL8-SIMPLIS computer output for the equations specified in the Relationships: command also provide R^2 values, which are interpreted as the reliabilities of the respective observed variables that define the latent variables in the measurement model. The R^2 values indicated for the structural equations indicate the amount of variance predicted by the latent independent variable(s).

Consequently, the measurement model equations provide valuable information (validity and reliability) for determining how well the latent variables are assessed. The structural equations indicate the coefficients for the independent latent predictor variables, and an R^2 value that indicates the amount of variance predicted in the dependent latent variable. The coefficients in the structural equations are tested for significance by dividing the coefficients by their respective standard errors, yielding a test statistic. For example, the coefficient for Home predicting Aspire is .51 with a standard error of .15. This yielded a test statistic of 3.29 (.51 divided by .15 = 3.4, due to rounding error), which is significant at the .05 level ($z = 1.96$).

A covariance matrix of independent latent variables used in the analysis and a covariance matrix of latent variables in the model are outputted next by default, unless otherwise specified in the program. The covariance values among the independent latent variables are indicated along with their standard errors and test statistics, which can be used to test them for significance.

Next are listed the various fit indices, which are used to assess model fit or model parsimony or to compare models, as discussed in chapter 7. The LISREL8-SIMPLIS program has provided an excellent set of indices for this purpose. As indicated before, appropriate indices should be reported and used as a subjective guide to interpret model fit (see chap. 7).

The LISREL8-SIMPLIS program will output a fitted covariance matrix (Σ), a fitted residual matrix, and a standardized residual matrix. This is accomplished by adding the command PRINT RESIDUALS before the END OF PROBLEM command line. Otherwise, only summary statistics are listed for the fit and standardized residuals, which include the smallest fitted residual, median fitted residual, and largest fitted residual. The stem–leaf plots indicate whether the residuals are normally distributed, as expected in large samples.

The LISREL8-SIMPLIS program will provide modification indices afterward to suggest adding additional paths or error covariances with associated estimated decreases in chi-square. As mentioned before, we recommend selecting the largest single modification index to respecify the model and then reanalyzing the model.

The use of the Path Diagram command will permit viewing several different diagrams in LISREL8-SIMPLIS running under Windows 3.11. The B diagram (basic model) displays the model with parameter estimates, but error terms are not included. The S diagram (structural model) displays the structural relationships among the latent variables. The X diagram displays the independent-latent-variable measurement model. The Y diagram displays the dependent-latent-variable measurement model. The R diagram displays the error covariances only. The T diagram will display the model with *t* values instead of parameter estimates. The M diagram will display modification indices. The E diagram displays models with parameter estimates. If running an analysis of a model for more than one group, use the N diagram function to obtain the model for the next group. Pressing F reveals the fit measures. Any path model selected can be printed by pressing P.

All of the different path diagrams are saved in a file with the extension .pdm; that is, the default file name is input.pdm. A separate command, PATHDIAG, will reproduce these diagrams again at a later date, should you desire. Up to 15 different diagrams are saved and can be retrieved by issuing the command PATHDIAG filename.pdm. Another handy feature of this path-diagramming capability is the use of a D function, which will display the output file.

Other optional commands that can be used in the LISREL8-SIMPLIS program can be listed separately or combined on an OPTIONS: command; for example:

```
Print Residuals
Wide Print
Number of Decimals = 3
Method of Estimation = Weighted Least Squares
Admissibility Check = off
Iterations = 100
Save Sigma in file asycov.mat
```

could be combined in a single command line:

```
OPTIONS: RS WP ND=3 ME=WLS AD=OFF IT=100 SI=asycov.mat
```

The LISREL8-SIMPLIS command language and associated options have provided a much easier method for the specification and testing of measurement and structural models. We encourage you to use three decimal places to prevent rounding errors, and use the Method of Estimation command to compare and/or select an appropriate estimation technique. The admissibility check is also recommended, because it will examine the various matrices to determine whether they have full column rank, whether they contain no rows of only zeros, and whether their covariance matrix is positive definite. If the admissibility check fails, then a poor model is suspect, possibly due to singular matrices, matrices with rows of zeros, a non-positive definite covariance matrix, or simply a marked disagreement between the model and the data.

8.6 SUMMARY

Each computer program offers certain unique features. EQS5 provides a statistical analysis package, outlier detection, and a *robust* estimation procedure, to name a few. EQS5 also provides a graphic user interface capable of diagramming models. An EQS5 version for Mac permits structural equation modeling programs to be run on the Apple Macintosh. The LM test (inclusion of significant parameters) and the W test (exclusion of nonsignificant parameters) provided for models in EQS5 also help guide the researcher in model respecification. The Bentler–Weeks representation system also simplifies specifying and analyzing theoretical models.

The LISREL8-SIMPLIS command language running in MS Windows provides ease of programming measurement and structural equation models, diagramming the model, conducting simulations, and comparing groups. LISREL8-SIMPLIS for Windows also provides PRELIS2 for handling different types of correlations as input data, and conducts statistical analysis of raw data, including skewness and kurtosis. In addition, the software provides modification indices for guidance in model respecification and permits the generation of sample variance–covariance matrices, and the computer printout can indicate the parameter to be estimated as elements within up to eight different matrices for the structural model (see chap. 11 for the LISREL matrix command language).

Each computer program permits the input of external raw data files or the inclusion of correlations, means, and standard deviations, and/or variance–covariance matrices. Other similarities include the calculation of initial estimates (not shown in this chapter), measurement and structural equation coefficients, and a standardized solution (also not shown). EQS5 and LISREL8-SIMPLIS both present the null-model chi-square and the model chi-square values. It is obvious that the programming in EQS5 and/or the SIMPLIS command language makes the specifying of models and the running of the analyses much easier, especially in comparison with earlier LISREL matrix command language programs in SPSS (1990). Once again, we find ourselves recommending the personal-computer versions of these software packages running in the Windows environment. The newer EQS5 version for Macintosh also provides for a greater use of the modeling software.

EXERCISES

Use the following information to complete the chapter problems:

Sample size = 500.

Observed X variables: ACT, CGPA, ENTRY (ACT scores; college grade point average; and company entry-level skills test score).

Observed Y variables: SALARY, PROMO (beginning salary, and current salary due to promotions).

Latent dependent variable: JOB (job success).

Latent independent variable: ACAD (academic success).

Covariance matrix:

ACT	1.002				
CGPA	.792	1.006			
ENTRY	1.027	.919	1.844		
SALARY	.756	.697	1.244	1.286	
PROMO	.567	.537	.876	.632	.852

Hypothesized model:

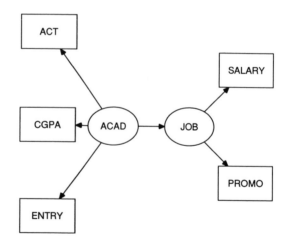

FIG. 8.1.

Research question: Does academic success predict job success?

Statistical hypothesis:

$$H_0: \text{ACAD} \rightarrow \text{JOB} = 0$$
$$H_a: \text{ACAD} \rightarrow \text{JOB} \neq 0$$

1. Write an EQS5 program to analyze the relationship specified in the diagrammed model.
2. Write a LISREL8-SIMPLIS program to analyze the relationship specified in the diagrammed model.
3. Does ACAD predict JOB, as hypothesized?

REFERENCES

Bentler, P. M., & Wu, E. J. C. (1993). *EQS/Windows user's guide.* Los Angeles: BMDP Statistical Software.

Collins, L. M., & Horn, J. L. (Eds.). (1992). *Best methods for the analysis of change: Recent advances, unanswered questions, future directions.* Washington, DC: American Psychological Association.

Rigdon, E. E. (1994). Demonstrating the effects of unmodeled random measurement error. *Structural Equation Modeling: A Multidisciplinary Journal, 1,* 375–380.

SPSS. (1990). *SPSS LISREL7 and PRELIS user's guide and reference.* Chicago: SPSS.

9

MODELS AND DIAGRAMS

Chapter Outline:

Key Concepts:

Types of models
Measurement error, reliability, and validity
Tests of group differences

The purpose of this chapter is to illustrate the one-to-one correspondence between models that can be hypothesized or diagrammed and the associated /EQUATIONS command in EQS5 and the Equations:, Relationships:, and Paths: commands in LISREL8-SIMPLIS. The examples cover several different types of models, both measurement and structural, as well as models with observed variables. This should help the reader to better understand how these models are specified for analysis in EQS5 and LISREL8-SIMPLIS. There are obviously other optional commands in the programs, as noted here and in the previous chapter, that permit the specification of input data type, estimation method, and type of output, but in this chapter our focus is solely on how various models are specified in the programs.

9.1 REGRESSION MODEL

Multiple regression models can be run using structural equation software; however, the models are always identified. The results will therefore be identical to those obtained in other statistical packages. The EQS5 program for Windows software, as mentioned before, does provide several features for handling missing data, outlier detection, and graphing, which overall help in the data analysis effort. The regression model takes the form of a linear, additive model of observed variables that does not consider measurement error per se, but does examine the errors of prediction or residual errors. The multiple regression model can be conceptualized as in Fig. 9.1.

The regression model would imply a specific set of observed variables as predictors of a dependent variable. The SIMPLIS command language for this regression model would be:

```
PREDICTION OF Y BY TWO VARIABLES
OBSERVED VARIABLES: Y X1 X2
COVARIANCE MATRIX:
 <covariance matrix here>
SAMPLE SIZE: <sample size here>
EQUATION:
 Y = X1 X2
Set covariance between X1 and X2 to zero
END OF PROBLEM
```

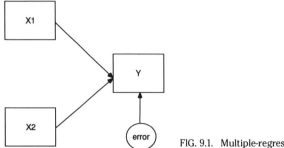

FIG. 9.1. Multiple-regression model.

The EQS5 program for the regression model would be:

```
/TITLE
 REGRESSION ANALYSIS MODEL
/SPECIFICATIONS
 CASES= <n size here>;VARIABLES=3; METHOD=GLS;
/EQUATIONS
 V1 = 1*V2 + 1*V3 + E1;
/VARIANCES
 V2,V3 = 1*;
 E1 = 1*;
/MATRIX
 <correlation matrix here>
/END
```

In the EQS5 program, V1 = Y, V2 = X_1, V3 = X_2, and E1 = error in the diagram in Fig. 9.1.

9.2 ANALYSIS-OF-COVARIANCE MODEL

Traditional analysis-of-covariance (ANCOVA) designs adjust the raw-score Y means, based on covariate variable(s), before testing for significant mean differences between groups. In structural equation modeling, the Y-variable scores can be adjusted for one or more covariates before testing is done for differences in group means. The basic ANCOVA model is shown in Fig. 9.2. In this model, X1 through X3 are covariates, Y is the dependent variable, and T1 and T2 represent dummy-coded group membership. The residual mean error for each group is tested for significant difference.

The SIMPLIS command language for this model would be:

```
GROUP T1: BOYS READING SCORES AND COVARIATES
OBSERVED VARIABLES: Y X1 X2 X3
COVARIANCE MATRIX: <file name here>
MEANS: <file name here>
SAMPLE SIZE: <sample size here>
```

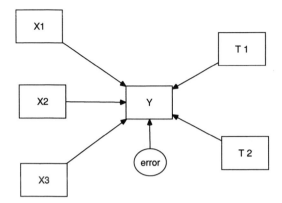

FIG. 9.2. ANCOVA model (two groups, three covariates).

```
EQUATION: Y = CONST X1 X2 X3
GROUP T2: GIRLS READING SCORES AND COVARIATES
OBSERVED VARIABLES: Y X1 X2 X3
COVARIANCE MATRIX: <file name here>
MEANS: <file name here>
SAMPLE SIZE: <sample size here>
Y = CONST
END OF PROBLEM
```

In EQS5, a V999 vector is created that contains the means. The EQS5 program syntax for the ANCOVA model is:

```
/TITLE
 ANALYSIS OF COVARIANCE MODEL
/SPECIFICATIONS
 CASES= <n size here>;VARIABLES=4; METHOD=ML;GROUPS=2;
 MATRIX=CORRELATION;ANALYSIS=MOMENT;
/EQUATIONS
 V1 = 1*V999 + 1*V2 + 1*V3 + 1*V4 + E1;
/VARIANCES
 V2,V3,V4 = 1*;
 E1 = 1*;
/COVARIANCES
 V2,V3,V4 = 1*;
/MATRIX
 <correlation matrix here>
/STANDARD DEVIATIONS
 <variable standard deviations here>
/MEANS
 <variable means here>
/END
```

9.3 PATH MODELS

Two basic types of path models are presented. The first represents a non-reciprocal model sometimes referred to as a *recursive* model. The second path model is a reciprocal model sometimes referred to as a *nonrecursive* model.

Nonreciprocal Path Model

The first diagram displays a nonreciprocal relationship with X1 and X2 covarying in the prediction of X3, which in turn predicts Y. This type of path model is diagrammed in Fig. 9.3a. The SIMPLIS command language for this path model would be:

```
PATH MODEL WITH NONRECIPROCAL RELATIONSHIP
OBSERVED VARIABLES: Y X1-X3
COVARIANCE MATRIX:
 <covariance matrix here>
SAMPLE SIZE: <sample size here>
EQUATIONS:
 X3 = X1 X2
 Y = X3
END OF PROBLEM
```

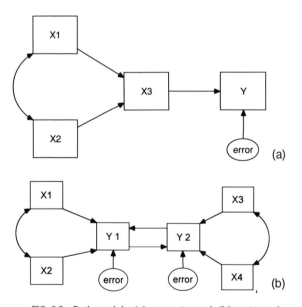

FIG. 9.3. Path models: (a) nonreciprocal; (b) reciprocal.

In EQS5, this path model would be written as:

```
/TITLE
  PATH ANALYSIS MODEL
/SPECIFICATIONS
  CASES= <n size here>;VARIABLES=4; METHOD=GLS;
/EQUATIONS
  V3 = 1*V1 + 1*V2 + E1;
  V4 = 1*V3 + E2;
/VARIANCES
  V1,V2 = 1*;
  E1,E2 = 1*;
/COVARIANCES
  V1,V2 = 1*;
/MATRIX
  <correlation matrix here>
/MEANS
  <variable means here>
/STANDARD DEVIATIONS
  <variable standard deviations here>
/END
```

Reciprocal Path Model

The second type of path model, displayed in Fig. 9.3b, indicates a reciprocal relationship between two dependent variables. This implies that two latent dependent variables influence each other. In SIMPLIS command language this would be written as:

```
RECIPROCAL PATH MODEL
OBSERVED VARIABLES: Y1-Y2 X1-X4
COVARIANCE MATRIX:
  <covariance matrix here>
SAMPLE SIZE: <sample size here>
EQUATION:
  Y1 = Y2 X1 X2
  Y2 = Y1 X3 X4
END OF PROBLEM
```

In EQS5, the model would be written as:

```
/TITLE
  PATH ANALYSIS RECIPROCAL MODEL
/SPECIFICATIONS
  CASES= <n size here>;VARIABLES=6; METHOD=ML;
/LABELS
  V1 = Y1; V2 = Y2; V3=X1; V4=X2; V5=X3; V6=X4;
```

```
/EQUATIONS
  V1 = 1*V2 + 1*V3 + 1*V4 + E1;
  V2 = 1*V1 + 1*V5 + 1*V6 + E2;
/VARIANCES
  V2,V3,V4 = 1*;
  V1,V5,V6 = 1*;
  E1,E2 = 1*;
/COVARIANCES
  V3 TO V6 = 1*;
/MATRIX
  <correlation matrix here>
/END
```

9.4 MEASUREMENT MODELS

In this section, several measurement-model diagrams will be presented. These include a single observed indicator of a factor, a measurement model for latent independent variables, a measurement model for latent dependent variables, a second-order latent-variable measurement model, a multidimensional model, and finally a multitrait multimethod model. The models serve to illustrate the complexity of the types of measurement errors possible.

Simple Measurement Model

Figure 9.4a indicates a simple measurement model that reflects a single indicator of a latent variable (as noted previously, this is not recommended in practice, but if included in a model, then the reliability of the observed variable should be specified). This model simply serves to illustrate that each observed variable is measured with error.

Single Measurement Model (X Variables)

Next, the single-factor measurement model for the X variables is displayed on the top of Fig. 9.4b. This indicates three observed variables that define a single latent independent variable. The model can be written in SIMPLIS program command language as follows:

```
SINGLE INDEPENDENT LATENT VARIABLE EXAMPLE
OBSERVED VARIABLES: X1 X2 X3
COVARIANCE MATRIX: <file name here>
SAMPLE SIZE: <sample size here>
LATENT VARIABLES: Factor1
RELATIONSHIPS:
  X1 = Factor1
  X2 = Factor1
  X3 = Factor1
END OF PROBLEM
```

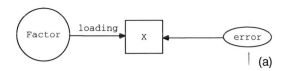

(a)

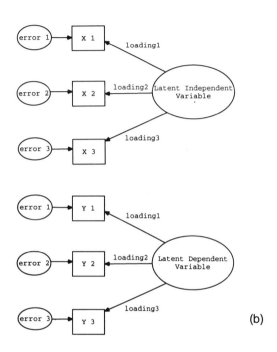

(b)

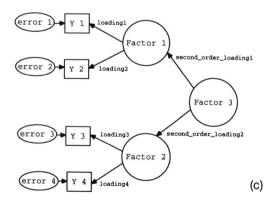

(c)

FIG. 9.4. *(Continued)*

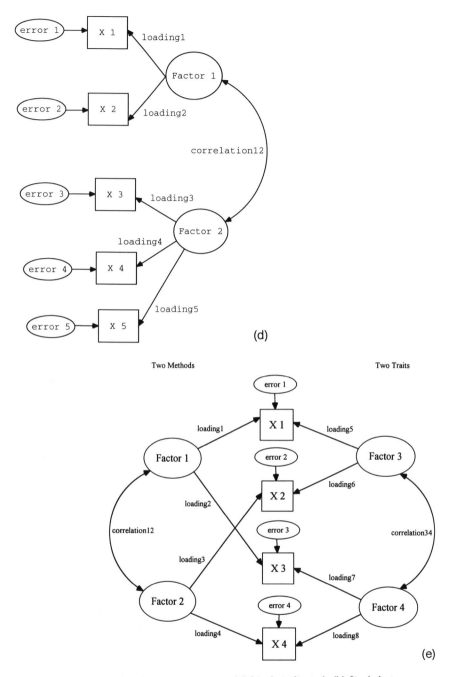

FIG. 9.4. (a) Simple measurement model (single indicator). (b) Single-factor measurement model: X variables (top); Y variables (bottom). (c) Second-order factor model. (d) Multidimensional factor model (correlated factors). (e) Simple multitrait multimethod model.

In EQS5, the single-independent-latent-variable model is written as:

```
/TITLE
 SINGLE INDEPENDENT LATENT VARIABLE MODEL
/SPECIFICATIONS
 CASES= <n size here>;VARIABLES=3; METHOD=ML;
/LABELS
 V1 = X1; V2 = X2; V3 = X3;
/EQUATIONS
 V1 = F1 + E1;
 V2 = F1 + E2;
 V3 = F1 + E3;
/VARIANCES
 F1 = 1.0;
 E1 TO E3 = 1*;
/MATRIX
 <correlation matrix here>
/END
```

Single Measurement Model (Y Variables)

A single latent dependent variable is diagrammed on the bottom of Fig. 9.4b. The Y_1 to Y_3 observed variables assess or define the single latent dependent variable. Notice that each observed variable has a unique error term and associated factor loading.

This single latent dependent variable can be defined in a SIMPLIS program as follows:

```
SINGLE DEPENDENT LATENT VARIABLE EXAMPLE
OBSERVED VARIABLES: Y1 Y2 Y3
COVARIANCE MATRIX: <file name here>
SAMPLE SIZE: <sample size here>
LATENT VARIABLES: Factor2
RELATIONSHIPS:
 Y1 = Factor2
 Y2 = Factor2
 Y3 = Factor2
END OF PROBLEM
```

In the EQS5 program, F2 is a latent dependent variable that is inferred or measured by the observed variables V4 to V6. In later EQS5 programs, the prefix D will be used to indicate the error term of a dependent latent variable that is predicted by one or more latent independent variables. The EQS5 program is specified as:

```
/TITLE
 SINGLE DEPENDENT LATENT VARIABLE MODEL
/SPECIFICATIONS
 CASES= <n size here> ;VARIABLES=3; METHOD=ML;
/LABELS
 V4 = Y1; V5 = Y2; V6 = Y3;
/EQUATIONS
 V4 = F2 + E4;
 V5 = F2 + E5;
 V6 = F2 + E6;
/VARIANCES
 F2 = 1.0;
 E4 TO E6 = 1*;
/MATRIX
 <correlation matrix here>
/END
```

Second-Order Factor Model

Figure 9.4c indicates a second-order factor analysis model. In this model, two observed dependent variables (Y_1 and Y_2) define a latent independent variable (Factor 1), and two other observed dependent variables (Y_3 and Y_4) define another latent independent variable (Factor 2). The first two *latent* variables then indicate a *third* latent variable (Factor 3).

The SIMPLIS command language program for the model in Fig. 9.4c would be:

```
SECOND ORDER LATENT VARIABLE MODEL
OBSERVED VARIABLES: Y1-Y4
COVARIANCE MATRIX: <file name here>
SAMPLE SIZE: <sample size here>
LATENT VARIABLES: Factor1 Factor2 Factor3
RELATIONSHIPS:
 Y1 = Factor1
 Y2 = Factor1
 Y3 = Factor2
 Y4 = Factor2
 Factor1 = Factor3
 Factor2 = Factor3
Let Path Factor 1 -> Factor3 = Path Factor2 -> Factor3
Set variance of Factor3 = 1
END OF PROBLEM
```

The EQS5 program would be:

```
/TITLE
 SECOND ORDER LATENT VARIABLE MODEL
/SPECIFICATION
 CASES = <sample size here>; VARIABLES = 4; METHOD=GLS;
/LABELS
 V1=Y1; V2=Y2; V3=Y3; V4=Y4;
/EQUATIONS
 V1 = 1*F1 + E1;
 V2 = F1 + E2;
 V3 = 1*F2 + E3;
 V4 = F2 + E4;
 F1 = 1*F3 + D1;
 F2 = F3 + D2;
/VARIANCES
 F3=1;
 D1,D2 = 1*;
 E1 TO E4 = 1*;
/CONSTRAINTS
 (F1,F3)=(F2,F3);
/MATRIX
 <covariance matrix here>
/END
```

In the SIMPLIS command language and EQS5 programs, two interesting points need to be made because of the simplified second-order factor model. First, any correlation or covariance between the factors is now explained by the third, second-order factor. Second, in order for the model to be identified, the SIMPLIS program must include a LET command to set the loadings equal and a SET command to fix the third-factor variance at 1. This is accomplished in the EQS5 program by including a /CONSTRAINTS command, which sets the second-order factor loadings equal, and by including F3 fixed at 1 on the /VARIANCE command (see Byrne, 1994, for further discussion about types of confirmatory factor models).

Multidimensional Models

The use of multidimensional models, or models with correlated latent variables (factors), is not uncommon in the research literature. The traditional approach in factor analysis would include a correlation between the first and second factor. This would result in different factor loadings in the pattern and structure matrices given by traditional factor analysis. In this example, however, we are specifically interested in assessing the amount of correlation between the two unidimensional factors. Figure 9.4d indicates the multidimensional factor model. This model is explicitly testing whether the factors are correlated.

In SIMPLIS command language format, the program can be written as:

```
MULTI-DIMENSIONAL LATENT VARIABLE MODEL
OBSERVED VARIABLES: X1-X5
COVARIANCE MATRIX: <file name here>
SAMPLE SIZE: <sample size here>
LATENT VARIABLES: Factor1 Factor2
RELATIONSHIPS:
  X1 = Factor1
  X2 = Factor1
  X3 = Factor2
  X4 = Factor2
  X5 = Factor2
END OF PROBLEM
```

The EQS5 program would be:

```
/TITLE
  MULTIDIMENSIONAL LATENT VARIABLE MODEL
/SPECIFICATION
  CASES = <sample size here>; VARIABLES = 5; METHOD=GLS;
/LABELS
  V1=X1; V2=X2; V3=X3; V4=X4; V5=X5;
/EQUATIONS
  V1 = 1*F1 + E1;
  V2 = F1 + E2;
  V3 = 1*F2 + E3;
  V4 = 1*F2 + E4;
  V5 = F2 + E5;
/VARIANCES
  F1,F2 = 1*;
  E1 TO E5 = 1*;
/COVARIANCES
  F1,F2= 1*;
/MATRIX
  <covariance matrix here>
/END
```

Multitrait Multimethod Models

The final type of measurement model presented indicates a simple multitrait multimethod (MTMM) model. The model in Fig. 9.4e reflects two traits and two methods with an indication of covariance (correlation) between either the methods or the traits. It might be helpful to conceptualize in the model that verbal ability and quantitative ability are the two traits (Factor 3, Factor 4) being measured by two methods (Factor 1, Factor 2): teacher ratings and parent ratings. This model represents a hypothesized model against which specific restricted models are tested to determine the presence of either convergent or discriminant validity.

The MTMM approach was proposed by Campbell and Fiske (1959). Their basic logic was that scores on similar tests, that is, tests that measure the same construct, should correlate, and scores on tests that do not measure the same construct should not correlate. This provided for an assessment of the correlation matrix among traits and methods. Obviously, different methods could be used to measure any given construct, and so which method(s) were better in assessing a construct was also of interest. This, however, required an examination of the specific loadings (parameters) for each method.

Widaman (1985) presented a set of steps by which to test specific restricted models for either convergent or discriminant validity in confirmatory factor analysis. Basically, each restricted model yields a chi-square value; therefore, a difference test in chi-square values for the models can be used to determine whether convergent and/or discriminant validity is present. This approach obviously examines the covariance (correlation) matrix for the presence of either convergent or discriminant validity. However, separate method parameters can also be examined to determine if one method assesses a given trait better. We first present the hypothesized model program setup, and then indicate the restricted model programs.

The SIMPLIS command program to analyze the hypothesized model is:

```
MULTITRAIT MULTIMETHOD MODEL
OBSERVED VARIABLES: X1 X2 X3 X4
COVARIANCE MATRIX: <file name here>
SAMPLE SIZE: <sample size here>
LATENT VARIABLES: Factor1 Factor2 Factor3 Factor4
RELATIONSHIPS:
  X1 = Factor1 Factor3
  X2 = Factor2 Factor3
  X3 = Factor1 Factor4
  X4 = Factor2 Factor4
Set covariances between Factor1-Factor3 and Factor1-Factor4 to 0
Set covariances between Factor2-Factor3 and Factor2-Factor4 to 0
END OF PROBLEM
```

In EQS5, the hypothesized model would be specified as:

```
/TITLE
  MULTITRAIT MULTIMETHOD MODEL
/SPECIFICATIONS
```

```
CASES= <sample size here>; VARIABLES=4;METHOD=ML;
MATRIX=COVARIANCE;DATA='file name here';
/LABELS
  V1=X1;V2=X2;V3=X3;V4=X4;
/EQUATIONS
  V1 = 1*F1 + 1*F3 + E1;
  V2 = 1*F2 + 1*F3 + E2;
  V3 = 1*F1 + 1*F4 + E3;
  V4 = 1*F2 + 1*F4 + E4;
/VARIANCE
  F1 TO F4 = 1;
  E1 TO E4 = 1*;
/COVARIANCE
  F1,F2 = 1*;
  F3,F4 = 1*;
/END
```

The Set command in the SIMPLIS command language restricts the correlations so that only traits correlate together and methods correlate together. In the EQS5 program, the /COVARIANCE command specifies that the two traits are to be correlated and the two methods are to be correlated. In the more restricted programs, either trait factors or method factors are eliminated, as can be seen in the /EQUATIONS and /COVARIANCES commands for EQS5, or the RELATIONSHIPS: and SET commands for the SIMPLIS command language.

Convergent validity relates to the extent that separate measures of the same trait are correlated, for example, teacher ratings and parent ratings of verbal ability. Evidence of convergent validity can be tested by comparing a restricted model in which *no* traits are specified with the previously hypothesized model, then conducting a chi-square difference test. A significant difference in the chi-square values of the two models indicates the presence of convergent validity.

The SIMPLIS command language restricted model with *no* traits indicated would be written as:

```
CONVERGENT VALIDITY MULTITRAIT MULTIMETHOD MODEL
OBSERVED VARIABLES: X1 X2 X3 X4
COVARIANCE MATRIX: <file name here>
SAMPLE SIZE: <sample size here>
LATENT VARIABLES: Factor1 Factor2
RELATIONSHIPS:
  X1 = Factor1
  X2 = Factor2
  X3 = Factor1
  X4 = Factor2
END OF PROBLEM
```

In EQS5, the hypothesized model would be specified as:

```
/TITLE
 CONVERGENT VALIDITY MULTITRAIT MULTIMETHOD MODEL
/SPECIFICATIONS
 CASES= <sample size here>; VARIABLES=4;METHOD=ML;
 MATRIX=COVARIANCE;DATA='file name here';
/LABELS
 V1=X1;V2=X2;V3=X3;V4=X4;
/EQUATIONS
 V1 = 1*F1 + E1;
 V2 = 1*F2 + E2;
 V3 = 1*F1 + E3;
 V4 = 1*F2 + E4;
/VARIANCE
 F1 TO F2 = 1;
 E1 TO E4 = 1*;
/COVARIANCE
 F1,F2 = 1*;
/END
```

The Set command is no longer needed in the SIMPLIS command language, because only methods are indicated and they are free to correlate by default. In the EQS5 program, the two trait factors (Factor 3, Factor 4) are also not indicated. The /EQUATIONS command indicates only the method factors, and the /COVARIANCES command has been altered to include only a correlation for the two methods. Evidence for convergent validity is therefore tested by comparing the previous model in which the traits were specified with this restricted model in which they are not.

Discriminant validity can be assessed for both traits and methods. This requires a comparison between the hypothesized model and two different restricted models. Discriminant validity for traits involves comparing the hypothesized model chi-square value with the chi-square value obtained when the traits are perfectly correlated. A significant difference in the chi-square values indicates the presence of discriminant validity. Similarly, the previous hypothesized-model chi-square value can be compared with a restricted-model chi-square value in which method factors are perfectly correlated. A nonsignificant difference indicates a lack of discriminant validity, and hence indicates common methods.

The restricted models that indicate either trait or method discriminant validity are presented next. For the SIMPLIS command language, the restricted model requires fixing the correlation between the trait factors to 1. This is accomplished using the Set command (boldface) as follows:

```
DIVERGENT TRAIT VALIDITY MODEL
OBSERVED VARIABLES: X1 X2 X3 X4
```

```
COVARIANCE MATRIX: <file name here>
SAMPLE SIZE: <sample size here>
LATENT VARIABLES: Factor1 Factor2 Factor3 Factor4
RELATIONSHIPS:
 X1 = Factor1 Factor3
 X2 = Factor2 Factor3
 X3 = Factor1 Factor4
 X4 = Factor2 Factor4
Set covariances between Factor1-Factor3 and Factor1-Factor4 to 0
Set covariances between Factor2-Factor3 and Factor2-Factor4 to 0
Set covariance between Factor3-Factor4 to 1
END OF PROBLEM
```

In EQS5, the trait restricted model would be specified as:

```
/TITLE
 MULTITRAIT MULTIMETHOD MODEL
/SPECIFICATIONS
 CASES= <sample size here>; VARIABLES=4;METHOD=ML;
 MATRIX=COVARIANCE;DATA='file name here';
/LABELS
 V1=X1;V2=X2;V3=X3;V4=X4;
/EQUATIONS
 V1 = 1*F1 + 1*F3 + E1;
 V2 = 1*F2 + 1*F3 + E2;
 V3 = 1*F1 + 1*F4 + E3;
 V4 = 1*F2 + 1*F4 + E4;
/VARIANCE
 F1 TO F4 = 1;
 E1 TO E4 = 1*;
/COVARIANCE
 F1,F2 = 1*;
 F3,F4 = 1.0;
/END
```

The second restricted-model chi-square value for method discriminant validity can be obtained by replacing the previous SET command with SET covariance between Factor1-Factor2 to 1. Similarly, in EQS5, change the /COVARIANCE command so that F1, F2 = 1.0; and F3, F4 = 1*;. The difference in chi-square values from this analysis and the hypothesized model is then tested.

In further examining MTMM models, it is important to inspect the individual factor loadings for the traits and methods, and the correlations among trait factors and among the method factors. This can be accomplished by examining the output from an original hypothesized model. Convergent validity is indicated by significant factor loadings for the traits across the methods. Discriminant validity is indicated by examining either the trait factor intercorrelations or the method factor intercorrelations. Obviously, if two traits are significantly correlated, we infer that they measure the same thing; and if two methods are significantly correlated, we infer that either method would yield similar measurements of the observed variable. This forms the basic logic behind examining the factor loadings and factor intercorrelations for traits and methods. Byrne (1994) provides an example of an MTMM model with associated output that includes the chi-square difference tests for convergent and discriminant validity. A more extensive treatment of the topic is beyond the scope of this book.

9.5 STRUCTURAL MODELS

The structural model, as previously mentioned, establishes relationships between or among the latent variables. This could imply paths that denote reciprocal relationships, covariance, and direct or indirect relationships. This section presents examples of a simple structural model, a direct reciprocal model (correlated errors), and an indirect reciprocal model that has correlated errors hypothesized with the latent dependent variables.

Simple Structural Model

Figure 9.5a presents a simple structural model wherein two latent independent variables predict a latent dependent variable. The structural equation implies an equation prediction error or disturbance term. Notice that the two latent independent variables are correlated or covary.

The SIMPLIS command language program that indicates this type of structural model with two indicators of each latent-variable (see the boldface equation) is specified as:

```
LATENT DEPENDENT VARIABLE PREDICTION
OBSERVED VARIABLES: X1-X4 Y1-Y2
COVARIANCE MATRIX: <file name here>
LATENT VARIABLES: Factor1 Factor2 Factor3
RELATIONSHIPS:
  X1-X2 = Factor1
  X3-X4 = Factor2
  Y1-Y2 = Factor3
  Factor3 = Factor1 Factor2
END OF PROBLEM
```

In EQS5 program syntax, the structural model (see the boldface equation) would be specified as:

```
/TITLE
  Latent dependent variable prediction
/SPECIFICATIONS
```

```
CASES= <sample size here>; VARIABLES=6;METHOD=ML;
MATRIX=COVARIANCE;DATA='file name here';
/LABELS
  V1=X1;V2=X2;V3=X3;V4=X4;V5=Y1;V6=Y2;
/EQUATIONS
  V1 = F1 + E1;
  V2 = F1 + E2;
  V3 = F2 + E3;
  V4 = F2 + E4;
  V5 = F3 + E5;
  V6 = F3 + E6;
  F3 = F1 + F2 + D1;
/VARIANCE
  F1 TO F2 = 1;
  E1 TO E6 = 1*;
  D1 = 1*;
/COVARIANCE
  F1,F2 = 1*;
/END
```

Direct Reciprocal Model

Figure 9.5b indicates reciprocal paths between two latent dependent variables. The test of interest may not be in just the significance of each path, but typically in whether the null hypothesis is true, H_0: Path 1 = Path 2. Notice that we are correlating the prediction errors because of the reciprocal relationship between the two latent dependent variables. This is an important consideration in establishing relationships among latent dependent variables. It has been demonstrated that not taking these errors into consideration in a reciprocal path model can lead to erroneous calculations of path values, as well as of the path values between the independent and dependent latent variables, such as those indicated in Fig. 9.5a (Rigdon, 1994).

Indirect Reciprocal Model

Figure 9.5c indicates the indirect reciprocal effects between latent variables with correlated-variable error included. This model could also be diagrammed to include a path from Factor 2 to Factor 1, such as that indicated in Fig. 9.5b. The important thing to note here is that correlated prediction-equation errors provide for the indirect reciprocal effects.

9.6 COMPLETE MEASUREMENT AND STRUCTURAL MODEL

A complete structural equation model that incorporates both the measurement model and the structural model is presented in Fig. 9.6. The model reflects five observed independent variables that define two latent inde-

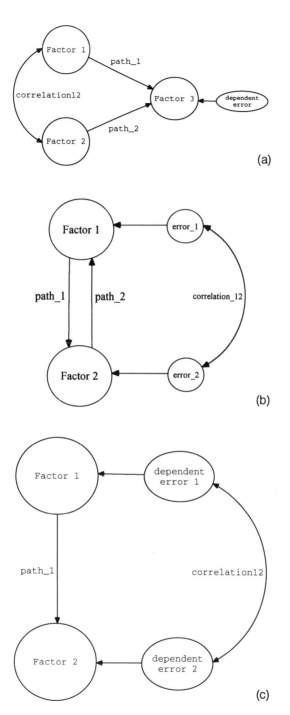

FIG. 9.5. (a) Simple structural model. (b) Direct reciprocal effects (correlated error). (c) Indirect reciprocal effects (correlated error).

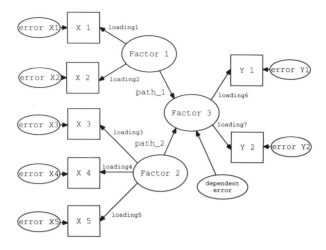

FIG. 9.6. Complete measurement and structural model.

pendent variables and two observed dependent variables that define a single latent dependent variable. Notice that the independent-observed-variable error terms and dependent-observed-variable error terms, as well as the latent-dependent-variable prediction error or disturbance term, are included in the diagram.

The SIMPLIS command language program for this complete model is:

```
COMPLETE STRUCTURAL EQUATION MODEL
OBSERVED VARIABLES: Y1-Y2 X1-X5
COVARIANCE MATRIX: <file name here>
SAMPLE SIZE: <sample size here>
LATENT VARIABLES: Factor1 Factor2 Factor3
RELATIONSHIPS:
  X1-X2 = Factor1
  X3-X5 = Factor2
  Y1-Y2 = Factor3
  Factor3 = Factor1 Factor2
END OF PROBLEM
```

In EQS5, the program would be:

```
/TITLE
 COMPLETE STRUCTURAL EQUATION MODEL
/SPECIFICATIONS
 CASES= <sample size here>; VARIABLES=7;METHOD=ML;
 MATRIX=COVARIANCE;DATA='SEM.DAT';
/LABELS
 V1=X1;V2=X2;V3=X3;V4=X4;V5=X5;V6=Y1;V7=Y2;
```

```
/EQUATIONS
  V1 = F1 + E1;
  V2 = F1 + E2;
  V3 = F2 + E3;
  V4 = F2 + E4;
  V5 = F2 + E5;
  V6 = F3 + E6;
  V7 = F3 + E7;
  F3 = 1*F1 + 1*F2 + D1;
/VARIANCE
  F1,F2 = 1;
  E1 TO E7 = 1*;
  D1 = 1*;
/COVARIANCE
  F1,F2 = 1*;
/END
```

9.7 SUMMARY

We hope that this chapter has helped you to better understand how EQS5 and SIMPLIS command languages specify measurement and structural equations in their programs for various diagrammed theoretical models. We encourage you to draw a model first and then write the corresponding program for it. By now you should have become familiar with the LISREL8-SIMPLIS command language and realized that the observed- and latent-variable measurement error terms do not need to be specified in the program. Likewise, by default, the independent latent variables are correlated, unless otherwise specified. In EQS5, the measurement and structural equation prediction errors do need to be specified, as well as any variances and covariances in the model. Our intent in this chapter was to also provide you with many of the basic models that are present in the research literature. As you will see in chapter 10, there are other advanced applications and topics in structural equation modeling.

Before leaving this chapter, it is important to remember the basic strategy you would use in developing measurement and structural models. The process begins with a sound theoretical basis. This can be developed by referencing substantive articles in your field that define the measurement variables or establish a theoretical structural relationship among latent variables.

As mentioned previously, we recommend establishing measurement models for each latent variable separately and then combining latent variables one at a time. Eventually, this will build two separate measurement models, one for the latent independent variables, and one for the latent dependent variables. Finally, the latent-variable relationships can be hypothesized on the basis of substantive theory. The resulting structural models can then be analyzed jointly with the measurement models, yielding the complete model. We have found that this approach permits a researcher to first focus on the validity and reliability of the latent variables before assessing any relationships among them.

Several available references provide more complete examples and discussion regarding types of confirmatory factor (measurement) models and structural equation models. Byrne (1994), for instance, provides extensive examples and discussion concerning confirmatory factor models, second-order models, and the testing for invariance in factor and mean structures. Jöreskog and Sörbom (1993), Bentler (1992), and Bollen (1989) also provide excellent examples and explanations of these topics. Many other excellent references were noted in the first chapter of the text. The software packages listed in chapter 1 also provide additional program setups and examples.

REFERENCES

Bentler, P. M. (1992). *EQS: Structural equations program manual.* Los Angeles: BMDP Statistical Software.

Bollen, K. A. (1989). *Structural equations with latent variables.* New York: Wiley.

Byrne, B. M. (1994). *Structural equation modeling with EQS and EQS/Windows: Basic concepts, applications, and programming.* Thousand Oaks, CA: Sage.

Campbell, D. T., & Fiske, D. W. (1959). Convergent and discriminant validation by the multitrait-multimethod matrix. *Psychological Bulletin, 56,* 81–105.

Jöreskog, K. G., & Sörbom, D. (1993). *LISREL8: Structural equation modeling with the SIMPLIS command language.* Hillsdale, NJ: Lawrence Erlbaum Associates.

Rigdon, E. E. (1994). Demonstrating the effects of unmodeled random measurement error. *Structural Equation Modeling: A Multidisciplinary Journal, 1,* 375–380.

Widaman, K. F. (1985). Hierarchically tested covariance structure models for multitrait-multimethod data. *Applied Psychological Measurement, 9,* 1–26.

10

ADVANCED TOPICS

Chapter Outline:

Key Concepts:

Cross validation of models: Replication, subsamples, CVI, and ECVI
Simulation concepts
Bootstrap concepts
Jackknife concepts
Multiple sample analyses
Interaction models: continuous and categorical variable

In the previous chapters of this book, we learned about the "basics" of structural equation modeling. In this chapter, we consider a selection of more advanced topics. However, you should be aware that our discussion will only scratch the surface of the many exciting new developments in structural equation modeling. Some of the new developments have already been included in the previous chapters, such as new methods of parameter estimation, new model fit indices, new methods for dealing with discrete and non-normally distributed variables, new computer software, and new methods for detecting misspecified models. Bollen and Long (1993), Marcoulides and Schumacker (1996), and the other references in this chapter provide more detail about the advanced topics discussed.

This chapter introduces the topics of cross validation, simulation, bootstrapping, jackknifing, multiple sample models, and interaction models (continuous variable and categorical variables) in structural equation modeling. Our intention is to provide a basic understanding of these topics to further your interest in the structural equation modeling approach. In some cases, we have added computer program examples to better illustrate the topic.

10.1 CROSS VALIDATION

Popular approaches to validating the results of a study are to replicate the study either by obtaining a second set of data (time, money, and resources permitting), or by splitting the existing sample, given that the sample size is sufficient, and running the analysis on the two smaller samples. In addition, certain other procedures examine estimates and models using a single sample of data. These techniques are called *expected cross validation, cross validation, bootstrap,* and *jackknife* in structural equation modeling.

ECVI

Browne and Cudeck (1989) proposed a single-sample expected cross validation index (ECVI) for comparing alternative models using only one sample of data. The alternative model that results in the *smallest* ECVI value should be the most stable in the population. The ECVI is a function of chi-square and degrees of freedom. It is computed in LISREL8 as ECVI $= (c/n) + 2(q/n)$, where c is the chi-square value for the overall fitted model, p = number of observed variables, and $n = N - 1$ (sample size). Browne and Cudeck (1989, 1993) also provided a confidence interval for ECVI, $(c_L; c_U) = [(\lambda_L + p + q)/n; (\lambda_U + p + q) /n]$, where c_L = lower limit, c_U = upper limit, λ_L = parameter estimate for lower limit, λ_U = parameter estimate for upper limit, and q is the number of independent parameters estimated. When sample size is small, it is important to compare the confidence intervals of the ECVI for the alternative competing models. The ECVI is also not very useful for choosing a parsimonious model when the sample size is large. In this instance, we recommend one of the parsimonious model fit indices and/or the comparative fit index (see chap. 7). Bandalos (1993), in a simulation study, further examined the use of the one-sample cross validation index and found it to be quite accurate in confirmatory factor models. Other research also indicated that the one-sample expected cross validation index yielded highly similar results to those of the two-sample approach (Benson & Bandalos, 1992; Benson & El-Zahhar, 1994; Benson, Moulin-Julian, Schwarzer, Seipp, & El-Zahhar, 1992). The ECVI is routinely printed among the fit indices reported on the LISREL8-SIMPLIS computer output.

CVI

Cudeck and Browne (1983) also proposed a cross validation index (CVI) for covariance structure analysis that incorporated splitting a sample into two subsamples. Subsample A is used as a *calibration* sample, and Subsample B is used as the *validation* sample. The reproduced model implied covariance matrix, Σ_a, from the calibration sample is then compared with the covariance matrix derived from Subsample B, S_b. A CVI value near zero indicates that the model cross-validates or is the same in the two subsamples. The cross validation index is denoted as CVI $= F(S_b, \Sigma_a)$. The choice among alternative models can also be based on the model that yields the smallest CVI value. One could further "double-cross-validate" by using Subsample B as the calibration sample and Subsample A as the validation sample. In this instance, the cross validation index is denoted as CVI $= F(S_a, \Sigma_b)$. If the same model holds regardless of which subsample is used as the calibration sample, greater confidence in the model is achieved. An obvious drawback to splitting a sample into two subsamples is that sufficient subsample sizes may not exist to provide stable parameter estimates. Obviously, this approach requires an initial large sample that can be randomly split into two subsamples of sufficient size.

The CVI can be computed using LISREL8-SIMPLIS command language, but requires two programs. In the following example, two LISREL8-SIMPLIS programs are run to compute the CVI and associated 90% confidence interval. The first program reads in the covariance matrix of the calibration sample

(S_a) and then generates and saves the implied model covariance matrix, Σ_a. The second program uses the covariance matrix of Subsample B and then outputs the CVI and the 90% confidence interval.

```
PROGRAM ONE CALIBRATION SAMPLE
OBSERVED VARIABLES: X1 X2 X3
COVARIANCE MATRIX FROM FILE SAMPLEA.COV
LATENT VARIABLES: Factor1
RELATIONSHIPS:
 X1-X3 = Factor1
SAMPLE SIZE: 200
SAVE SIGMA IN FILE MODEL1C
END OF PROBLEM
PROGRAM TWO VALIDATION SAMPLE AND COMPUTE CVI
OBSERVED VARIABLES: X1 X2 X3
COVARIANCE MATRIX FROM FILE SAMPLEB.COV
SAMPLE SIZE: 200
CROSSVALIDATE FILE MODEL1C
END OF PROBLEM
```

This CVI cross validation example involved randomly splitting an original sample of size 400 and calculating two covariance matrices, which were saved in separate files. The covariance matrix in the file SAMPLEA.COV was:

```
 5.86
 3.12    3.32
35.28   23.85   622.09
```

The covariance matrix in the file SAMPLEB.COV was:

```
 5.74
 3.47    4.36
45.65   22.58   611.63
```

In our measurement-model example, a single factor with three indicator variables is being tested to see if it cross-validates. The low CVI value and associated 90% confidence interval indicate that the measurement model holds for both subsamples. The reduced computer output from the CVI cross validation program is:

```
PROGRAM ONE CALIBRATION SAMPLE
COVARIANCE MATRIX TO BE ANALYZED
```

	X1	X2	X3
X1	5.86		
X2	3.12	3.32	
X3	35.28	23.85	622.09

```
SI was written to file MODEL1C
PROGRAM TWO VALIDATION SAMPLE AND COMPUTE CVI
COVARIANCE MATRIX TO BE ANALYZED
```

	X1	X2	X3
X1	5.74		
X2	3.47	4.36	
X3	45.65	22.58	611.63

MATRIX SIGMA

	X1	X2	X3
X1	5.86		
X2	3.12	3.32	
X3	35.28	23.85	622.09

```
CROSS-VALIDATION INDEX (CVI) = 0.32
90 PERCENT CONFIDENCE INTERVAL FOR CVI = (0.16 ; 0.56)
```

Summary

The ECVI and CVI are most useful when a theoretically implied model is sufficiently indicated by the appropriate fit indices—in other words, when a plausible model is fitted and the parameter estimates are meaningful given a specified sample size. The number of parameters, model complexity, and sample size affect these cross validation indices; therefore, you should not routinely discard other modeling considerations when you select the smaller ECVI of two competing models, report the CVI from two subsamples, or report the CVI across samples taken from a population. Currently, we know of only two software packages, LISREL8-SIMPLIS and SEPATH in STATISTICA, that compute these cross validation indices.

10.2 SIMULATION, BOOTSTRAP, JACKKNIFE METHODS

Simulation

EQS5 provides a very easy-to-use method for conducting simulation studies, including bootstrap and jackknife output (Bentler, 1992). Simulation studies afford the opportunity to study models when data are randomly sampled from a population under known conditions. They require the specification of a population (model-generated or matrix input), a sampling method (simple random sampling or resampling of input raw data), an estimation method

(GLS, ML, etc.), the number of samples to be simulated, and file name(s) if we wish to save the outputted files. A basic EQS5 simulation program that uses a specific path model, the maximum-likelihood estimation method, simple random sampling, and outputs five data files with the prefix `SIM` would be:

```
/TITLE
 SIMULATION EXAMPLE
/SPECIFICATIONS
 CASES=30;VARIABLES=4;METHOD=ML;
/EQUATION
 V1 = 1*V2 + 1*V3 + E1;
 V4 = 1*V1 + E2;
/SIMULATION
 SEED = 12345;
 REPLICATIONS=5;
 POPULATION=MODEL;
 DATA_PREFIX = 'SIM';
 SAVE=SEPARATE;
/OUTPUT
 LISTING;COVARIANCE MATRIX;
/END
```

In conducting simulations, it is important to remember that changing the value on the REPLICATIONS subcommand would increase the number of sample data sets simulated and thus could easily cause existing disk space to become exhausted. The path model specified in the /EQUATIONS command is analyzed for each of the five generated data sets due to the POPULATION = MODEL; subcommand, which is the program default specification. The researcher can examine the overall model fit across the five samples, as well as the path coefficients, which for our example are in the computer output listing. In addition to all program output appearing by use of the LISTING; subcommand, the /OUTPUT command can specify that only certain technical information appear in a default file named EQSOUT.DAT. In this example, only the covariance matrix for each data set was requested to be outputted in the file. Other choices for technical output could include, for example, parameter estimates, standard errors, residual matrix, and/or weight matrix. However, please note that other specific technical information is outputted before each simulation request in the program. In our example, the covariance matrix we requested is printed after the technical information for each simulation. We know that this has been accomplished when we see the following computer output information in the listing file:

```
THE FOLLOWING TECHNICAL INFORMATION HAS BEEN STORED IN EQSOUT.DAT

PARAMETERS TO BE PRINTED ARE:

 V2,V2 V3,V3 E1,E1 E2,E2 V1,V2 V1,V3 V4,V1
```

NOTE: SAMPLE COVARIANCE MATRIX AND RESIDUAL MATRIX IN THIS
      TECHNICAL OUTPUT HAVE BEEN ARRANGED IN THE SEQUENCE
      OF ALL DEPENDENT VARIABLES FOLLOWED BY ALL INDEPENDENT
      VARIABLES 10 ELEMENTS OF MODEL STATISTICS, THEY ARE:

      ESTIMATION METHOD (LS,GLS,ML,ELS,EGLS,ERLS,AGLS)
      CONDITION CODE (0 FOR NORMAL CONDITION)
      CONVERGENCE (0 FOR MODEL CONVERGED)
      NULL MODEL CHI-SQUARE
      MODEL CHI-SQUARE
      DEGREES OF FREEDOM
      PROBABILITY LEVEL
      BENTLER-BONETT NORMED FIT INDEX
      BENTLER-BONETT NON-NORMED FIT INDEX
      COMPARATIVE FIT INDEX

      4 BY 4 SAMPLE COVARIANCE MATRIX

      OUTPUT FORMAT FOR INFORMATION SECTION IS: (8D16.8)

      TOTAL NUMBER OF LINES PER SET OF INFORMATION IS: 5

The five covariance matrices generated from the randomly sampled data
for each simulation were:

Simulation 1:

```
3.518
1.585   1.408
 .992    .012    .881
4.133   1.623   1.088   5.479
```

Simulation 2:

```
2.414
 .554    .639
 .849   -.082    .843
2.521    .596    .898   3.950
```

Simulation 3:

```
2.225
 .709    .925
 .821    .045    .803
2.133    .472    .879   3.411
```

Simulation 4:

```
4.150
1.583   1.508
1.479    .098   1.234
3.911   1.479   1.462   4.858
```

Simulation 5:

```
2.118
 .507    .738
1.075   -.136   1.228
2.114    .600   1.232   3.093
```

The parameter estimates for our example were taken from the computer output listing but could have been outputted in the five simulation files along with the covariance matrices by simply changing the /OUTPUT command to LISTING;COVARIANCE MATRIX;PARAMETER ESTIMATES;. The path coefficients in the standardized solution for each simulation were:

Simulation 1:

```
V1 = .709*V2 + .558*V3 + .431 E1
V4 = .941*V1 + .339 E2
```

Simulation 2:

```
V1 = .500*V2 + .630*V3 + .594 E1
V4 = .826*V1 + .563 E2
```

Simulation 3:

```
V1 = .470*V2 + .598*V3 + .649 E1
V4 = .770*V1 + .638 E2
```

Simulation 4:

```
V1 = .605*V2 + .628*V3 + .490 E1
V4 = .865*V1 + .501 E2
```

Simulation 5:

```
V1 = .486*V2 + .703*V3 + .520 E1
V4 = .839*V1 + .544 E2
```

Simulation programs are typically run to examine covariance matrices and/or parameter estimates to determine how much they fluctuate or change under certain conditions, for example, different sample sizes. More complex simulation programs are possible that use other optional commands. For example, a simulation using a covariance matrix could be conducted. The covariance matrix could be included in the program after the /MATRIX command, or read from an input data file specified as DA='<file name>'; on the /SPECIFICATION command line. The simulation of a covariance matrix also requires the changing of the POPULATION subcommand to POPULATION=MATRIX;. A computer output listing file can also be named as an alternative to using the default name EQSOUT.DAT. This is accomplished by including in the /OUTPUT command the subcommand DATA = '<file name>';. These and other optional commands are found in the *EQS Structural Equations Program Manual* (Bentler, 1992), but we provide the program setup for modeling a covariance matrix to further illustrate the ease of performing simulations in EQS5. The following EQS5 simulation program generates five simulations based on the input covariance matrix:

```
/TITLE
 COVARIANCE MATRIX SIMULATION EXAMPLE
/SPECIFICATIONS
 CASES=30;VARIABLES=4;METHOD=ML;
/EQUATION
 V1 = 1*V2 + 1*V3 + E1;
 V4 = 1*V1 + E2;
/SIMULATION
 SEED = 12345;
 REPLICATIONS=5;
 DATA_PREFIX = 'COV';
 SAVE=SEPARATE;
 POPULATION = MATRIX;
/MATRIX
 3.518
 1.585 1.408
  .992  .012  .881
 4.133 1.623 1.088 5.479
/OUTPUT
 LISTING;COVARIANCE MATRIX;
/END
```

The reduced computer output from the listing file is as follows:

```
TITLE: SIMULATION EXAMPLE
SIMULATION DEFINITIONS
```

```
NUMBER OF REPLICATIONS : 5
SAMPLE DATA GENERATED FROM: MATRIX
SAMPLE SIZE : 30
DATA IS NORMAL ? YES
DATA TO BE CONTAMINATED ? NO
ORIGINAL SEED = 12345.
DATA FILE TO BE SAVED ? YES
IN WHICH TYPE ? SEPARATED
```

DATA GENERATED BASED ON FOLLOWING CORRELATION MATRIX

```
        V1      V2      V3      V4
V 1   1.000
V 2   0.712   1.000
V 3   0.563   0.011   1.000
V 4   0.941   0.584   0.495   1.000
```

SIMULATION PROCEED IN REPLICATION 1, SEED IS 12345.00

INPUT DATA FILE NAME IS COV001.DAT
COVARIANCE MATRIX TO BE ANALYZED:

```
        V1      V2      V3      V4
V 1   4.954
V 2   2.251   1.634
V 3   1.562   0.373   0.891
V 4   5.735   2.412   1.934   6.849
```

GOODNESS OF FIT SUMMARY

INDEPENDENCE MODEL CHI-SQUARE = 181.459 ON 6 DEGREES OF FREEDOM

INDEPENDENCE AIC = 169.45948 INDEPENDENCE CAIC = 155.05229
    MODEL AIC = 7.27969   MODEL CAIC = 0.07610

CHI-SQUARE = 13.280 BASED ON 3 DEGREES OF FREEDOM
PROBABILITY VALUE FOR THE CHI-SQUARE STATISTIC IS 0.00407
THE NORMAL THEORY RLS CHI-SQUARE FOR THIS ML SOLUTION IS 8.990.

BENTLER-BONETT NORMED FIT INDEX= 0.927
BENTLER-BONETT NONNORMED FIT INDEX= 0.883
COMPARATIVE FIT INDEX = 0.941

STANDARDIZED SOLUTION:

V1 = .699*V2 + .622*V3 + .354 E1
V4 = .981*V1 + .196 E2

              E N D   O F   M E T H O D

SIMULATION IN REPLICATION 2, SEED IS 267464470.
INPUT DATA FILE NAME IS COV002.DAT

COVARIANCE MATRIX TO BE ANALYZED:

```
        V1      V2      V3      V4
V 1   2.249
V 2   0.886   0.926
V 3   0.711  -0.040   0.703
V 4   2.738   0.878   0.772   4.045
```

GOODNESS OF FIT SUMMARY

INDEPENDENCE MODEL CHI-SQUARE = 98.647 ON 6 DEGREES OF FREEDOM

INDEPENDENCE AIC = 86.64701 INDEPENDENCE CAIC = 72.23982
    MODEL AIC = 4.07089   MODEL CAIC = -3.13270

CHI-SQUARE = 10.071 BASED ON 3 DEGREES OF FREEDOM
PROBABILITY VALUE FOR THE CHI-SQUARE STATISTIC IS 0.01797
THE NORMAL THEORY RLS CHI-SQUARE FOR THIS ML SOLUTION IS 8.430.

BENTLER-BONETT NORMED FIT INDEX= 0.898
BENTLER-BONETT NONNORMED FIT INDEX= 0.847
COMPARATIVE FIT INDEX = 0.924

STANDARDIZED SOLUTION:

V1 = .631*V2 + .586*V3 + .508 E1
V4 = .911*V1 + .413 E2

             E N D   O F   M E T H O D

SIMULATION IN REPLICATION 3, SEED IS 1011473914.
INPUT DATA FILE NAME IS COV003.DAT

COVARIANCE MATRIX TO BE ANALYZED:

```
        V1      V2      V3      V4
V1    3.253
V2    1.536   1.281
V3    0.593  -0.075   0.634
V4    3.716   1.605   0.574   4.918
```

GOODNESS OF FIT SUMMARY

INDEPENDENCE MODEL CHI-SQUARE = 112.322 ON 6 DEGREES OF FREEDOM

INDEPENDENCE AIC = 100.32230 INDEPENDENCE CAIC = 85.91512
    MODEL AIC = 2.84846   MODEL CAIC = -4.35513

CHI-SQUARE = 8.848 BASED ON 3 DEGREES OF FREEDOM
PROBABILITY VALUE FOR THE CHI-SQUARE STATISTIC IS 0.03138
THE NORMAL THEORY RLS CHI-SQUARE FOR THIS ML SOLUTION IS 7.543.

BENTLER-BONETT NORMED FIT INDEX= 0.921
BENTLER-BONETT NONNORMED FIT INDEX= 0.890
COMPARATIVE FIT INDEX = 0.945

STANDARDIZED SOLUTION:

    V1 = .769*V2 + .464*V3 + .440 E1
    V4 = .933*V1 + .360 E2

———

E N D   O F   M E T H O D

———

SIMULATION IN REPLICATION 4, SEED IS 131472437.
INPUT DATA FILE NAME IS COV004.DAT

COVARIANCE MATRIX TO BE ANALYZED:

         V1   V2   V3   V4
    V1 5.304
    V2 2.543   2.071
    V3 1.375   0.196   0.919
    V4 6.074   2.563   1.509   7.756

GOODNESS OF FIT SUMMARY

INDEPENDENCE MODEL CHI-SQUARE = 139.995 ON 6 DEGREES OF FREEDOM

INDEPENDENCE AIC = 127.99537 INDEPENDENCE CAIC = 113.58819
    MODEL AIC = 11.49616   MODEL CAIC = 4.29257

CHI-SQUARE = 17.496 BASED ON 3 DEGREES OF FREEDOM
PROBABILITY VALUE FOR THE CHI-SQUARE STATISTIC IS LESS THAN 0.001
THE NORMAL THEORY RLS CHI-SQUARE FOR THIS ML SOLUTION IS 13.524.

BENTLER-BONETT NORMED FIT INDEX= 0.875
BENTLER-BONETT NONNORMED FIT INDEX= 0.784
COMPARATIVE FIT INDEX = 0.892

STANDARDIZED SOLUTION:

    V1 = .731*V2 + .554*V3 + .398 E1
    V4 = .941*V1 + .337 E2

———

E N D   O F   M E T H O D

———

SIMULATION IN REPLICATION 5, SEED IS 2082996961.
INPUT DATA FILE NAME IS COV005.DAT

COVARIANCE MATRIX TO BE ANALYZED:

```
      V1       V2       V3       V4
V1  2.596
V2  0.957   1.188
V3  0.763  -0.258   0.782
V4  3.301   1.032   0.862   4.820
```

GOODNESS OF FIT SUMMARY

INDEPENDENCE MODEL CHI-SQUARE = 126.420 ON 6 DEGREES OF FREEDOM

INDEPENDENCE AIC = 114.42036 INDEPENDENCE CAIC = 100.01317
    MODEL AIC = 14.60023   MODEL CAIC = 7.39664

CHI-SQUARE = 20.600 BASED ON 3 DEGREES OF FREEDOM
PROBABILITY VALUE FOR THE CHI-SQUARE STATISTIC IS LESS THAN 0.001
THE NORMAL THEORY RLS CHI-SQUARE FOR THIS ML SOLUTION IS 14.998.

BENTLER-BONETT NORMED FIT INDEX= 0.837
BENTLER-BONETT NONNORMED FIT INDEX= 0.708
COMPARATIVE FIT INDEX = 0.854

STANDARDIZED SOLUTION:

V1 = .653*V2 + .646*V3 + .396 E1
V4 = .947*V1 + .321 E2

          E N D   O F   M E T H O D

The simulation of an inputted covariance matrix permits a comparison with replicated covariance matrices under certain known conditions, as well as an examination of the parameter estimates from the implied model. The variation in the covariance matrices, parameter estimates, and fit indices is readily apparent from just these five simulated replications.

Bootstrap

The bootstrapping approach treats a random sample of data as a substitute for the population and resamples from it a specified number of times to generate sample bootstrap estimates and standard errors. These sample bootstrap estimates and standard errors are averaged and used to obtain a confidence interval around the average of the bootstrap estimates. This average is termed a *bootstrap estimator*. The bootstrap estimator and associated confidence interval are used to determine how stable or good the sample statistic is as an estimate of the population parameter. Obviously, if the random sample initially drawn from the population is not representative, then the sample statistic and corresponding bootstrap estimator obtained from resampling will yield misleading results. The bootstrap approach is used in research situations where replication (in which additional samples are obtained) and cross validation (in which the sample is split or a single sample is used) are not practical.

To obtain bootstrap estimates of parameters, one simply uses the subcommand BOOTSTRAP = <n of cases>; which replaces the POPULATION subcommand in the previous EQS5 program. The POPULATION subcommand is no longer valid in this instance, because the bootstrap method uses a resampling strategy given the number of cases specified. A raw-data file, DA = `SAMPLE.DAT`;, is also specified in the following example; it contains 4 variables and 30 cases. The raw scores in the file are:

```
50 33 14 02
64 28 56 22
65 28 46 15
67 31 56 24
63 28 51 15
46 34 14 03
69 31 51 23
62 22 45 15
59 32 48 18
46 36 10 02
61 30 46 14
60 27 51 16
65 30 52 20
56 25 39 11
65 30 55 18
58 27 51 19
68 32 59 23
51 33 17 05
57 28 45 13
62 34 54 23
77 38 67 22
63 33 47 16
67 33 57 25
76 30 66 21
49 25 45 17
55 35 13 02
67 30 52 23
70 32 47 14
64 32 45 15
61 28 40 13
```

The following bootstrap program serves to illustrate the basic EQS5 bootstrap program setup:

```
/TITLE
 BOOTSTRAP EXAMPLE
/SPECIFICATIONS
 CASES=30;VARIABLES=4;METHOD=ML; DA='SAMPLE.DAT';
/EQUATION
 V1 = 1*V2 + 1*V3 + E1;
 V4 = 1*V1 + E2;
/SIMULATION
 SEED = 12345;
 REPLICATIONS = 5;
 DATA_PREFIX = 'BOOT';
 BOOTSTRAP = 30;
 SAVE = SEPARATE;
/OUTPUT
 LISTING;
/END
```

This EQS5 bootstrap program inputs a raw-data file with 30 individual cases and 4 variables. Using the sample data and a maximum-likelihood estimation technique, path coefficients are generated for the path model specified in the /EQUATION command. The /SIMULATION command, using a seed number as a start value, computes five separate bootstrap estimates of the path model, based on a bootstrap sampling of 30 cases from the raw-data file each time. The bootstrap samples are obviously not based on the same 30 cases, because each sample is selected at random with replacement. The bootstrap samples are outputted for each replication and saved in a separate file with the prefix 'Boot'—for example, BOO001.dat to BOO005.dat. The EQS5 standard computer output for all the replications is also provided because of the LISTING; option specified in the /OUTPUT command.

To compute the bootstrap estimator for a path coefficient, we would first list all five bootstrap estimates for the coefficients, average them, and compute a standard deviation. The difference between this average bootstrap estimate for a given coefficient and the original sample coefficient indicates the amount of bias present. A comparison of each of these average bootstrap estimates, their standard errors, and their confidence intervals with the original sample path coefficient estimates indicates the stability or confidence in the original sample path coefficient estimates. In addition, the fit indices of the path model for each of the five replications could be compared. Notice that with 100 replications, a more stable bootstrap estimator of a sample statistic is possible; however, this may require ample disk space if we are saving the files separately, or even using the other option, which is SAVE = CONCATENATE;, to place all output into one file. In this case, the DATA_PREFIX command is not needed, because all output is placed in the default file EQSOUT.DAT. However, as previously mentioned, another file name can be selected by specifying DATA = '<file name>'; in the /OUTPUT command.

An abbreviated computer output listing of the bootstrap results is as follows:

```
TITLE: BOOTSTRAP EXAMPLE


SIMULATION DEFINITIONS
      BOOTSTRAP SIMULATION IS ELECTED
      NUMBER OF REPLICATIONS : 5
      SAMPLE DATA GENERATED FROM: EXIST
      SAMPLE SIZE : 30
      ORIGINAL SEED = 12345.
      DATA FILE TO BE SAVED ? YES
      IN WHICH TYPE ? SEPARATED


SIMULATION IN REPLICATION 1, SEED IS 12345.
INPUT DATA FILE NAME IS BOO001.DAT


COVARIANCE MATRIX TO BE ANALYZED:

            V1         V2        V3        V4
      V1    78.944
      V2   -14.013    12.737
      V3   145.201   -40.787   332.764
      V4    55.594   -15.870   133.523   57.689


STANDARDIZED SOLUTION:

    V1 = .176*V2 + .911*V3 + .372 E1
    V4 = .852*V1 + .524 E2


SIMULATION IN REPLICATION 2, SEED IS 424962143.
INPUT DATA FILE NAME IS BOO002.DAT


COVARIANCE MATRIX TO BE ANALYZED:

            V1         V2        V3        V4
      V1    64.838
      V2    -4.966    11.310
      V3   117.524   -21.931   266.947
      V4    45.676    -8.862   108.680   48.547


STANDARDIZED SOLUTION:

    V1 = .192*V2 + .906*V3 + .378 E1
    V4 = .834*V1 + .552 E2
```

SIMULATION IN REPLICATION 3, SEED IS 1431563226.
INPUT DATA FILE NAME IS BOO003.DAT

COVARIANCE MATRIX TO BE ANALYZED:

```
        V1       V2       V3       V4
V1   45.357
V2   -1.238   10.838
V3   80.055   -8.834   174.372
V4   35.451   -1.683    73.076   36.257
```

STANDARDIZED SOLUTION:

V1 = .130*V2 + .905*V3 + .406 E1
V4 = .879*V1 + .477 E2

SIMULATION IN REPLICATION 4, SEED IS 910484867.
INPUT DATA FILE NAME IS BOO004.DAT

COVARIANCE MATRIX TO BE ANALYZED:

```
        V1       V2       V3       V4
V1   57.817
V2    9.897   13.310
V3   91.962   10.931   177.597
V4   34.107    6.207    73.438   36.838
```

STANDARDIZED SOLUTION:

V1 = .166*V2 + .900*V3 + .403 E1
V4 = .728*V1 + .686 E2

SIMULATION IN REPLICATION 5, SEED IS 267464470.
INPUT DATA FILE NAME IS BOO005.DAT

COVARIANCE MATRIX TO BE ANALYZED:

```
        V1       V2       V3       V4
V1   69.454
V2    7.937   10.171
V3   95.707   -1.038   190.231
V4   38.293   -0.652    78.252   40.852
```

STANDARDIZED SOLUTION:

V1 = .316*V2 + .835*V3 + .450 E1
V4 = .721*V1 + .693 E2

TABLE 10.1
Bootstrap Estimates of Path Coefficients

Sample	V2	V3	E1	V1	E2
Original	.252	.859	.446	.789	.524
Bootstrap 1	.176	.911	.372	.852	.524
Bootstrap 2	.192	.906	.378	.834	.552
Bootstrap 3	.130	.905	.406	.879	.477
Bootstrap 4	.166	.900	.403	.728	.686
Bootstrap 5	.316	.835	.450	.721	.693
Bootstrap estimator	.196	.891	.402	.803	.586
Standard error	.005	.001	.001	.005	.009
90% Confidence Interval					
V2	(.188, .204)				
V3	(.889, .893)				
E1	(.400, .404)				
V1	(.795, .811)				
E2	(.571, .601)				

The bootstrap estimates in the standardized solutions are tabled for ease of comparison with the original sample data parameter estimates (see Table 10.1). A bootstrap estimator and standard error are given for each path coefficient in the equations. When reporting bootstrap estimators and standard errors, one should report confidence intervals. The bootstrap estimates for the two path model equations, V1= *V2 + *V3 + *E1 and V4= *V1 + * E2, are in Table 10.1.

The bootstrap estimators do indicate more bias than one would normally encounter because only five replications are examined, that is, .252 versus .196, .859 versus .891, .446 versus .402, .789 versus 803, and .524 versus .586. Obviously, if more replications were requested, it would behoove the researcher to input the data files into another statistics program and generate summary statistics on the parameter estimates, standard errors, and fit indices of interest. EQS5 does not readily produce the summary statistics in Table 10.1.

The LISREL8-SIMPLIS software program does not provide bootstrap capabilities. However, bootstrapping can be accomplished using PRELIS2 and LISREL8 (Jöreskog & Sörbom, 1993a). In our bootstrap example, the researcher would first run a LISREL8 program using the original sample data. The raw-data file, efficacy.raw, used in the example is provided with the PRELIS2/LISREL8 program and used in other examples in the *PRELIS2 User's Reference Guide* (Jöreskog & Sörbom, 1993d). A two-factor model is specified in the example with six factor-loading estimates, three for each of the factors (see the MO and FR command lines). The LISREL8 program is written as:

```
Estimate original factor loadings for model from file efficacy.raw

DA NI=6 NO=297 ME=GLS
RA=efficacy.raw FO;(6F1.0)
CO ALL
MO NX=6 NK=2
FR LX(1,1) LX(2,1) LX(3,1) LX(4,2) LX(5,2) LX(6,2)
OU MA=CM
```

The variance–covariance matrix to be analyzed is indicated as:

```
VAR1    0.60
VAR2    0.16    0.59
VAR3    0.11    0.14    0.59
VAR4    0.23    0.14    0.21    0.57
VAR5    0.16    0.08    0.14    0.30    0.49
VAR6    0.19    0.11    0.17    0.34    0.27    0.53
```

The six factor loadings for the two-factor model specified are estimated as:

	Estimate	Standard Error
LX(1,1)	0.43	0.05
LX(2,1)	0.30	0.05
LX(3,1)	0.37	0.05
LX(4,2)	0.63	0.04
LX(5,2)	0.48	0.04
LX(6,2)	0.55	0.04

Then, to compute bootstrap estimates of the factor loadings for the two-factor model with three indicators per factor, the raw-data file is read into a PRELIS2 program with the number of variables, number of cases, and estimation method specified (DA NI=6 NO=297 ME=GLS). In our example, the program reads in a raw-data file containing 6 variables and 297 cases with the generalized least-squares estimation method selected [RA=effi-cacy.raw FO;(6F1.0)]. The PRELIS2 program then generates 10 covariance matrices using the generalized least-squares estimation method. The number of bootstrap samples to be taken is specified (BS=10), and these samples are randomly drawn from the raw-data file with replacement. A 100% resampling (SF=100) of the raw-data file is specified. The 10 covariance matrices are outputted into a bootstrap save file (BM=efficacy.cm) for further analysis by a LISREL8 program. This output file is in ASCII format and can be examined. The PRELIS2 program is:

```
Generate 10 covariance matrices from file efficacy.raw
DA NI=6 NO=297 ME=GLS
RA=efficacy.raw FO;(6F1.0)
OU MA=CM BS=10 SF=100 BM=efficacy.cm
```

The first two variance–covariance matrices outputted into the file `effi-cacy.cm` are:

```
VAR1    1.00
VAR2    0.27    1.00
VAR3    0.26    0.26    1.00
VAR4    0.46    0.25    0.42    1.00
VAR5    0.38    0.16    0.27    0.64    1.00
VAR6    0.43    0.26    0.36    0.72    0.63    1.00


VAR1    1.00
VAR2    0.32    1.00
VAR3    0.11    0.22    1.00
VAR4    0.40    0.26    0.45    1.00
VAR5    0.35    0.18    0.36    0.68    1.00
VAR6    0.34    0.22    0.32    0.72    0.68    1.00
```

Notice that the diagonal values indicate variances equal to 1.0, whereas the off-diagonal values indicate the covariance terms. The manipulation of raw data (recoding variables, selecting cases, transformations) and the treatment of missing data (imputation method and/or deleting cases listwise) should be specified and handled in this program prior to bootstrap or Monte Carlo estimation. The researcher can also specify the type of matrix and estimation method desired in this PRELIS2 program.

The saved file, `efficacy.cm`, is next read by a LISREL8 program (`CM=efficacy.cm`) to estimate 10 sets of six factor loadings for the two-factor model. The output from this program indicates the 10 different bootstrap sampled covariance matrices read from the file, as well as parameter estimates, fit indices, and so forth. (The output is no different from running 10 separate stacked programs.) The LISREL8 program is written as:

```
Estimate 10 sets of 6 factor loadings for two factor model using
  efficacy.cm file
DA NI=6 NO=297 RP=10
CM=efficacy.cm
MO NX=6 NK=2
FR LX(1,1) LX(2,1) LX(3,1) LX(4,2) LX(5,2) LX(6,2)
OU LX=efficacy.lx
```

The LISREL8 program indicates that 6 variables and 297 cases were used to compute the 10 covariance matrices that are read in from the saved file (`CM = efficacy.cm`). The program is run 10 times (`RP=10`), once for each covariance matrix saved in the file. The model specifies six variables and two factors (`MO NX=6 NK=2`). The parameters (factor loadings) to be estimated indicate that the first three variables define one factor and the last three variables define a second factor (see the FR command line, which indicates elements in the matrix to be free or estimated). The 10 sets of six factor loadings are computed and outputted in a saved file (OU LX=effi-cacy.lx).

The saved file is then read by the following PRELIS2 program to generate the bootstrap estimates and standard errors for six factor loadings in the model:

```
Analyze 10 sets of 6 factor loadings from efficacy.lx file
DA NI=6
LA
'LX(1,1)' 'LX(2,1)' 'LX(3,1)' 'LX(4,2)' 'LX(5,2)' 'LX(6,2)'
RA=efficacy.lx
CO ALL
OU MA=CM
```

The PRELIS2 program analyzes the 10 sets of six factor-loading bootstrap estimates and outputs summary statistics. For our example, the bootstrap estimator and standard deviation for the six factor loadings were:

UNIVARIATE SUMMARY STATISTICS FOR CONTINUOUS VARIABLES

VARIABLE	MEAN	S. D.
LX(1,1)	0.298	0.322
LX(2,1)	0.447	0.459
LX(3,1)	0.207	0.230
LX(4,2)	0.373	0.384
LX(5,2)	0.251	0.260
LX(6,2)	0.403	0.415

These values can be used to form confidence intervals around the original-sample factor loading estimates to indicate how stable or good the estimates are given the representativeness of the original sample to the population. Rather than further discuss the PRELIS2 and LISREL8 matrix program setups for bootstrapping and Monte Carlo experiments, we refer you to the manual for various straightforward data set examples and output explanations.

These examples were intended only to provide a basic presentation of the bootstrap method in structural equation modeling. Lunneborg (1987) provides additional software to compute bootstrap estimates for means, correlations (bivariate, multivariate, part, and partial), regression weights, and analysis-of-variance designs, to name a few. Stine (1990) provides a basic introduction to bootstrapping methods, and Bollen and Stine (1993) give a more in-depth discussion of bootstrapping in structural equation modeling. Mooney and Duval (1993) also provide an overview of bootstrapping methods, give a basic algorithm and program for bootstrapping, and indicate other statistical packages that have bootstrap routines. The AMOS (1995) program provides an exceptional set of programs for bootstrap estimation and summary statistics. We therefore refer you to these references, as well as others presented in this section, for a better coverage of the background, rationale, and appropriateness of using bootstrap techniques.

Jackknife

The jackknife approach provides sample estimates of a population parameter wherein each estimate is based upon $n - 1$ fewer data points. For example, if a sample mean of 50 were based on $n = 20$ data points, then 20 additional jackknife sample means would be calculated on the basis of a sample size of $n = 19$. Each sample mean, however, would be based on omission of a different data point. The jackknife approach is useful in determining if an influential data point exists that drastically changes the sample statistic. To obtain jackknife estimates of parameters in a model, the subcommand JACKNIFE; replaces the BOOTSTRAP = <n of cases> subcommand in EQS5. This simulation method reuses the data file but excludes one observation on each replication. The number of replications must therefore be less than or equal to the sample size, but is typically set to the sample size for purposes of examining the influence of each data point on the sample statistic. The SAVE command in this instance is not applicable, although you can examine the influence of data points on the population matrices generated in each replication. The following EQS5 jackknife program inputs a raw-data file, SAMPLE.TXT, which consists of the same data as before, but put in an ASCII file with spaces between the data points. Notice that the path coefficients from the original model are used as start values, to avoid potential iterative convergence problems. The program outputs 30 estimates of the path coefficients in the /EQUATIONS command that represent the path model.

```
/TITLE
 JACKNIFE PATH MODEL EXAMPLE
/SPECIFICATIONS
 CASES=30;VARIABLES=4;METHOD=GLS;DATA_FILE = 'SAMPLE.TXT';
/EQUATION
 V1 = .252*V2 + .859*V3 + E1;
 V4 = .789*V1 + E2;
/SIMULATION
 SEED = 12345;
 REPLICATIONS=30;
 JACKNIFE;
/END
```

We are interested in examining the 30 parameter estimates for each path coefficient outputted by the jackknife program and comparing them to determine the influence of any individual set of scores on the covariance matrix and hence the path model. Although not examined here, a comparison of the 30 covariance matrices and fit indices on the computer output listing would indicate potential effects on the overall model fit. The reduced computer output is not presented here; instead, only the 30 jackknife estimates for each path coefficient are compared. The results from the jackknife program are as follows:

```
TITLE: JACKNIFE PATH MODEL EXAMPLE
SIMULATION DEFINITIONS
          JACKNIFE SIMULATION IS ELECTED
          NUMBER OF REPLICATIONS : 30
          SAMPLE DATA GENERATED FROM: EXIST
          SAMPLE SIZE : 29
          ORIGINAL SEED = 12345.
          DATA FILE TO BE SAVED ? NO
```

The 30 jackknife path estimates for the two path model equations are listed in Table 10.2. Subjects 21 and 25 had the highest and the lowest path coefficient, respectively, for V2, with Subject 21 overall obtaining coefficients out of bounds with other subjects. Although this is a limited and simplistic example, it should serve to show how the influence of one subject's data points can affect estimates in a model. The use of the jackknife approach to determine whether influential or outlier cases are present can be assisted further in EQS5 by examining the univariate statistics (skewness, kurtosis) and multivariate statistics (Mardia's coefficient, normalized estimate) provided on the computer output listing. EQS5 computer output also lists the case numbers of those subjects with the largest multivariate kurtosis values. Obviously, a further inspection of such data is warranted. As previously mentioned in chapter 1, a first step in data collection and analysis is to edit data and examine summary statistics—for example, mean, standard deviation, skewness, and kurtosis—to avoid potential problems in structural equation modeling.

Summary

The LISREL8-SIMPLIS software program does not provide simulation, bootstrap, and jackknife capabilities. However, bootstrapping and Monte Carlo experiments can be accomplished in PRELIS2 and LISREL8 (Jöreskog & Sörbom, 1993a). The bootstrap or Monte Carlo data sets are generated using the PRELIS2 software and are then saved in a single file. This saved file is then inputted into LISREL8 for analysis given the specified model. The

TABLE 10.2
Jackknife Estimates of Path Coefficients

Samples	V2	V3	E1	V1	E2
Original	.252	.859	.446	.789	.615
1	.158	.955	.250	.931	.366
2	.151	.960	.237	.938	.346
3	.148	.961	.233	.940	.341
4	.145	.961	.236	.938	.347
5	.135	.964	.229	.944	.330
6	.158	.957	.245	.937	.350
7	.151	.965	.213	.943	.331
8	.163	.960	.228	.938	.346
9	.150	.961	.234	.939	.345
10	.148	.960	.239	.944	.331
11	.147	.961	.234	.939	.344
12	.135	.964	.230	.940	.341
13	.150	.960	.238	.937	.350
14	.134	.960	.247	.930	.367
15	.149	.961	.234	.939	.345
16	.144	.961	.236	.938	.348
17	.151	.957	.246	.931	.366
18	.151	.958	.243	.936	.353
19	.138	.963	.229	.939	.345
20	.134	.962	.237	.942	.337
21	**.205**	**.942**	**.266**	**.905**	**.424**
22	.153	.959	.238	.936	.352
23	.133	.961	.241	.937	.351
24	.147	.959	.243	.944	.331
25	**.129**	**.964**	**.235**	**.937**	**.351**
26	.144	.961	.234	.937	.349
27	.154	.963	.222	.943	.334
28	.145	.960	.237	.941	.338
29	.149	.960	.238	.937	.350
30	.151	.960	.237	.936	.351

LISREL8 program outputs the results in another saved file for each of the data sets generated. A second PRELIS2 run then calculates the summary statistics. The PRELIS2 and LISREL8 program setups for bootstrapping and Monte Carlo experiments are presented in the *PRELIS2 User's Reference Guide* (Jöreskog & Sörbom, 1993d).

10.3 MULTIPLE-SAMPLE MODELS

A nice feature of structural equation modeling, although not frequently used, is the possibility of studying a theoretical model with more than one sample simultaneously. For example, Lomax (1985) examined a model for schooling using the High School and Beyond (HSB) database. The model included home background, academic orientation, extracurricular activity, achievement, and educational and occupational aspirations as latent variables. The research determined the extent to which the measurement and structural equation models "fit" both a sample of public school students and a sample of private school students, as well as examining whether model differences existed between the two groups. Theoretical models can also be examined across samples to determine the degree of invariance in fit indices, parameter estimates, and standard errors.

The multiple-sample approach can also be used in the analysis of quasi-experimental, experimental, cross-sectional, and/or longitudinal data. With multiple samples it is possible to (a) estimate separately the parameters for each of G independent samples, (b) test whether specified parameters or parameter matrices are equivalent across these groups (i.e., for any of the parameters in the measurement and/or structural equation models), and (c) test whether there are group mean differences for the indicator variables and/or for any of the structural equations.

In Case a, we can obviously use all of the previously described procedures in dealing with each group separately. The researcher can then "eyeball" the results (i.e., parameter estimates, goodness-of-fit indices, etc.) across the groups. However, statistical comparisons of the equivalence of parameters cannot be made among the groups, nor can mean differences be estimated. Case a is not strictly multiple sample modeling, because only one sample is evaluated at a time; thus, we do not consider it further.

In Case b, one can statistically determine whether certain specified parameters or parameter matrices are equivalent across the groups. For instance, one may be interested in whether the factor loadings are the same for the public and private school samples. That is, are different indicators better for the public school sample as compared with the private school sample? We refer to Case b as simple multiple-sample analysis.

In Case c, one can statistically determine whether there are mean differences for the indicator variables and/or the structural equations. For instance, one might be interested in whether there is a mean group difference in the structural equation for student achievement. We refer to Case c as structured means analysis (i.e., analysis of mean differences in the covariance structure).

EQS5 Example

Case b essentially examines the equivalence of matrices or parameter estimates across several samples taken randomly from a population. In the EQS5 program, a researcher would indicate the specific hypothesis to be tested. For a measurement model, we could test whether the factor loadings are equal across the samples, whether the factor variances and covariances are equal across the samples, whether the factor residual variances and covariances are equal across the samples, or even whether the unique error variances and covariances are equal across the samples. For a structural model, we could test whether the structure coefficients are equal across the samples. For a combined structural equation model, all parameters—and hence the entire model—are tested for equivalence across the samples. Obviously, in this instance both the covariance matrix and the coefficients are tested for equality across the samples.

The basic EQS5 multiple-sample program setup would include individual "stacked" programs for each sample of data, but with minor modifications to the first and last programs. For illustration, the following EQS5 multiple-sample program tests the equality of factor loadings for a unidimensional factor across three samples:

```
/TITLE
 SAMPLE 1
/SPECIFICATIONS
 CASES=200;VARIABLES=4;GROUPS=3;
/EQUATIONS
 V1 = 3*F1 + E1;
 V2 = 3*F1 + E2;
 V3 = 3*F1 + E3;
 V4 = 3*F1 + E4;
/VARIANCES
 F1 = 1.0;
 E1 TO E4 = 5*;
/MATRIX
 100.25
 60.24 98.15
 40.56 45.32 78.89
 45.12 55.64 67.00 90.25
/END
/TITLE
 SAMPLE 2
/SPECIFICATIONS
 CASES=150;VARIABLES=4;
/EQUATIONS
 V1 = 3*F1 + E1;
 V2 = 3*F1 + E2;
 V3 = 3*F1 + E3;
 V4 = 3*F1 + E4;
/VARIANCES
 F1 = 1.0;
 E1 TO E4 = 5*;
```

```
/MATRIX
  98.25
  61.20 90.10
  45.50 44.35 80.90
  42.00 50.40 65.00 94.25
/END
/TITLE
  SAMPLE 3
/SPECIFICATIONS
  CASES=300;VARIABLES=4;
/EQUATIONS
  V1 = 3*F1 + E1;
  V2 = 3*F1 + E2;
  V3 = 3*F1 + E3;
  V4 = 3*F1 + E4;
/VARIANCES
  F1 = 1.0;
  E1 TO E4 = 5*;
/MATRIX
  99.55
  64.70 93.30
  47.30 40.65 87.75
  41.00 52.45 63.76 91.67
/CONSTRAINTS
  (1,V1,F1) = (2,V1,F1) = (3,V1,F1)
  (1,V2,F1) = (2,V2,F1) = (3,V2,F1)
  (1,V3,F1) = (2,V3,F1) = (3,V3,F1)
  (1,V4,F1) = (2,V4,F1) = (3,V4,F1)
/LMTEST
/END
```

Certain commands have been boldfaced in the first and third individual programs of the EQS5 multiple-sample analysis. In the first program, the GROUPS = 3; subcommand indicates that comparisons will be made across three groups. Notice that within each individual program the sample size can vary; however, the model specified in the /EQUATIONS command must be the same—that is, must use the same start values—and correspond to the same number and type of variables. The covariance matrices by definition, however, are different in each of the individual programs, as expected. The third individual program specifies the equality of the factor loadings in the model. This is accomplished by using the /CONSTRAINTS command and including statements indicating that the sample, observed variable, and factor of each sample are equal. In other words, the equality (1,V1,F1)= (2,V1,F1) = (3,V1,F1) tests whether the factor loading from V1 to F1 is the same in samples 1, 2, and 3. The equality statement is repeated for the other three factor loadings specified in the measurement model in the /EQUATIONS command. The /LMTEST command invokes individual Lagrange multiplier tests on the constraints specified in the third program. For each equality tested, a chi-square and a probability value are reported. It is important to examine these individual tests of equality, especially if chi-square goodness of fit indicates a lack of model fit, because it may be due to a specific constraint in the model. Also, the EQS5 fit indices are printed only once for the multiple-sample analysis, and not for each individual program run. The fit indices are therefore testing whether the specified model holds across the samples. In our example, we are testing whether the factor loadings are the same in the samples.

LISREL8-SIMPLIS Example

In LISREL8-SIMPLIS, any model can be specified and tested across data samples. The SIMPLIS program also "stacks" individual programs, but assumes by default that the models are identical in subsequent individual programs and therefore do not have to be restated in later program setups. Only the differences between the individual programs need to be specified, for example, sample sizes and covariance matrices. Using the previous example, the LISREL8-SIMPLIS multiple-sample analysis of equal factor loadings across three samples would be:

```
Group 1: Testing equality of factors
Model: Factor loadings invariant
Observed Variables: V1-V4
Covariance Matrix:
100.25
 60.24 98.15
 40.56 45.32 78.89
 45.12 55.64 67.00 90.25
Sample size: 200
Latent Variables: Factor1
Relationships:
 V1-V4 = Factor1
Group 2: Testing equality of factors
Covariance matrix:
98.25
61.20 90.10
45.50 44.35 80.90
42.00 50.40 65.00 94.25
Sample size: 150
Group 3: Testing equality of factors
Covariance matrix:
```

```
99.55
64.70 93.30
47.30 40.65 87.75
41.00 52.45 63.76 91.67
Sample size: 300
End of Problem
```

In this example, only the sample sizes and covariance matrices needed to be entered in subsequent programs. More complex programs beyond this basic example are also possible. For example, one might wish to test the equality of both factor loadings and error variances in a program, or specify that factor loadings, error variances, and correlations between two or more factors exist.

Summary

Many different measurement and structural models using the multiple-sample approach are illustrated in software manuals and books. The interested reader is referred to Jöreskog and Sörbom (1989), Muthén (1987), and Bentler (1992), as well as texts by Hayduk (1987) and Bollen (1989), for more detail on running these various multiple-sample models. Other empirical examples using multiple-sample models are given by Lomax (1983, 1985), Cole and Maxwell (1985), Faulbaum (1987), and McArdle and Epstein (1987). A suggested strategy for testing models in the multiple-sample case is also given by Lomax (1983). We have included a LISREL8 matrix language program example in chapter 11 for those who wish to use the LISREL OUTPUT command in the LISREL8-SIMPLIS program and compare results.

10.4 INTERACTION MODELS

Until now, we have assumed that the relationships in all models have been linear—that is, that the relationships among all variables, observed and latent, could be represented by linear equations. Although the use of non-linear and interaction effects is popular in regression analysis (Aiken & West, 1991; Lewis & Mouw, 1978), the inclusion of interaction hypotheses in path analysis has been minimal (Newman, Marchant, & Ridenour, 1993). And although McDonald (1967) developed a nonlinear factor analysis model (for a newer version, see Etezadi-Amoli & McDonald, 1983), few studies have been conducted using interactive structural equation models. Examples have been presented, however, by Kenny and Judd (1984), Hayduk (1987), Wong and Long (1987), Bollen (1989), Higgins and Judd (1990), Cole, Maxwell, Arvey, and Salas (1993), Mackenzie and Spreng (1992), and Ping (1993, 1994, 1995).

In structural equation modeling, one could postulate that there is an interactive effect between two latent variables. Such an effect can be assumed when the variables are either *continuous* variables or *categorical* variables. In both instances, we are testing to see whether there is an additional effect above and beyond the direct effects of the two individual latent variables.

Some preliminary background is needed, however, before discussing in depth the inclusion of nonlinear and interactive effects in structural equation modeling, both among observed variables and among latent variables. First, consider the case of such effects among observed variables. If a nonlinear relationship is found to exist between two observed variables (e.g., if X_1 and X_2 are curvilinearly related), one can transform one or both of the variables so that the relationship becomes a linear one. One can alternatively use quadratic (nonlinear) terms in the model, such as including a squared term (e.g., $X_2 = X_1^2$), although insidious errors have been noted where observed variables worked better than latent variables (Pohlmann, 1993). If one desires an interactive effect among two observed variables (e.g., $X_3 = X_1X_2$), then a product term can be included in the model. These types of interactive effects involve *continuous* variables. If the interaction effects involve using *categories* (groups), much as the analysis-of-variance procedure does, one is employing the multiple-sample approach previously discussed, but including an interaction term. The two types of interaction—continuous and categorical—are presented separately.

Continuous-Variable Approach

Kenny and Judd (1984) developed a procedure to test the interaction between latent variables based on the products of observed variables. Their procedure allowed one to include both quadratic and interaction terms among latent variables by rewriting the system of equations to include product terms among the observed variables, for example, X_1X_3. For example, if F_1 was defined by the observed variables X_1 and X_2 and F_2 was defined by the observed variables X_3 and X_4, then the interaction of the latent variables, denoted as F_3, could be specified by the products of their respective observed variables: X_1X_3, X_1X_4, X_2X_3, and X_2X_4. In this approach, the interaction latent variable, F_3, can be represented, along with the "main-effect" latent variables, F_1 and F_2, in the structural equation $F_4 = F_1 + F_2 + F_3 + D_4$, where F_4 is the latent dependent variable and D_4 represents the error term.

Also, under certain conditions, Kenny and Judd indicated that the variance of these observed-variable products could be determined using their respective factor loadings and error terms along with the variance of the latent variables. For one observed variable product, X_1X_3, this would be given as $\sigma^2_{X_1X_3} = $ var $(X_1X_3) = $ var $[(\lambda_{X_1}F_1 + \varepsilon_{X_1})(\lambda_{X_3}F_2 + \varepsilon_{X_3})]$, where the λs represent the observed variable's factor loading and the εs represent each observed variable's unique error term. The latent-variable interaction effect, F_3, is then specified by fixing each of the observed variable's factor loadings and error terms. For the one observed-variable product, X_1X_3, the factor loading and error term would be specified as $\lambda_{X_1X_3} = \lambda_{X_1}\lambda_{X_3}$, with var $(\varepsilon_{X_1X_3}) = \lambda^2_{X_1}$ var (F_1) var $(\varepsilon_{X_3}) + \lambda^2_{X_3}$ var (F_2) var (ε_{X_1}), where the respective factor loadings are squared and multiplied by the variance term of the latent variable and the variance error term of the other observed variable. For additional information on their procedure and its limitations (i.e., the non-normality of distributions and the use of WLS as the method of estimation to obtain proper tests of significance), the interested reader is referred to Kenny and Judd (1984), Bollen (1989), Hayduk (1987), Schumacker and Rigdon (1995), or Jöreskog and Yang (1996) for illustrative examples.

When we consider the continuous-variable approach with interaction effects among latent variables, the equations are not necessarily straightforward. Part of the problem is that nonlinear constraints cannot be directly estimated in EQS5 and LISREL8-SIMPLIS (Jöreskog & Sörbom, 1993c), although the LISREL matrix command language has been used for these types of tests (see chap. 11). Ping (1993), however, has introduced a variation of the Kenny and Judd technique that can be implemented in LISREL8-SIMPLIS and EQS5. The method incorporates Anderson and Gerbing's two-step approach (1988), where the measurement parameters for the linear latent variables are estimated and then fixed in the structural model. Basically, the measurement-model parameters are used to calculate the loadings and error variances for the observed product variables, which are used to define the latent interaction variable effect. The interaction effect is then added to the structural model with the loadings and error variances fixed for the observed-product variables. The Ping method, therefore, does not estimate the factor loadings and error terms in the interaction structural model for the observed product variables, which define the latent-variable interaction effect.

Ping (1994) basically outlined the technique as follows:

1. Verify indicator normality.

2. Assume that the latent variables are independent of the error terms and the error terms are independent of each other.

3. Unidimensionalize each latent variable.

4. Center the observed variables at zero by subtracting the mean of each variable from each case value for that variable.

5. Estimate loadings and error variances for the linear independent variable indicators in a measurement model.

6. Use these estimates to calculate estimates of loadings and error variances for the nonlinear latent-variable indicators.

7. Fix loadings and error variances of nonlinear latent-variable indicators in a structural model, and then estimate the structural model.

8. Repeat Steps 6 and 7 to assess any change in measurement parameters between the two structural models.

The technique permits models with latent-variable "main effects" to be tested against models with "interaction effects" added using the incremental fit index (IFI) and the chi-square difference test for a nested model. The degrees of freedom for the structural model with the "interaction effect" added would be reduced by the number of fixed observed product variable loadings and error variances. In addition, since the observed product variables in a structural model cause it to be non-normal, maximum-likelihood estimation (which assumes multivariate normality) and standard errors for the structural coefficients are not appropriate (Hu, Bentler, & Kano, 1992). Because estimates appear to be robust to departures from normality but standard errors and chi-square statistics may not be, the EQS5 Robust estimator (which is less dependent on multivariate normality) is recommended.

EQS5 Example. In our EQS5 example, we have first determined that our observed variables are normally distributed, and we have standardized them. We have also determined that the factors and error terms are independent. Three undimensional factors are indicated in Fig. 10.1 with two observed variables indicating each. The latent variable F1 is a dependent latent variable with F2 and F3 latent independent variables. We consequently need to demonstrate the three following EQS5 programs: Measurement Model, Main Effects Structural Model, and Interaction Effects Structural Model. (It may also be important to check a model that has both the initial measurement-model and structural-model estimates in it against the measurement model, to determine if the loadings and error variances are markedly different. This should not be the case unless unidimensional latent variables are not clearly indicated; then, the observed product variable loadings and error terms will be different depending on which model values are used.)

The measurement model is analyzed in the following EQS5 program:

```
/TITLE
 MEASUREMENT MODEL
/SPECIFICATIONS
 CASES=300;VARIABLES=10;METHOD=ML;DA='INTERACT.DAT';
/EQUATIONS
 V1 = *F1 + E1;
 V2 = *F1 + E2;
```

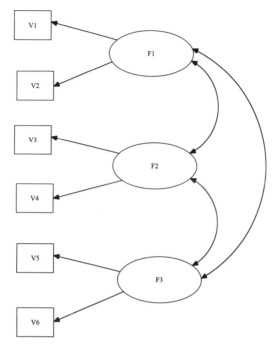

FIG. 10.1. Three unidimensional latent variables (measurement model).

```
V3 = *F2 + E3;
V4 = *F2 + E4;
V5 = *F3 + E5;
V6 = *F3 + E6;
/VARIANCES
 F1, F3 = 1.0;
 E1 TO E6 = *;
/COVARIANCES
 F1,F3 = *;
/END
```

The main-effects structural model, with this measurement model already specified, would be indicated by simply adding F1 = *F2 + *F3 + D1; as the last statement in the /EQUATIONS command and changing the /CO-VARIANCES command to F2,F3 =*;. This would yield the structural co-efficients for the direct effects of F2 and F3 on F1, the dependent latent variable, and permit the latent independent variables F2 and F3 to covary (see Fig. 10.2). A comparison between the factor loadings and error variances of the latent independent variables in the previous measurement-model program and this structural-model program should not be markedly different.

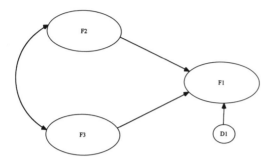

FIG. 10.2. Main-effects structural model.

Because there was little difference in the values between the measurement model and the main-effect structural model, we used the observed-variable factor loadings and error variances from the previous measurement-model program to compute the factor loadings and error terms of the product variables that define the latent-variable interaction effect for F4. The factor loadings and error terms in the measurement model were V1 = .80, E1 = .15; V2 = .76, E2 = .22; V3 = .79, E3 = .16; V4 = .88, E4 = .13; V5 = .87, E5 = .12; and V6 = .94, E6 = .10. The factor loadings and error terms for our product indicator variables were then computed as V(3,5) = .687, E(3,5) = .215; V(3,6) = .743, E(3,6) = .219; V(4,5) = .766, E(4,5) = .207; and V(4,6) = .827, E(4,6) = .205. We next included the original factor loadings and error terms, structure coefficients for F2 and F3, the covariance term for F2 and F3, and these product variable factor loadings and error terms in an interaction model program. The interaction model, as diagrammed in Fig. 10.3, is absent the structure coefficient from F4 to F1 and the resultant prediction error, D1, which is to be estimated in the program.

The following EQS5 program includes the added interaction term as a function of the product variables in the input data file, and outputs robust statistics for the parameter estimates. The Robust option in EQS5 provides the Satorra–Bentler scaled chi-square test statistic and standard errors that are distributionally freer, that is, when the normal distribution assumption may not be met. Please note that robust statistics can be computed only if raw-score data are inputted.

```
/TITLE
INTERACTION EFFECTS STRUCTURAL MODEL
/SPECIFICATIONS
CASES=300;VARIABLES=10;METHOD=ML,ROBUST;DA='INTERACT.DAT';
/EQUATIONS
V1 = .80F1 + .15E1;
V2 = .76F1 + .22E2;
V3 = .79F2 + .16E3;
V4 = .88F2 + .13E4;
```

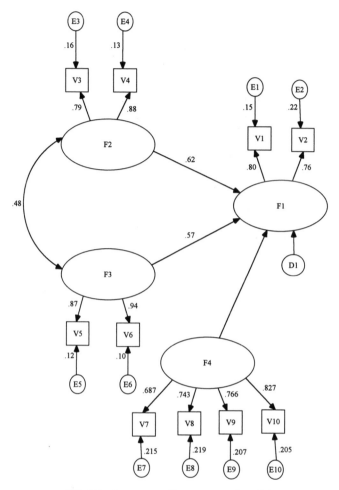

FIG. 10.3. Interaction-effects structural model.

```
V5 = .87F3 + .12E5;
V6 = .94F3 + .10E6;
V7 = .687F4 + .215E7;
V8 = .743F4 + .219E8;
V9 = .766F4 + .207E9;
V10 = .827F4 + .205E10;
F1 = .62F2 + .57F3 + *F4 + D1;
/VARIANCES
 F1, F4 = 1.0;
/COVARIANCES
 F2,F3 = .48;
/END
```

Categorical-Variable Approach

In the categorical-variable approach, the different samples are defined by the different levels of the interacting variables. The basic logic is that if interaction effects are present, then certain parameters should have different values in different samples. Both main effects and interaction effects can be determined by using different samples to estimate the intercept and regression slopes. A χ^2 difference test can determine whether a main-effect difference in the groups exists, as well as whether regression coefficients are equal or parallel. Since the two models are nested, a χ^2 difference test with one degree of freedom is computed.

LISREL8-SIMPLIS Example. The following LISREL8-SIMPLIS program analyzes data from two groups: high-motivation versus low-motivation students, where group represents the categorical variable. Separate covariance matrices and means on the dependent and independent variables are inputted to estimate the prediction of a math score given a pretest score. The means are required; otherwise, the intercept values will be zero. The SIMPLIS program is specified as follows:

```
Group HIGHACH: Math and Pretest Scores
Observed Variables: Math Pretest
Covariance Matrix:
181.349
 84.219 182.821
Means: 82.15 78.35
Sample Size: 373
Equation: Math = CONST Pretest
Group LOWACH: Math and Pretest Scores
Covariance Matrix:
174.485
 34.468 161.869
Means: 48.75 46.98
Sample Size: 249
Equation: Math = CONST Pretest
End of Problem
```

The expression CONST is used in the program to denote the intercept term. The command EQUATION: is used to specify the regression equations for each group. Selected results from the LISREL8-SIMPLIS computer output for the high- and low-motivation subjects were:

High-motivation group:

```
Math = 46.06 + 0.46*Pretest, Errorvar.= 154.85, R2 = 0.20
       (3.80)  (0.048)               (8.80)
       12.13    9.65                 17.59
```

Low-motivation group:

```
Math = 38.75 + 0.21*Pretest, Errorvar.= 154.85, R2 = 0.045
       (3.03)  (0.062)                   (8.80)
       12.81    3.43                     17.59
```

The main effect for group differences in math exam scores is given by the difference in the CONST values: 46.06 − 38.75 = 7.31. The interaction effect is given by the difference in the slope estimates of pretest values for the two groups: .46 − .21 = .25. The χ^2 difference test with one degree of freedom was 1.98, p = .16, indicating a significant difference in the slope estimates.

Summary

A categorical-variable interaction model can represent a wide variety of interaction effects, including higher-order interactions, without requiring any substantial new methodological developments. This approach can also be used regardless of whether the interaction intensifies or mutes the effects of the individual variables. Because the interaction effect is represented in the difference between samples, the researcher is also able to test linear relations of variables within each sample, thus avoiding any potential complications in fitting the model. Finally, most of the structural equation modeling programs permit restrictions across samples, thereby making use of this approach.

A weakness of the categorical approach, however, is that smaller subsamples of the total sample size are used. This could be a serious problem if some groups have low sample sizes that affect group parameter estimates. This reduction in sample size could also affect the results of the χ^2 difference tests. MacCallum, Roznowski, and Necowitz (1992) noted a substantial degree of instability in the fit indices in even moderately sized samples. Thus, it is possible that the categorical-variable approach may yield group samples that are too small, resulting in a χ^2 test statistic that misleads the researcher into believing that an interaction effect exists, whether it does or not. A possible solution is to minimize the number of distinct parameters being compared in the model by fixing certain parameters to be invariant across the samples being compared.

In our example, main effects for group differences holding slopes constant can be accomplished in the following program:

```
Group HIGHACH: Math and Pretest Scores
Observed Variables: Math Pretest
Covariance Matrix:
181.349
 84.219 182.821
```

```
Means: 82.15 78.35
Sample Size: 373
Equation: Math = CONST Pretest
Group LOWACH: Math and Pretest Scores
Covariance Matrix:
174.485
 34.468 161.869
Means: 48.75 46.98
Sample Size: 249
Equation: Math = CONST
End of Problem
```

The specifying of Equation: Math = CONST permits different CONST values to be estimated in the two regression equations with the slopes equal. The outputted equations from the LISREL8-SIMPLIS program indicate that the slope values are identical. Notice, however, that this main-effect difference with equal slopes was not a good fit. Obviously, the previous model, which indicated differences in both intercepts and slopes, had a better model fit.

High-motivation group:

```
Math = 53.26 + 0.37*Pretest, Errorvar.= 155.07, R2 = 0.14
      (3.04) (0.038)                (8.81)
      17.53    9.73                 17.59
```

Low-motivation group:

```
Math = 31.43 + 0.37*Pretest, Errorvar.= 155.07, R2 = 0.12
      (1.95) (0.038)                (8.81)
      16.13    9.73                 17.59
```

```
CHI-SQUARE WITH 2 DEGREES OF FREEDOM = 11.99 (P = 0.0025)
```

We do *not* recommend the categorical-variable approach when hypothesizing interaction involving two continuous variables. The basic logic is that there is a loss of information when reducing a continuous variable to a categorical variable, for purposes of defining a group (Russell & Bobko, 1992). Also, where does one choose the point for dividing a continuous variable into a categorical variable to form the groups? How do we justify the arbitrary value, that is, mean, median, or quartile? Random-sampling error also ensures that some cases would be misclassified, violating some basic assumptions about subject membership in a particular group.

The testing of interaction effects can present problems in structural equation modeling. First, we may have the problem of model specification. Linear models simplify the task of determining relationships to investigate and distributional assumptions to consider—not necessarily the situation in testing latent-variable interactions. Second, discarding the linearity assumption opens up the possibility of several interactive combinations, but this also serves to magnify the critical role of theory in focusing the research effort. Third, a researcher who seeks to model interaction effects must also collect data that span the range of values in which interaction effects are likely to be evident in the raw data, and must collect a sample of large enough size that subsample sizes are sufficient. Fourth, we have noted that the statistical output (fit indices, standard errors) is based on linearity and normality assumptions, and we may not have robust results to recognize the presence of an interaction effect unless it is substantial.

The continuous-variable approach does have its good points. It is possible to check for normality of variables and to standardize them, and the approach does not require creating subsamples or groups into which observations could possibly be misclassified, nor does it require the researcher to categorize a variable and thereby lose information. Moreover, the continuous-variable approach is parsimonious. Basically, all but one of the additional parameters involved in the interaction-model are exact functions of the "main-effects" parameters—the only new parameters to be estimated being the coefficient for the latent interaction independent variable and the prediction-equation error.

The continuous-variable approach also has several drawbacks. First, only a few software programs can perform the necessary nonlinear constraints, and the programming for testing interaction "effect" hypotheses in the traditional sense is not easy. Second, if you include too many indicator variables of your latent independent variables, this approach can become very cumbersome. For example, if one latent independent variable, Factor 1, has n_1 measures and the other latent independent variable, Factor 2, has n_2 measures, then the interaction term, Factor 1 × Factor 2, will have $n_1 \times n_2$ measures. If each independent latent variable had five indicator variables, then the multiplicative latent independent variable interaction would involve 25 indicators. Including the five measures for each of the two "main-effect" latent independent variables and two indicators of a latent dependent variable, the model would have 37 indicator variables before any other latent-variable relationships were considered. Third, the functional form of the interaction needs to be specified. The simple multiplicative interaction presented here hardly covers other types of interactions, and for these other types of interactions there is little prior research or available examples to guide the researcher.

A fourth problem to consider is multicollinearity. It is very likely that the interaction factor will be highly correlated with the observed variables used to construct it. This multicollinearity in the measurement model causes the interaction latent independent variable to be more highly correlated with the observed variables of other "main-effect" latent independent variables than each set of observed variables are with their own respective "main-effect" latent independent variables. For multiplicative interactions between normally distributed variables, Smith and Sasaki (1979) demonstrated how multicollinearity could be eliminated by centering the observed variables (using scores expressed as deviations from their means) before computing the product variable. However, centering the variables alters the form of the interaction relationship. Smith and Sasaki noted that centering the variables turns the original multiplicative interaction into a type of "consistency effect," in which interaction values take on values similar to the main-effect values when either both are above their respective means or both are below their respective means. Researchers who want to model other types of interactions may find no easy answer to the problem of multicollinearity.

A fifth concern relates to distributional problems, which are more serious than those associated with linear modeling techniques using observed variables only. If the observed variables are non-normal, then the variance of the product variable can be very different from the values implied by the basic measurement model, and the interaction "effect" will perform poorly. Of course, permissible transformations, as mentioned in earlier chapters, may result in a suitable, normal distribution for the observed variables. The resultant non-normality, however, in the observed variables violates the distributional assumptions associated with the estimation methods used, for example, maximum likelihood. Furthermore, estimation methods that do not make distributional assumptions may not work for interaction models. Basically, the asymptotic weight matrix associated with the covariance matrix for an interaction model may be non-positive definite because of dependencies between moments of different observed variables that are implied by the interaction model.

Structural equation models that include interaction effects are not prevalent in the research literature, in part, because of all the concerns mentioned here. The categorical-variable approach using multiple samples and constraints has been used more often. The Ping (1993) technique may provide a more plausible and user-friendly approach to modeling a continuous-variable interaction effect, under certain conditions. Jöreskog and Yang (1996), however, do provide additional insights into modeling interaction effects, given the problems and concerns discussed here. Suffice it to say that until the software programs include interaction capabilities and appropriate techniques, the task of including latent-variable interaction effects will continue to be researched.

10.5 SUMMARY

In this chapter, we considered several important advanced topics: cross validation; simulation, including bootstrap and jackknife techniques; multiple-sample models; and interaction models. The chapter began with a look at cross validation techniques and then introduced simulation programs including bootstrap and jackknife approaches to assessing parameter estimate invariance. Next, both a model in which multiple samples are considered simultaneously and the structured means model, in which mean differences and intercepts can be evaluated across groups, were presented. We then concluded the chapter by discussing interaction models and a newer plausible approach to modeling continuous-variable interaction effects.

We hope that our discussion of these more advanced topics in structural equation modeling has provided you with a basic overview and introduction to these methods. We encourage you to read the references provided at the end of the chapter and run some of the program setups provided in the chapter. We further hope that the basic introduction in this chapter will permit you to read the research literature and better understand the resulting models presented, which should support various theoretical perspectives. Attempting a few basic models will help you better understand the approach; afterward, you may wish to attempt more advanced models.

REFERENCES

Aiken, L. S., & West, S. G. (1991). *Multiple regression: Testing and interpreting interactions.* Newbury Park, CA: Sage.

AMOS user's guide. (1995). Chicago: SmallWaters Corporation.

Anderson, J. C., & Gerbing, D. W. (1988). Structural equation modeling in practice: A review and recommended two-step approach. *Psychological Bulletin, 103,* 411–423.

Bandalos, D. (1993). Factors influencing the cross-validation of confirmatory factor analysis models. *Multivariate Behavioral Research, 28,* 351–374.

Benson, J., & Bandalos, D. (1992). Second-order confirmatory factor analysis of the reactions to tests' scale with cross-validation. *Multivariate Behavioral Research, 27,* 459–487.

Benson, J., & El-Zahhar, N. (1994). Further refinement and validation of the revised test anxiety scale. *Structural Equation Modeling: A Multidisciplinary Journal, 1*(3), 203–221.

Benson, J., Moulin-Julian, M., Schwarzer, C., Seipp, B., & El-Zahhar, N. (1992). Cross-validation of a revised test anxiety scale using multi-national samples. In K. Hagtvet (Ed.), *Advances in test anxiety research: Vol. 7* (pp. 62–83). Lisse, Netherlands: Swets & Zeitlinger.

Bentler, P. M. (1992). *EQS structural equations program manual.* Los Angeles: BMDP Statistical Software, Inc.

Bollen, K. A. (1989). *Structural equations with latent variables.* New York: Wiley.

Bollen, K. A., & Long, J. S. (Eds.). (1993). *Testing structural equation models.* Newbury Park, CA: Sage.

Bollen, K. A., & Stine, R. A. (1993). Bootstrapping goodness-of-fit measures in structural equation models. In K. A. Bollen & J. S. Long (Eds.), *Testing structural equation models* (pp. 66–110). Newbury Park, CA: Sage.

Browne, M., & Cudeck, R. (1989). Single sample cross-validation indices for covariance structures. *Multivariate Behavioral Research, 24,* 445–455.

Browne, M., & Cudeck, R. (1993). Alternative ways of assessing model fit. In K. A. Bollen & J. S. Long (Eds.), *Testing structural equation models.* Newbury Park, CA: Sage.

Cole, D. A., & Maxwell, S. E. (1985). Multitrait-multimethod comparisons across populations: A confirmatory factor analytic approach. *Multivariate Behavioral Research, 20,* 389–417.

222 CHAPTER 10

Cole, D. A., Maxwell, S. E., Arvey, R., & Salas, E. (1993). Multivariate group comparisons of variable systems: MANOVA and structural equation modeling. *Psychological Bulletin, 114*, 174–184.

Cudeck, R., & Browne, M. W. (1983). Cross-validation of covariance structures. *Multivariate Behavioral Research, 18*, 147–167.

Etezadi-Amoli, J., & McDonald, R. P. (1983). A second generation nonlinear factor analysis. *Psychometrika, 48*, 315–342.

Faulbaum, F. (1987). Intergroup comparisons of latent means across waves. *Sociological Methods and Research, 15*, 317–335.

Hayduk, L. A. (1987). *Structural equation modeling with LISREL: Essentials and advances*. Baltimore: Johns Hopkins University Press.

Higgins, L. F., & Judd, C. M. (1990). Estimation of non-linear models in the presence of measurement error. *Decision Sciences, 21*, 738–751.

Hu, L., Bentler, P. M., & Kano, Y. (1992). Can test statistics in covariance structure analysis be trusted? *Psychological Bulletin, 112*, 351–362.

Jöreskog, K. G., & Sörbom, D. (1989). *LISREL7: A guide to the program and applications* (2nd ed.). Chicago: SPSS.

Jöreskog, K. G., & Sörbom, D. (1993a). *Bootstrapping and Monte Carlo experimenting with PRELIS2 and LISREL8*. Chicago: Scientific Software International.

Jöreskog, K. G., & Sörbom, D. (1993b). *LISREL8 user's reference guide*. Chicago: Scientific Software International.

Jöreskog, K. G., & Sörbom, D. (1993c). *LISREL8: Structural equation modeling with the SIMPLIS command language*. Hillsdale, NJ: Lawrence Erlbaum Associates.

Jöreskog, K. G., & Sörbom, D. (1993d). *PRELIS2 user's reference guide*. Chicago: Scientific Software International.

Jöreskog, K. G., & Yang, F. (1996). Non-linear structural equation models: The Kenny-Judd model with interaction effects. In G. A. Marcoulides & R. E. Schumacker (Eds.), *Advanced structural equation modeling: Issues and techniques*. Mahwah, NJ: Lawrence Erlbaum Associates.

Kenny, D. A., & Judd, C. M. (1984). Estimating the non-linear and interactive effects of latent variables. *Psychological Bulletin, 96*, 201–210.

Lewis, E. L., & Mouw, J. T. (1978). *The use of contrast coefficients*. Carbondale: Southern Illinois University Press.

Lomax, R. G. (1983). A guide to multiple sample equation modeling. *Behavior Research Methods and Instrumentation, 15*, 580–584.

Lomax, R. G. (1985). A structural model of public and private schools. *Journal of Experimental Education, 53*, 216–226.

Lunneborg, C. E. (1987). *Bootstrap applications for the behavioral sciences: Vol. 1*. Psychology Department, University of Washington, Seattle.

MacCallum, R. C., Roznowski, M., & Necowitz, L. B. (1992). Model modifications in covariance structure analysis: The problem of capitalization on chance. *Psychological Bulletin, 111*, 490–504.

Mackenzie, S. B., & Spreng, R. A. (1992). How does motivation moderate the impact of central and peripheral processing on brand attitudes and intentions? *Journal of Consumer Research, 18*, 519–529.

Marcoulides, G., & Schumacker, R. E. (Eds.). (1996). *Advanced structural equation modeling: Issues and techniques*. Mahwah, NJ: Lawrence Erlbaum Associates.

McArdle, J. J., & Epstein, D. (1987). Latent growth curves within developmental structural equation models. *Child Development, 58*, 110–133.

McDonald, R. P. (1967). Nonlinear factor analysis. *Psychometric Monograph*, No. 15.

Mooney, C. Z., & Duval, R. D. (1993). *Bootstrapping: A nonparametric approach to statistical inference*. Sage University Series on Quantitative Applications in the Social Sciences, 07-097. Beverly Hills, CA: Sage.

Muthén, B. (1987). *LISCOMP: Analysis of linear structural equations with a comprehensive measurement model.* Mooresville, IN: Scientific Software.

Newman, I., Marchant, G. J., & Ridenour, T. (1993, April). *Type VI errors in path analysis: Testing for interactions.* Paper presented at the annual meeting of the American Educational Research Association, Atlanta.

Ping, R. A., Jr. (1993). *Latent variable interaction and quadratic effect estimation: A suggested approach* (Tech. Rep.). Dayton, OH: Wright State University.

Ping, R. A., Jr. (1994). Does satisfaction moderate the association between alternative attractiveness and exit intention in a marketing channel? *Journal of the Academy of Marketing Science, 22*(4), 364–371.

Ping, R. A., Jr. (1995). A parsimonious estimating technique for interaction and quadratic latent variables. *Journal of Marketing Research, 32*(3), 336–347.

Pohlmann, J. T. (1993). Insidious structural errors in latent variable models. *Mid-Western Educational Researcher, 6*(3), 29–32.

Russell, C. J., & Bobko, P. (1992). Moderated regression analysis and Likert scales: Too coarse for comfort. *Journal of Applied Psychology, 77*, 336–342.

Schumacker, R. E., & Rigdon, E. (1995, April). *Testing interaction effects in structural equation modeling.* Paper presented at the annual meeting of the American Educational Research Association, San Francisco.

Smith, K. W., & Sasaki, M. S. (1979). Decreasing multicollinearity: A method for models with multiplicative functions. *Sociological Methods and Research, 8*, 35–56.

Stine, R. (1990). An introduction to bootstrap methods: Examples and ideas. In J. Fox & J. S. Long (Eds.), *Modern methods of data analysis* (pp. 325–373). Beverly Hills, CA: Sage.

Wong, S. K., & Long, J. S. (1987). *Parameterizing non-linear constraints in models with latent variables.* Unpublished manuscript, Department of Sociology, Indiana University, Bloomington.

11

TECHNICAL SECTION: MATRIX APPROACH TO MODELING

Chapter Outline:

11.1 General Overview of Matrix Notation

In this chapter we consider the technical matrix notation associated with the LISREL matrix command language. As described in Jöreskog and Sörbom (1993), the structural model is written in the following matrix equation:

$$\eta = B\eta + \Gamma\xi + \zeta \tag{1}$$

The latent dependent variables are denoted by η (eta) as a vector ($m \times 1$) of m such variables. The latent independent variables are denoted by ξ (xi) as a vector ($n \times 1$) of n such variables. A matrix Φ contains the variances and covariances among these latent independent variables. The relationships among the latent variables are denoted by B (capital beta) and Γ (capital gamma), the elements of which are denoted by $[\beta]$ (lowercase beta) and $[\gamma]$ (lowercase gamma), respectively. B is an $m \times m$ matrix of structure coefficients that relate the latent dependent variables to one another. Γ is an $m \times n$ matrix of structure coefficients that relate the latent independent variables to the latent dependent variables. The error term ζ in the structural model equation is a vector that contains the equation prediction errors or disturbance terms. The matrix Ψ contains the variances and covariances among these latent dependent prediction-equation errors.

As described in Jöreskog and Sörbom (1993), the measurement models are written in the following set of matrix equations:

$$Y = \Lambda_y\eta + \varepsilon \tag{2}$$

for the latent dependent variables and

$$X = \Lambda_x\xi + \delta \tag{3}$$

for the latent independent variables. The observed variables are denoted by the vector Y ($p \times 1$) for the measures of the latent dependent variables η ($m \times 1$), and by the vector X ($q \times 1$) for the measures of the latent independent variables ξ ($n \times 1$). The relationships between the observed variables and the latent variables (typically referred to as *factor loadings*) are denoted by the ($p \times m$) matrix Λ_y (capital lambda sub y) for the Ys, the elements of which are denoted by $[\lambda_y]$ (lowercase lambda sub y); and by the $q \times n$ matrix Λ_x (capital lambda sub x) for the Xs, the elements of which are denoted by $[\lambda_x]$ (lowercase lambda sub x). Finally, the measurement errors for the Ys are denoted by the $p \times 1$ vector ε (lowercase epsilon) and for the Xs by the $q \times 1$ vector δ (lowercase delta). The matrix θ_ε contains the variances and covariances among the errors for the observed dependent variables. The matrix θ_δ contains the variances and covariances among the errors for the observed independent variables.

A graphic summary of the general structural equation model in matrix format has been depicted by Hayduk (1987) and is reproduced in Fig. 11.1. The three equations diagrammed in matrix format correspond respectively to the structural equation model (equation 1), the measurement model for the Y latent dependent variables (equation 2), and the measurement model for the X latent independent variables (equation 3).

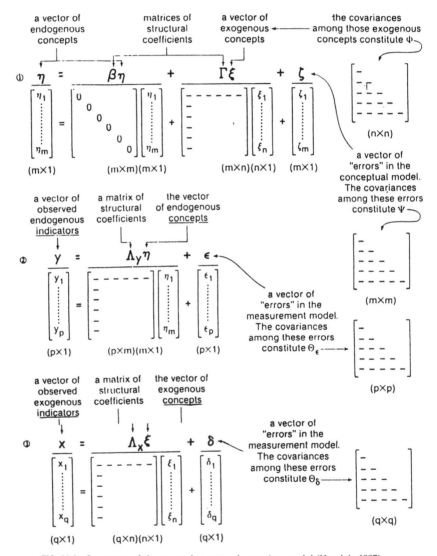

FIG. 11.1. Summary of the general structural equation model (Hayduk, 1987).

Obviously, not all of the eight matrices are necessary in a given model—for example, the confirmatory factor model. Our basic example in chapter 6 is presented here to illustrate the matrix notation. In our first example in chapter 6 (see Fig. 6.1), there were two structure coefficients of interest. The first involved the influence of *intelligence* on *achievement₁*. The structure coefficient for this influence would reside in the matrix Γ, because it represents the relationship between the latent independent variable *intelligence* and the latent dependent variable *achievement₁*. The second structure coefficient involved the influence of *achievement₁* on *achievement₂*. This coefficient would reside in the matrix B, because it represents the relationship between the latent dependent variable *achievement₁* and the latent dependent variable *achievement₂*. The final term in the structural model of equation 1 is ζ (zeta), which is an $m \times 1$ vector of m equation errors or disturbances, which represent that portion of each latent dependent variable that is not explained or predicted by the model.

In LISREL notation, our equations would be written as

$$\eta_1 = \gamma_{11}\,\xi_1 + \zeta_1$$

and

$$\eta_2 = \beta_{21}\,\eta_1 + \zeta_2\,,$$

respectively, or in the complete matrix equation as:

$$\begin{bmatrix} \eta_1 \\ \eta_2 \end{bmatrix} = \begin{bmatrix} 0 & 0 \\ \beta_{21} & 0 \end{bmatrix} \begin{bmatrix} \eta_1 \\ \eta_2 \end{bmatrix} + \begin{bmatrix} \gamma_{11} \\ 0 \end{bmatrix} [\xi_1] + \begin{bmatrix} \zeta_1 \\ \zeta_2 \end{bmatrix},$$

where the subscripts on β represent the rows for a latent dependent variable being predicted and columns for a latent dependent variable as the predictor, respectively. The subscripts for the γ vector represents the rows for a latent dependent variable being predicted and columns for a latent independent variable as the predictor, respectively.

The values of 0 shown in the matrix equations for B and Γ represent structure coefficients that we hypothesize to be equal to 0. For example, because we did not specify that intelligence influenced achievement₂, rather than estimate γ_{21}, we set that value to 0. Likewise, we did not specify that achievement₂ influenced achievement₁, and we set β_{12} to 0. Finally, notice that the diagonal values of B are also 0, that is, β_{11} and β_{22}. The diagonal values of B are always set to 0 because they would indicate the extent to which a latent dependent variable influences itself. These influences are never of interest to the applied researcher. In summary, our matrix equation suggests that there are potentially four structure coefficients of interest, β_{12},

β_{21}, γ_{11}, and γ_{21}; however, our model included only two of these coefficients. Other structural models of these same latent variables could be developed that contain different configurations of structure coefficients.

We now need to provide a more explicit definition of the measurement models in our example. We have two different measurement models in our example, one for the latent dependent variables and one for the latent independent variables. In LISREL matrix notation, these equations would be written for the *Y*s as:

$$y_1 = \lambda_{y_{11}} \eta_1 + \varepsilon_1$$

$$y_2 = \lambda_{y_{21}} \eta_1 + \varepsilon_2$$

$$y_3 = \lambda_{y_{32}} \eta_2 + \varepsilon_3$$

$$y_4 = \lambda_{y_{42}} \eta_2 + \varepsilon_4$$

and for the *X*s as

$$x_1 = \lambda_{x_{11}} \xi_1 + \delta_1$$

$$x_2 = \lambda_{x_{21}} \xi_1 + \delta_2.$$

The factor loadings and error terms would also appear in their respective error variance–covariance matrices. The complete matrix equation for the *Y*s would be written as:

$$\begin{bmatrix} y_1 \\ y_2 \\ y_3 \\ y_4 \end{bmatrix} = \begin{bmatrix} \lambda_{y_{11}} & 0 \\ \lambda_{y_{21}} & 0 \\ 0 & \lambda_{y_{32}} \\ 0 & \lambda_{y_{42}} \end{bmatrix} \begin{bmatrix} \eta_1 \\ \eta_2 \end{bmatrix} + \begin{bmatrix} \varepsilon_1 \\ \varepsilon_2 \\ \varepsilon_3 \\ \varepsilon_4 \end{bmatrix}$$

and for the *X*s as:

$$\begin{bmatrix} x_1 \\ x_2 \end{bmatrix} = \begin{bmatrix} \lambda_{x_{11}} \\ \lambda_{x_{21}} \end{bmatrix} [\xi_1] + \begin{bmatrix} \delta_1 \\ \delta_2 \end{bmatrix},$$

where the subscripts in λ_y represent the rows for an observed *Y* variable and columns for a latent dependent variable and those in λ_x represent the rows for an observed *X* variable and columns for a latent independent variable, respectively.

The values of 0 shown in the matrix equations for Λ_y (and theoretically for Λ_x, although not for this model) represent factor loadings that we hypothesize to be equal to 0. For example, since we did not specify that California$_1$ was an indicator of *achievement*$_2$, rather than estimate $\lambda_{y_{12}}$, we set that value to 0. Likewise, we specified that $\lambda_{y_{22}}$, $\lambda_{y_{31}}$, and $\lambda_{y_{41}}$ were set to 0.

There are several covariance terms that we need to define. From the structural model, there are two covariance terms to consider. First, we define Φ (capital phi) as an $n \times n$ covariance matrix of the n latent independent variables, the elements of which are denoted by $[\phi]$ (lowercase phi). The diagonal elements of Φ contain the variances of the latent independent variables. In our example model, Φ contains only one element, the variance of *intelligence* (denoted by ϕ_{11}).

Second, let us define Ψ (capital psi) as an $m \times m$ covariance matrix of the m equation errors ζ, the elements of which are denoted by $[\psi]$ (lowercase psi). The diagonal elements of Ψ contain the variances of the equation errors, that is, the amount of unexplained variance for each equation. In our example model, Ψ contains two diagonal elements, one for each equation (denoted by ψ_{11} and ψ_{22}).

From the measurement model, there are two additional covariance terms to be concerned with. First, we define Θ_ε (capital theta sub epsilon) as a $p \times p$ covariance matrix of the measurement errors for the Ys (that is, ε), the elements of which are denoted by $[\theta_\varepsilon]$ (lowercase theta sub epsilon). The diagonal elements of Θ_ε contain the variances of the measurement errors for the Ys. In our example model, Θ_ε contains four diagonal elements, one for each Y. Second, let us define Θ_δ (capital theta sub delta) as a $q \times q$ covariance matrix of the measurement errors for the Xs (that is, δ), the elements of which are denoted by $[\theta_\delta]$ (lowercase theta sub delta). The diagonal elements of Θ_δ contain the variances of the measurement errors for the Xs. In our example model, Θ_δ contains two diagonal elements, one for each X.

There is one more covariance term that we need to define, and it really represents the ultimate covariance term. To this point, we have defined eight different matrices, B, Γ, Λ_y, Λ_x, Φ, Ψ, Θ_ε, and Θ_δ. From these matrices we can generate an ultimate matrix of covariances that the overall model implies, and this matrix is denoted by Σ (capital sigma). Officially, Σ is a supermatrix composed of four submatrices, as follows:

$$\Sigma = \begin{bmatrix} \Sigma_{yy} & \Sigma_{yx} \\ \Sigma_{xy} & \Sigma_{xx} \end{bmatrix} \qquad (4)$$

This supermatrix certainly looks imposing, but it can be easily understood. First consider the submatrix in the upper left portion of Σ. It deals with the covariances among the Ys, and in terms of our model can be written as:

$$\Sigma_{yy} = \left[\Lambda_y [(I - B)^{-1} (\Gamma \Phi \Gamma' + \Psi)(I - B')^{-1}] \Lambda_y' + \Theta_\varepsilon \right], \qquad (5)$$

where I is an $m \times m$ identity matrix (i.e., a matrix having 1s on the diagonal and 0s elsewhere). You can see in Equation 5 that all of the matrices are involved except for those of the measurement model in the Xs. That is, (5) contains the matrices for the structural model and for the measurement model in the Ys.

Consider next the submatrix in the lower right portion of Σ. It deals with the covariances among the Xs and in terms of our model can be written as:

$$\Sigma_{xx} = \left[\Lambda_x \Phi \Lambda_x' + \Theta_\delta \right].$$ (6)

As shown in Equation 6, the only matrices included are those that involve the X side of the model. This particular portion of the model is the same as the common factor analysis model, which you may recognize from that context.

Finally, consider the submatrix in the lower left portion of Σ. It deals with the covariances between the Xs and the Ys and in terms of our model can be written as:

$$\Sigma_{xy} = \left[\Lambda_x \Phi \Gamma' (I - B')^{-1} \Lambda_y' \right].$$ (7)

As shown in Equation 7, this portion of the model includes all of our matrices except for the error terms, that is, Θ_ε, Θ_δ, and Ψ. The submatrix in the upper right portion of Σ is the transposed version of Equation 7 (i.e., the matrix of Equation 7 with rows and columns switched), and we need not concern ourselves with it.

11.2 FREE, FIXED, AND CONSTRAINED PARAMETERS

Let us return for a moment to our eight parameter matrices B, Γ, Λ_x, Λ_y, Φ, Ψ, Θ_ε, and Θ_δ. In the structural model there are structure coefficients in matrices B and Γ. The covariances among structural equation errors are in the matrix Ψ. In the measurement models for latent independent and dependent variables, there are factor loadings in the matrices Λ_x and Λ_y, respectively. The covariances of measurement errors for the latent independent and dependent variables are in the matrices Θ_δ, and Θ_ε, respectively. The covariances among the latent independent variables are in the matrix Φ. Each and every element in these eight matrices, if used in a particular model, must be specified to be a free parameter, a fixed parameter, or a constrained parameter. A free parameter is a parameter that is unknown and thus is one that you wish to estimate. A fixed parameter is a parameter that is not free but rather is fixed to a specified value, typically either 0 or

1. A constrained parameter is a parameter that is unknown, but is constrained to equal one or more other parameters.

For example, consider the following matrix B such that:

$$B = \begin{bmatrix} 0 & \beta_{12} \\ \beta_{21} & 0 \end{bmatrix}.$$

The βs represent values in B that might be parameters of interest and thus would constitute free parameters. The 0s represent values in B that are fixed or constrained to be equal to 0. These diagonal values of B represent the influence of a latent dependent variable on itself, and by definition are always fixed to 0. If our hypothesized model included only β_{21}, then β_{12} would also be fixed to 0. For the model specified in Fig. 6.1 and discussed in the chapter, B would take the following form:

$$B = \begin{bmatrix} 0 & 0 \\ \beta_{21} & 0 \end{bmatrix}.$$

For another example, consider the following matrix Λ_y with the factor loadings for the latent dependent variable measurement model, such that:

$$\Lambda_y = \begin{bmatrix} \lambda_{y_{11}} & \lambda_{y_{12}} \\ \lambda_{y_{21}} & \lambda_{y_{22}} \\ \lambda_{y_{31}} & \lambda_{y_{32}} \\ \lambda_{y_{41}} & \lambda_{y_{42}} \end{bmatrix}.$$

Here the λ_ys represent values in Λ_y that might be parameters of interest and would constitute free parameters. This specifies that we are allowing all of the parameters in Λ_y to be free so that each of our four indicator variables (the Ys) loads on each of our two latent dependent variables (the ηs). However, in order to solve the identification problem for Λ_y, some constraints are usually placed on this matrix whereby some of the parameters are fixed. We might specify that the first two indicator variables are allowed to load only on the first latent dependent variable (η_1) and the latter two indicators on the second latent dependent variable (η_2). Then Λ_y would appear as:

$$\Lambda_y = \begin{bmatrix} \lambda_{y_{11}} & 0 \\ \lambda_{y_{21}} & 0 \\ 0 & \lambda_{y_{32}} \\ 0 & \lambda_{y_{42}} \end{bmatrix}.$$

Additional constraints in Λ_y are also necessary for identification purposes.
For the example in chapter 6, the following structural equations were specified:

$$\text{Aspirations} = \text{home background} + \text{ability} + \text{error}$$
$$\text{Achievement} = \text{aspirations} + \text{home background} + \text{ability} + \text{error}$$

The matrix equation would be $\eta = B\eta + \Gamma\xi + \varsigma$, and the elements of the matrices would be:

$$\begin{bmatrix} \eta_1 \\ \eta_2 \end{bmatrix} = \begin{bmatrix} 0 & 0 \\ \beta_{21} & 0 \end{bmatrix} \begin{bmatrix} \eta_1 \\ \eta_2 \end{bmatrix} + \begin{bmatrix} \gamma_{11} & \gamma_{12} \\ \gamma_{21} & \gamma_{22} \end{bmatrix} \begin{bmatrix} \xi_1 \\ \xi_2 \end{bmatrix} + \begin{bmatrix} \varsigma_1 \\ \varsigma_2 \end{bmatrix}.$$

The matrix equation for the latent dependent variable measurement model is $Y = \Lambda_y\eta + \varepsilon$, and the elements of the matrices are:

$$\begin{bmatrix} y_1 \\ y_2 \\ y_3 \\ y_4 \end{bmatrix} = \begin{bmatrix} 1 & 0 \\ \lambda_{y_{21}} & 0 \\ 0 & 1 \\ 0 & \lambda_{y_{42}} \end{bmatrix} \begin{bmatrix} \eta_1 \\ \eta_2 \end{bmatrix} + \begin{bmatrix} \varepsilon_1 \\ \varepsilon_2 \\ \varepsilon_3 \\ \varepsilon_4 \end{bmatrix}.$$

The matrix equation for the latent independent variable measurement model is $X = \Lambda_x\xi + \delta$ and the elements of the matrices are:

$$\begin{bmatrix} x_1 \\ x_2 \\ x_3 \\ x_4 \\ x_5 \end{bmatrix} = \begin{bmatrix} 1 & 0 \\ \lambda_{x_{21}} & 0 \\ \lambda_{x_{31}} & 0 \\ 0 & 1 \\ 0 & \lambda_{x_{52}} \end{bmatrix} \begin{bmatrix} \xi_1 \\ \xi_2 \end{bmatrix} + \begin{bmatrix} \delta_1 \\ \delta_2 \\ \delta_3 \\ \delta_4 \\ \delta_5 \end{bmatrix}.$$

Note that for each dependent and independent latent variable, one factor loading for an observed variable has been fixed to 1. This is necessary to identify the model and to fix the scale for the latent variables.

The covariance terms are written next. The covariance matrix for the latent independent variables is:

$$\Phi = \begin{bmatrix} \phi_{11} & \\ \phi_{21} & \phi_{22} \end{bmatrix}.$$

The covariance matrix for the structural equation errors is:

$$\Psi = \begin{bmatrix} \psi_{11} & \\ \psi_{21} & \psi_{22} \end{bmatrix}.$$

The covariance matrices for the measurement errors are written as follows, first for the indicators of the latent independent variables by:

$$\Theta_\delta = \begin{bmatrix} \theta_{\delta_{11}} & & & & \\ 0 & \theta_{\delta_{22}} & & & \\ 0 & \theta_{\delta_{32}} & \theta_{\delta_{33}} & & \\ 0 & 0 & 0 & \theta_{\delta_{44}} & \\ 0 & 0 & 0 & 0 & \theta_{\delta_{55}} \end{bmatrix},$$

and second for the indicators of the latent dependent variables by:

$$\Theta_\varepsilon = \begin{bmatrix} \theta_{\varepsilon_{11}} & & & \\ 0 & \theta_{\varepsilon_{22}} & & \\ 0 & 0 & \theta_{\varepsilon_{33}} & \\ 0 & 0 & 0 & \theta_{\varepsilon_{44}} \end{bmatrix}.$$

Note: In the LISREL8-SIMPLIS program for the model in chapter 6, simply include the LISREL OUTPUT command to produce these matrices and associated values on the computer printout.

11.3 LISREL8 MATRIX PROGRAM

The LISREL8 matrix command language program works directly from the matrix notation previously discussed and is presented here for the example in chapter 6. The basic LISREL8 matrix command language program includes TITLE, DATA (DA), INPUT, MODEL CONSTRUCTION (MO), and OUTPUT (OU) program statements. The TITLE lines are optional. The user's guide provides an excellent overview of the various commands and their purpose (Jöreskog & Sörbom, 1993). The DA statement identifies the number of input variables in the variance–covariance matrix, the NO statement indicates the number of observations, and MA identifies the kind of matrix to be *analyzed*, not the kind of matrix to be *inputted*: MA=cm, covariance matrix; MA=km, correlation matrix based on raw scores or normal scores; MA=mm, matrix of moments about zero; MA=am, augmented moment matrix; MA=om, special correlation matrix of optimal scores from PRELIS2; and MA=pm, correlation matrix of polychoric or polyserial correlations. The SE statement must be used to select and/or reorder variables used in the analysis of a model (note:

Y variables must be listed first). An external raw-score data file can be read using the RA statement with the FI and FO subcommands (RA FI= raw.dat FO). The FO subcommand permits the specification of how observations are to be read (for fixed, a FORMAT statement must be enclosed in parentheses; for free-field, an asterisk is placed in in the first column, which appears on the line following the RA command). If FI or UN (logical unit number of a FORTRAN file) subcommands are not used, then the data must directly follow the RA command and be included in the program.

In the following LISREL8 matrix command language program, a lower diagonal variance–covariance matrix is inputted; hence, the use of the CM statement. The SY subcommand, which reads only the lower diagonal elements of a matrix, has been omitted because it is the default option for matrix input. The LA statement provides for up to eight characters for variable labels, with similar subcommand options for input and specifications as with the RA command for data input. A lowercase c permits line continuation for various commands. The LE command permits variable labels for the latent dependent variables, and the LK command permits variable labels for the latent independent variables.

The MO command specifies the model for LISREL analysis. The subcommands specify the number of *Y* variables (ny), number of *X* variables (nx), number of latent dependent variables (ne), and number of latent independent variables (nk). The form and mode of the eight LISREL8 parameter matrices must be specified and are further explained in the user's guide (Jöreskog & Sörbom, 1993). The FU parameter indicates a full nonsymmetric matrix form, and FI indicates a fixed matrix mode, in contrast to a free mode (FR). The DI statement indicates a diagonal matrix form, and the SY statement indicates a symmetric matrix form. It is strongly recommended that any designation of a LISREL8 model for analysis include the presentation of the eight matrices in matrix form. This will greatly ease the writing of the MO command and the identification of fixed or free parameters in the matrices on the FR and VA commands. The VA command assigns numerical values to the fixed parameters. The OU command permits the selection of various output procedures. One feature of interest on the OU command is the AM option, which provides for automatic model specification by freeing at each step the fixed or constrained parameters with the largest modification indices—although, as previously noted, this should not be the sole criterion for model respecification.

The LISREL8 matrix command language program used to analyze the model in Fig. 6.1 (chapter 6), using a maximum-likelihood method, is as follows:

```
Model 2 in Figure 6.1
da ni=9 no=200 ma=cm
cm sy
```

```
1.024
 .792  1.077
1.027   .919  1.844
 .756   .697  1.244  1.286
 .567   .537   .876   .632   .852
 .445   .424   .677   .526   .518   .670
 .434   .389   .635   .498   .475   .545   .716
 .580   .564   .893   .716   .546   .422   .373   .851
 .491   .499   .888   .646   .508   .389   .339   .629   .871
la
 EDASP OCASP VERBACH QUANTACH FAMINC FAED MOED VERBAB QUANTAB
mo ny=4 nx=5 ne=2 nk=2 be=fu,fi ga=fu,fi ph=sy,fi ps=di,fi      c
   ly=fu,fi lx=fu,fi td=fu,fi te=fu,fi
le
 aspire achieve
lk
 home ability
fr be(2,1) ga(1,1) ga(1,2) ga(2,1) ga(2,2)                      c
   ly(2,1) ly(4,2) lx(2,1) lx(3,1) lx(5,2)                      c
   te(1,1) te(2,2) te(3,3) te(4,4) td(1,1) td(2,2) td(3,3)      c
   td(4,4) td(5,5)                                              c
   ps(1,1) ps(2,2) ph(1,1) ph(2,2) ph(2,1) td(3,2)
va 1.0 ly(1,1) ly(3,2) lx(1,1) lx(4,2)
ou me=ml all
```

We have found that the LISREL8 matrix command language requires the user to specifically understand the nature, form, and mode of the eight matrices, and thereby fully comprehend the model being specified for analysis, even though not all eight matrices are necessarily used in a given model. We present the LISREL8 output from this program next, but in an edited and condensed format.

LISREL8 Matrix Program Output (Edited and Condensed)

```
Model 2 in Fig. 6.1
                    NUMBER OF INPUT VARIABLES    9
                    NUMBER OF Y - VARIABLES      4
                    NUMBER OF X - VARIABLES      5
                    NUMBER OF ETA - VARIABLES    2
                    NUMBER OF KSI - VARIABLES    2
                    NUMBER OF OBSERVATIONS     200


        COVARIANCE MATRIX TO BE ANALYZED

              EDASP    OCASP   VERBACH  QUANTACH  FAMINC    FAED
              -----    -----   -------  --------  ------    -----
       EDASP   1.02
```

```
       OCASP    0.79    1.08
     VERBACH    1.03    0.92    1.84
    QUANTACH    0.76    0.70    1.24    1.29
      FAMINC    0.57    0.54    0.88    0.63    0.85
        FAED    0.45    0.42    0.68    0.53    0.52    0.67
        MOED    0.43    0.39    0.64    0.50    0.48    0.55
      VERBAB    0.58    0.56    0.89    0.72    0.55    0.42
     QUANTAB    0.49    0.50    0.89    0.65    0.51    0.39
```

COVARIANCE MATRIX TO BE ANALYZED

	MOED	VERBAB	QUANTAB
MOED	0.72		
VERBAB	0.37	0.85	
QUANTAB	0.34	0.63	0.87

PARAMETER SPECIFICATIONS

LAMBDA-Y

	aspire	achieve
EDASP	0	0
OCASP	1	0
VERBACH	0	0
QUANTACH	0	2

LAMBDA-X

	home	ability
FAMINC	0	0
FAED	3	0
MOED	4	0
VERBAB	0	0
QUANTAB	0	5

BETA

	aspire	achieve
aspire	0	0
achieve	6	0

GAMMA

	home	ability
aspire	7	8
achieve	9	10

PHI

	home	ability
home	11	
ability	12	13

PSI

aspire	achieve
14	15

THETA-EPS

EDASP	OCASP	VERBACH	QUANTACH
16	17	18	19

THETA-DELTA

	FAMINC	FAED	MOED	VERBAB	QUANTAB
FAMINC	20				
FAED	0	21			
MOED	0	22	23		
VERBAB	0	0	0	24	
QUANTAB	0	0	0	0	25

INITIAL ESTIMATES (TSLS)

LAMBDA-Y

	aspire	achieve
EDASP	1.00	—
OCASP	0.94	—
VERBACH	—	1.00
QUANTACH	—	0.75

LAMBDA-X

	home	ability
FAMINC	1.00	—
FAED	0.92	—
MOED	0.88	—
VERBAB	—	1.00
QUANTAB	—	0.90

BETA

	aspire	achieve
aspire	—	—
achieve	0.50	—

GAMMA

	home	ability
aspire	—	—
achieve	0.50	—

COVARIANCE MATRIX OF ETA AND KSI

	aspire	achieve	home	ability
aspire	0.85			
achieve	1.00	1.66		
home	0.52	0.79	0.55	
ability	0.58	0.94	0.49	0.70

PHI

	home	ability
home	0.55	
ability	0.49	0.70

PSI

aspire	achieve
0.30	0.23

SQUARED MULTIPLE CORRELATIONS FOR STRUCTURAL EQUATIONS

aspire	achieve
0.64	0.86

THETA-EPS

EDASP	OCASP	VERBACH	QUANTACH
0.18	0.34	0.19	0.35

THETA-DELTA

	FAMINC	FAED	MOED	VERBAB	QUANTAB
FAMINC	0.30				
FAED	—	0.20			
MOED	—	0.10	0.29		
VERBAB	—	—	—	0.15	
QUANTAB	—	—	—	—	0.30

Number of Iterations = 9

LISREL ESTIMATES (MAXIMUM LIKELIHOOD)

LAMBDA-Y

	aspire	achieve
EDASP	1.00	—
OCASP	0.92	—
	(0.06)	
	14.34	
VERBACH	—	1.00
QUANTACH	—	0.75
		(0.04)
		18.13

LAMBDA-X

	home	ability
FAMINC	1.00	—
FAED	0.78	—
	(0.06)	
	12.18	
MOED	0.72	—
	(0.07)	
	10.37	
VERBAB	—	1.00
QUANTAB	—	0.95
		(0.07)
		14.10

BETA

	aspire	achieve
aspire	—	—
achieve	0.53	—
	(0.12)	
	4.56	

GAMMA

	home	ability
aspire	0.51	0.45
	(0.15)	(0.15)
	3.29	2.96
achieve	0.30	0.69
	(0.16)	(0.16)
	1.87	4.27

COVARIANCE MATRIX OF ETA AND KSI

	aspire	achieve	home	ability
aspire	0.86			
achieve	1.02	1.65		
home	0.57	0.87	0.66	
ability	0.57	0.91	0.54	0.66

PHI

	home	ability
home	0.66	
	(0.09)	
	7.32	
ability	0.54	0.66
	(0.07)	(0.09)
	7.64	7.51

PSI

aspire	achieve
0.32	0.23
(0.06)	(0.06)
5.61	3.97

SQUARED MULTIPLE CORRELATIONS FOR STRUCTURAL EQUATIONS

aspire	achieve
0.63	0.86

THETA-EPS

EDASP	OCASP	VERBACH	QUANTACH
0.16	0.35	0.19	0.35
(0.04)	(0.05)	(0.05)	(0.04)
3.88	7.36	3.81	7.95

SQUARED MULTIPLE CORRELATIONS FOR Y - VARIABLES

EDASP	OCASP	VERBACH	QUANTACH
0.84	0.67	0.90	0.73

THETA-DELTA

	FAMINC	FAED	MOED	VERBAB	QUANTAB
FAMINC	0.19				
	(0.04)				
	4.74				

```
FAED          —         0.27
                       (0.03)
                        7.66
MOED          —         0.17      0.37
                       (0.03)    (0.04)
                        5.28      8.50
VERBAB        —          —         —        0.19
                                          (0.03)
                                           5.41
QUANTAB       —          —         —         —       0.27
                                                    (0.04)
                                                     7.20
```

SQUARED MULTIPLE CORRELATIONS FOR X - VARIABLES

FAMINC	FAED	MOED	VERBAB	QUANTAB
0.78	0.60	0.48	0.78	0.69

GOODNESS OF FIT STATISTICS

CHI-SQUARE WITH 20 DEGREES OF FREEDOM = 19.17 (P = 0.51)
ESTIMATED NON-CENTRALITY PARAMETER (NCP) = 0.0
90 PERCENT CONFIDENCE INTERVAL FOR NCP = (0.0 ; 13.53)

MINIMUM FIT FUNCTION VALUE = 0.096
POPULATION DISCREPANCY FUNCTION VALUE (F0) = 0.0
90 PERCENT CONFIDENCE INTERVAL FOR F0 = (0.0 ; 0.068)
ROOT MEAN SQUARE ERROR OF APPROXIMATION (RMSEA) = 0.0
90 PERCENT CONFIDENCE INTERVAL FOR RMSEA = (0.0 ; 0.058)
P-VALUE FOR TEST OF CLOSE FIT (RMSEA < 0.05) = 0.90

EXPECTED CROSS-VALIDATION INDEX (ECVI) = 0.35
90 PERCENT CONFIDENCE INTERVAL FOR ECVI = (0.35 ; 0.42)
ECVI FOR SATURATED MODEL = 0.45
ECVI FOR INDEPENDENCE MODEL = 7.16

CHI-SQUARE FOR INDEPENDENCE MODEL WITH
36 DEGREES OF FREEDOM = 1407.10
INDEPENDENCE AIC = 1425.10
MODEL AIC = 69.17
SATURATED AIC = 90.00
INDEPENDENCE CAIC = 1463.78

MODEL CAIC = 176.63
SATURATED CAIC = 283.42

ROOT MEAN SQUARE RESIDUAL (RMR) = 0.015
STANDARDIZED RMR = 0.015
GOODNESS OF FIT INDEX (GFI) = 0.98
ADJUSTED GOODNESS OF FIT INDEX (AGFI) = 0.95
PARSIMONY GOODNESS OF FIT INDEX (PGFI) = 0.44

NORMED FIT INDEX (NFI) = 0.99
NON-NORMED FIT INDEX (NNFI) = 1.00
PARSIMONY NORMED FIT INDEX (PNFI) = 0.55
COMPARATIVE FIT INDEX (CFI) = 1.00
INCREMENTAL FIT INDEX (IFI) = 1.00
RELATIVE FIT INDEX (RFI) = 0.98

CRITICAL N (CN) = 391.00

FITTED COVARIANCE MATRIX

	EDASP	OCASP	VERBACH	QUANTACH	FAMINC	FAED
EDASP	1.02					
OCASP	0.79	1.08				
VERBACH	1.02	0.93	1.84			
QUANTACH	0.77	0.70	1.24	1.29		
FAMINC	0.57	0.53	0.87	0.66	0.85	
FAED	0.45	0.41	0.68	0.51	0.52	0.67
MOED	0.41	0.38	0.63	0.47	0.48	0.54
VERBAB	0.57	0.52	0.91	0.69	0.54	0.42
QUANTAB	0.54	0.49	0.87	0.65	0.51	0.40

FITTED COVARIANCE MATRIX

	MOED	VERBAB	QUANTAB
MOED	0.72		
VERBAB	0.39	0.85	
QUANTAB	0.37	0.63	0.87

FITTED RESIDUALS

	EDASP	OCASP	VERBACH	QUANTACH	FAMINC	FAED
EDASP	0.00					
OCASP	0.00	0.00				
VERBACH	0.01	−0.01	0.00			
QUANTACH	−0.01	−0.01	0.00	0.00		

FAMINC	−0.01	0.01	0.01	−0.02	0.00
FAED	0.00	0.01	0.00	0.01	0.00	0.00
MOED	0.02	0.01	0.01	0.03	0.00	0.00
VERBAB	0.01	0.04	−0.02	0.03	0.01	0.00
QUANTAB	−0.05	0.00	0.02	−0.01	0.00	−0.01

FITTED RESIDUALS

	MOED	VERBAB	QUANTAB
	-----	------	--------
MOED	0.00		
VERBAB	−0.01	0.00	
QUANTAB	−0.03	0.00	0.00

SUMMARY STATISTICS FOR FITTED RESIDUALS
SMALLEST FITTED RESIDUAL = −0.05
 MEDIAN FITTED RESIDUAL = 0.00
LARGEST FITTED RESIDUAL = 0.04

STEMLEAF PLOT

```
− 4 | 8
− 3 |
− 2 | 842
− 1 | 4400
− 0 | 886542100000000000000
  0 | 2469999
  1 | 1123
  2 | 0067
  3 |
  4 | 3
```

STANDARDIZED RESIDUALS

	EDASP	OCASP	VERBACH	QUANTACH	FAMINC	FAED
	-----	-----	--------	--------	------	-----
EDASP	0.00					
OCASP	0.00	0.00				
VERBACH	1.26	−0.01	0.00			
QUANTACH	−0.52	−0.23	0.00	0.00		
FAMINC	−0.64	0.45	0.55	−1.17	0.00	
FAED	−0.25	0.45	−0.23	0.58	0.15	0.00
MOED	0.82	0.30	0.36	0.91	−0.15	0.00
VERBAB	0.88	1.93	−2.34	1.50	0.72	0.10
QUANTAB	−2.53	0.16	1.59	−0.38	−0.13	−0.50

STANDARDIZED RESIDUALS

	MOED	VERBAB	QUANTAB
MOED	0.00		
VERBAB	−0.63	0.00	
QUANTAB	−1.10	0.00	0.00

SUMMARY STATISTICS FOR STANDARDIZED RESIDUALS
SMALLEST STANDARDIZED RESIDUAL = −2.53
 MEDIAN STANDARDIZED RESIDUAL = 0.00
 LARGEST STANDARDIZED RESIDUAL = 1.93

STEMLEAF PLOT

```
 − 2 | 5
 − 2 | 3
 − 1 |
 − 1 | 210
 − 0 | 6655
 − 0 | 4322210000000000000
   0 | 122344
   0 | 5567899
   1 | 3
   1 | 569
```

MODIFICATION INDICES AND EXPECTED CHANGE

MODIFICATION INDICES FOR LAMBDA-Y

	aspire	achieve
EDASP	−	0.30
OCASP	−	0.30
VERBACH	0.32	−
QUANTACH	0.32	−

EXPECTED CHANGE FOR LAMBDA-Y

	aspire	achieve
EDASP	−	0.28
OCASP	−	−0.26
VERBACH	0.12	−
QUANTACH	−0.09	−

STANDARDIZED EXPECTED CHANGE FOR LAMBDA-Y

	aspire	achieve
EDASP	−	0.36
OCASP	−	−0.33

```
VERBACH        0.11              —
QUANTACH      -0.09              —
```

MODIFICATION INDICES FOR LAMBDA-X

	home	ability
FAMINC	—	0.40
FAED	—	0.11
MOED	—	0.49
VERBAB	0.63	—
QUANTAB	0.63	—

EXPECTED CHANGE FOR LAMBDA-X

	home	ability
FAMINC	—	0.18
FAED	—	0.04
MOED	—	-0.08
VERBAB	0.16	—
QUANTAB	-0.16	—

STANDARDIZED EXPECTED CHANGE FOR LAMBDA-X

	home	ability
FAMINC	—	0.15
FAED	—	0.03
MOED	—	-0.06
VERBAB	0.13	—
QUANTAB	-0.13	—

NO NON-ZERO MODIFICATION INDICES FOR BETA

NO NON-ZERO MODIFICATION INDICES FOR GAMMA

NO NON-ZERO MODIFICATION INDICES FOR PHI

NO NON-ZERO MODIFICATION INDICES FOR PSI

MODIFICATION INDICES FOR THETA-EPS

	EDASP	OCASP	VERBACH	QUANTACH
EDASP	—			
OCASP	—	—		
VERBACH	2.32	1.91	—	
QUANTACH	0.17	0.01	—	—

EXPECTED CHANGE FOR THETA-EPS

	EDASP	OCASP	VERBACH	QUANTACH
EDASP	—			
OCASP	—	—		
VERBACH	0.05	-0.05	—	
QUANTACH	-0.01	0.00	—	—

MODIFICATION INDICES FOR THETA-DELTA-EPS

	EDASP	OCASP	VERBACH	QUANTACH
FAMINC	0.12	0.06	0.86	2.09
FAED	0.62	0.32	0.30	0.15
MOED	1.13	0.40	0.02	0.37
VERBAB	0.51	1.13	8.44	3.03
QUANTAB	4.92	0.30	5.47	0.94

EXPECTED CHANGE FOR THETA-DELTA-EPS

	EDASP	OCASP	VERBACH	QUANTACH
FAMINC	-0.01	0.01	0.03	-0.04
FAED	-0.01	0.01	-0.01	0.01
MOED	0.02	-0.02	0.00	0.01
VERBAB	0.02	0.03	-0.09	0.05
QUANTAB	-0.06	0.02	0.07	-0.03

MODIFICATION INDICES FOR THETA-DELTA

	FAMINC	FAED	MOED	VERBAB	QUANTAB
FAMINC	—				
FAED	0.02	—			
MOED	0.02	—	—		
VERBAB	0.15	0.14	0.36	—	
QUANTAB	0.02	0.05	0.59	—	—

EXPECTED CHANGE FOR THETA-DELTA

	FAMINC	FAED	MOED	VERBAB	QUANTAB
FAMINC	—				
FAED	0.00	—			
MOED	0.00	—	—		
VERBAB	0.01	0.01	-0.01	—	
QUANTAB	0.00	0.00	-0.02	—	—

MAXIMUM MODIFICATION INDEX IS 8.44 FOR ELEMENT (4, 3) OF THETA-DELTA-EPSILON

CORRELATIONS OF ESTIMATES

	LY 2,1	LY 4,2	LX 2,1	LX 3,1	LX 5,2	BE 2,1
LY 2,1	1.00					
LY 4,2	0.00	1.00				
LX 2,1	0.00	0.00	1.00			
LX 3,1	0.00	0.00	0.71	1.00		
LX 5,2	0.00	0.00	0.00	0.00	1.00	
BE 2,1	0.21	−0.06	−0.02	−0.02	−0.02	1.00
GA 1,1	−0.06	0.00	0.17	0.14	−0.03	0.03
GA 1,2	−0.06	0.00	−0.07	−0.06	0.12	−0.11
GA 2,1	−0.04	−0.02	0.10	0.09	−0.03	−0.38
GA 2,2	−0.04	−0.06	−0.03	−0.03	0.18	−0.33
PH 1,1	0.00	0.00	−0.43	−0.37	0.00	0.03
PH 2,1	0.00	0.00	−0.19	−0.16	−0.21	0.02
PH 2,2	0.00	0.00	0.00	0.00	−0.44	0.04
PS 1,1	−0.36	0.00	−0.03	−0.02	−0.01	−0.17
PS 2,2	−0.04	−0.26	−0.01	−0.01	−0.02	−0.01
TE 1,1	0.45	0.00	0.00	0.00	0.00	0.33
TE 2,2	−0.33	0.00	0.00	0.00	0.00	−0.07
TE 3,3	0.00	0.35	0.00	0.00	0.00	−0.02
TE 4,4	0.00	−0.23	0.00	0.00	0.00	0.01
TD 1,1	0.00	0.00	0.39	0.34	0.00	−0.07
TD 2,2	0.00	0.00	−0.29	−0.21	0.00	−0.01
TD 3,2	0.00	0.00	−0.26	−0.27	0.00	−0.01
TD 3,3	0.00	0.00	−0.16	−0.23	0.00	0.00
TD 4,4	0.00	0.00	0.00	0.00	0.35	−0.10
TD 5,5	0.00	0.00	0.00	0.00	−0.29	−0.03

CORRELATIONS OF ESTIMATES

	GA 1,1	GA 1,2	GA 2,1	GA 2,2	PH 1,1	PH 2,1
GA 1,1	1.00					
GA 1,2	−0.88	1.00				
GA 2,1	0.06	−0.02	1.00			
GA 2,2	−0.08	0.11	−0.64	1.00		
PH 1,1	−0.20	0.09	−0.12	0.04	1.00	
PH 2,1	−0.05	−0.05	−0.07	−0.04	0.76	1.00
PH 2,2	0.05	−0.14	0.06	−0.21	0.36	0.77
PS 1,1	−0.05	0.03	0.05	0.04	0.03	0.02
PS 2,2	0.01	−0.01	0.09	−0.11	0.01	0.01
TE 1,1	−0.03	−0.03	−0.10	−0.09	0.00	0.00
TE 2,2	0.02	0.02	0.01	0.01	0.00	0.00
TE 3,3	0.00	0.00	−0.01	−0.02	0.00	0.00
TE 4,4	0.00	0.00	0.01	0.01	0.00	0.00
TD 1,1	0.29	−0.21	0.19	−0.09	−0.34	−0.08
TD 2,2	0.00	−0.02	0.00	−0.01	0.09	0.06

TD 3,2	0.00	-0.02	0.00	-0.01	0.09	0.05
TD 3,3	0.00	-0.01	0.00	0.00	0.06	0.04
TD 4,4	-0.13	0.19	-0.15	0.30	0.00	-0.07
TD 5,5	-0.04	0.02	-0.04	0.05	0.00	0.06

CORRELATIONS OF ESTIMATES

	PH 2,2	PS 1,1	PS 2,2	TE 1,1	TE 2,2	TE 3,3
PH 2,2	1.00					
PS 1,1	0.02	1.00				
PS 2,2	0.04	0.05	1.00			
TE 1,1	0.00	-0.45	-0.10	1.00		
TE 2,2	0.00	0.12	0.01	-0.33	1.00	
TE 3,3	0.00	0.00	-0.53	0.00	0.00	1.00
TE 4,4	0.00	0.00	0.08	0.00	0.00	-0.25
TD 1,1	0.00	-0.08	-0.03	0.00	0.00	0.00
TD 2,2	0.00	-0.01	0.00	0.00	0.00	0.00
TD 3,2	0.00	-0.01	0.00	0.00	0.00	0.00
TD 3,3	0.00	0.00	0.00	0.00	0.00	0.00
TD 4,4	-0.28	-0.04	-0.10	0.00	0.00	0.00
TD 5,5	0.08	-0.01	-0.03	0.00	0.00	0.00

CORRELATIONS OF ESTIMATES

	TE 4,4	TD 1,1	TD 2,2	TD 3,2	TD 3,3	TD 4,4
TE 4,4	1.00					
TD 1,1	0.00	1.00				
TD 2,2	0.00	-0.21	1.00			
TD 3,2	0.00	-0.20	0.76	1.00		
TD 3,3	0.00	-0.14	0.41	0.75	1.00	
TD 4,4	0.00	0.00	0.00	0.00	0.00	1.00
TD 5,5	0.00	0.00	0.00	0.00	0.00	-0.19

CORRELATIONS OF ESTIMATES

	TD 5,5
TE 5,5	1.00

COVARIANCES

Y - ETA

	EDASP	OCASP	VERBACH	QUANTACH
aspire	0.86	0.79	1.02	0.77
achieve	1.02	0.93	1.65	1.24

Y - KSI

	EDASP	OCASP	VERBACH	QUANTACH
home	0.57	0.53	0.87	0.66
ability	0.57	0.52	0.91	0.69

X - ETA

	FAMINC	FAED	MOED	VERBAB	QUANTAB
aspire	0.57	0.45	0.41	0.57	0.54
achieve	0.87	0.68	0.63	0.91	0.87

X - KSI

	FAMINC	FAED	MOED	VERBAB	QUANTAB
home	0.66	0.52	0.48	0.54	0.51
ability	0.54	0.42	0.39	0.66	0.63

STANDARDIZED SOLUTION

LAMBDA-Y

	aspire	achieve
EDASP	0.93	—
OCASP	0.85	—
VERBACH	—	1.29
QUANTACH	—	0.97

LAMBDA-X

	home	ability
FAMINC	0.81	—
FAED	0.64	—
MOED	0.59	—
VERBAB	—	0.81
QUANTAB	—	0.77

BETA

	aspire	achieve
aspire	0.93	—
achieve	0.85	—

GAMMA

	home	ability
aspire	0.44	0.39
achieve	0.19	0.43

CORRELATION MATRIX OF ETA AND KSI

	aspire	achieve	home	ability
aspire	1.00			
achieve	0.85	1.00		
home	0.76	0.83	1.00	
ability	0.75	0.87	0.81	1.00

PSI

aspire	achieve
0.37	0.14

REGRESSION MATRIX ETA ON KSI (STANDARDIZED)

	home	ability
aspire	0.44	0.39
achieve	0.36	0.58

TOTAL AND INDIRECT EFFECTS

TOTAL EFFECTS OF KSI ON ETA

	home	ability
aspire	0.51	0.45
	(0.15)	(0.15)
	3.29	2.96
achieve	0.57	0.92
	(0.17)	(0.18)
	3.26	5.20

INDIRECT EFFECTS OF KSI ON ETA

	home	ability
aspire	—	—
achieve	0.27	0.23
	(0.10)	(0.09)
	2.63	2.62

TOTAL EFFECTS OF ETA ON ETA

	aspire	achieve
aspire	—	—
achieve	0.53	—
	(0.12)	
	4.56	

LARGEST EIGENVALUE OF B*B' (STABILITY INDEX) IS 0.276

TOTAL EFFECTS OF ETA ON Y

	aspire	achieve
EDASP	1.00	—
OCASP	0.92	—
	(0.06)	
	14.34	
VERBACH	0.53	1.00
	(0.12)	
	4.56	
QUANTACH	0.40	0.75
	(0.09)	(0.04)
	4.48	18.13

INDIRECT EFFECTS OF ETA ON Y

	aspire	achieve
EDASP	—	—
OCASP	—	—
VERBACH	0.53	—
	(0.12)	
	4.56	
QUANTACH	0.40	—
	(0.09)	
	4.48	

TOTAL EFFECTS OF KSI ON Y

	home	ability
EDASP	0.51	0.45
	(0.15)	(0.15)
	3.29	2.96
OCASP	0.46	0.41
	(0.14)	(0.14)
	3.25	2.93
VERBACH	0.57	0.92
	(0.17)	(0.18)
	3.26	5.20
QUANTACH	0.43	0.69
	(0.13)	(0.14)
	3.23	5.09

STANDARDIZED TOTAL AND INDIRECT EFFECTS

        STANDARDIZED TOTAL EFFECTS OF KSI ON ETA

	home	ability
aspire	0.44	0.39
achieve	0.36	0.58

        STANDARDIZED INDIRECT EFFECTS OF KSI ON ETA

	home	ability
aspire	—	—
achieve	0.17	0.15

        STANDARDIZED TOTAL EFFECTS OF ETA ON ETA

	aspire	achieve
aspire	—	—
achieve	0.38	—

        STANDARDIZED TOTAL EFFECTS OF ETA ON Y

	aspire	achieve
EDASP	0.93	—
OCASP	0.85	—
VERBACH	0.49	1.29
QUANTACH	0.37	0.97

        STANDARDIZED INDIRECT EFFECTS OF ETA ON Y

	aspire	achieve
EDASP	—	—
OCASP	—	—
VERBACH	0.49	—
QUANTACH	0.37	—

        STANDARDIZED TOTAL EFFECTS OF KSI ON Y

	home	ability
EDASP	0.41	0.36
OCASP	0.38	0.33
VERBACH	0.46	0.75
QUANTACH	0.35	0.56

At this point, we leave it up to the reader to extract the factor loadings, error variances, structure coefficients, and disturbance terms from the various matrices indicated in the standardized solution. It is also helpful to determine the direct and indirect "effects" indicated in the model and compare them to the values presented here. The fit indices do indicate that the data fit the model!

11.4 ADVANCED MODELS IN MATRIX NOTATION

This section presents a basic multiple-sample model, a structured-means model, and two types of interaction models in structural equation modeling. The reader is referred to the references in the book for further detail and explanation of these types of models.

Simple Multiple Sample Model

Using LISREL notation, the *measurement* model is written as: $Y = \Lambda_y^{(g)}\eta + \varepsilon$ (for the latent dependent indicator variables); and $X = \Lambda_x^{(g)}\xi + \delta$ (for the latent independent indicator variables), where $g = 1, \ldots, G$ indicates the group and the other terms are as previously defined. The *structural* model can be written as $\eta = B^{(g)}\eta + \Gamma^{(g)}\xi + \zeta$. The four covariance matrices that you are already familiar with are written as: $\Phi^{(g)}$, $\Psi^{(g)}$, $\Theta_\varepsilon^{(g)}$, and $\Theta_\delta^{(g)}$. The net result is that estimates can be obtained for each of the eight parameter matrices for each group—that is, for $B^{(g)}$, $\Gamma^{(g)}$, $\Lambda_y^{(g)}$, $\Lambda_x^{(g)}$, $\Phi^{(g)}$, $\Psi^{(g)}$, $\Theta_\varepsilon^{(g)}$, and $\Theta_\delta^{(g)}$.

For instance, with two groups, one may be interested in testing whether the factor loadings are equivalent. These hypotheses for the latent dependent variables would be written as:

$$\Lambda_y^{(1)} = \Lambda_y^{(2)}$$

and for the latent independent variables as:

$$\Lambda_x^{(1)} = \Lambda_x^{(2)}.$$

One might also hypothesize that any of the other matrices are equivalent so that:

$$\Theta_\varepsilon^{(1)} = \Theta_\varepsilon^{(2)}$$

$$\Theta_\delta^{(1)} = \Theta_\delta^{(2)}$$

$$B^{(1)} = B^{(2)}$$

$$\Gamma^{(1)} = \Gamma^{(2)}$$

$$\Phi^{(1)} = \Phi^{(2)}$$

$$\Psi^{(1)} = \Psi^{(2)}$$

Thus, a series of models may be evaluated to determine which matrices are equivalent.

Structured Means Model

Using LISREL notation, the *measurement* model for the latent dependent indicator variables is now written as $Y = \tau_y^{(g)} + \Lambda_y^{(g)}\eta + \varepsilon$, and for the latent independent indicator variables, written as $X = \tau_x^{(g)} + \Lambda_x^{(g)}\xi + \delta$. We denote τ_y and τ_x as vectors of constant-intercept terms for the indicator variables, and the other terms are as previously defined. Although τ is the current way that Jöreskog & Sörbom (1993) denote these intercept terms, most publications have used υ instead. The structural model is now written as $\eta = \alpha^{(g)} + B^{(g)}\eta + \Gamma^{(g)}\xi + \zeta$, where α is a vector of constant-intercept terms for the structural equations and the other terms are as previously defined. In all previous models, the intercept terms were assumed to be zero and thus were not denoted. In the structured-means model, the intercept terms need not be zero and therefore can be estimated.

In addition, various means can also be estimated. The mean of each latent independent variable ξ is given by κ. Thus, κ_1 would denote the mean for ξ_1. The mean of each latent dependent variable is given by $(I - B)^{-1}(\alpha + \Psi\kappa)$.

In addition to the hypotheses given previously for the simple multiple-sample model, the structured-means model can also examine α, the group effects for each structural equation; and κ, the group effects for each latent independent variable. Here we constrain the value for one group to be zero and estimate the difference between that group and a second group, which we refer to as *group effects*.

In the following LISREL8 matrix language program, the first program specifies the number of groups (NG=2), the group sample size (NO=200), the number of observed variables (NI=6) and the type of matrix (MA=CM); while the second program need only define the sample size (NO=160) and input the specific group's covariance matrix (CM) and variable means (ME), in order to test for different values in the two groups:

```
FIRST PROGRAM INTERCEPT FOR BOYS
GROUP: BOYS
DA NI=6 NO=200 MA=CM NG=2
CM FI = <boys covariance matrix file name>
ME FI = <boys variable means file name>
LA
  V1 V2 V3 V4 V5 V6
LE
  ETA1 ETA2
```

```
MO NY=6 NE=2                             C
FR LY(2,1) LY(3,1) LY(5,2) LY(6,2) C
VA 1 LY(1,1) LY(4,2)                     C
FR BE(2,1)
OU AD=OFF

SECOND PROGRAM INTERCEPT FOR GIRLS
GROUP: GIRLS
DA NO=160
CM FI = <girls covariance matrix file name>
ME FI = <girls variable means file name>
LA
  V1 V2 V3 V4 V5 V6
MO LY=IN BE=PS TE=PS PS=PS TY=IN AL=FR
OU
```

The model parameters are set free (FR) in the first group, and the intercepts are defined for the two groups. The intercept for the first group is fixed to 0. Then the estimate of the intercept in the second group is evaluated relative to the 0 intercept in the first group. The structural model is represented as $\eta_2 = \alpha_2 + \beta_2\eta_1 + \zeta_2$, for both groups separately with a test of H_0: $\alpha_{boys} = \alpha_{girls}$.

Interaction Models

Continuous-Variable Approach. The interaction structural equation model in LISREL8 matrix notation for the example discussed in the chapter would be $\eta_1 = \gamma_1\xi_1 + \gamma_2\xi_2 + \gamma_3\xi_3 + \zeta_1$, where η_1 is the latent dependent variable, ξ_1 and ξ_2 are the main-effect latent independent variables, ξ_3 is the interaction effect formed by multiplying ξ_1 by ξ_2, γ_1 and γ_2 are the structure coefficients for the main-effect latent independent variables, γ_3 is the structure coefficient for the interaction-effect latent independent variable, and ζ_1 is the error term in the structural equation. Notice that the relationship between η_1 and ξ_3 is itself linear. The structure of the interaction model emerges as a logical extension of the measurement model for ξ_1 and ξ_2. The basic measurement model would be $X = \Lambda\xi + \delta$, where X is a vector of observed variables, Λ is a matrix of factor loadings, and δ is a vector of measurement error terms. The covariance matrices of these common and unique factors are Φ, and Θ_δ, respectively.

Kenny and Judd (1984) used simple algebraic substitution to develop their model of multiplicative interaction effects. Basically, given two latent independent variables, the models would be $X_1 = \lambda_1\xi_1 + \delta_1$ and $X_2 = \lambda_2\xi_2 + \delta_2$. The interaction "effect," or product, would be $X_3 = X_1X_2$, indicated in the model as $X_3 = \lambda_1\lambda_2\xi_1\xi_2 + \lambda_1\xi_1\delta_2 + \lambda_2\xi_2\delta_1 + \delta_1\delta_2$, or $X_3 = \lambda_3\xi_3 + \lambda_1\xi_4 + \lambda_2\xi_5 + \delta_3$, where $\xi_3 = \xi_1\xi_2$, $\xi_4 = \xi_1\delta_2$, $\xi_5 = \xi_2\delta_1$, $\delta_3 = \delta_1\delta_2$, and $\lambda_3 = \lambda_1\lambda_2$. All of these new latent variables are mutually uncorrelated and uncorrelated with all other latent variables in the model.

In order to incorporate this interaction effect into the structural equation model, we need to specify X_3 as a function of latent variables whose variances and covariances reflect these relationships. This involves specifying some model parameters as nonlinear functions of other parameters.

In the LISREL8 program, these types of nonlinear constraints are indicated by using the VA (value), EQ (equality), and CO (constraint) commands. For example, the Kenny–Judd interaction model implies that $\sigma^2(\xi_3) = \sigma^2(\xi_1)\sigma^2 (\xi_2) + \sigma(\xi_1, \xi_2)^2$. This relationship using the CO command line can be specified as CO PH(3,3) = PH(1,1) * PH(2,2) + PH(2,1) * * 2. Similarly, the model implies that $\sigma^2(\xi_4) = \sigma^2(\xi_1) \, \sigma^2(\delta_2)$, and this relationship can be specified as: CO PH(4,4) = PH(1,1) * TD(2,2).

The Kenny and Judd approach is indicated in the following LISREL8 program:

```
Title card: Kenny-Judd interaction model
DA NI=9 NO=500 MA=CM
LA; x1 x2 z1 z2 x1_z1 x1_z2 x2_z1 x2_z2 y
SE; 9 1 2 3 4 5 6 7 8
CM <covariance matrix here>
MO NY=1 NE=1 NX=8 NK=7 PS=SY TE=FI PH=SY,FI TD=SY,FI GA=FI
LE; ETA_Y
LK; KSI_X KSI_Z KSI_XZ X_TD3 X_TD4 Z_TD1 Z_TD2
VA 1.0 LY(1,1) LX(1,1) LX(3,2)
FR GA(1,1) GA(1,2) PH(1,1) PH(2,2) PH(2,1)
FR LX(2,1) LX(4,2) TD(1,1) TD(2,2) TD(3,3) TD(4,4)
FR GA(1,3)
VA 1.0 LX(5,3)
CO LX(6,3) = LX(4,2)
CO LX(7,3) = LX(2,1)
CO LX(8,3) = LX(2,1) * LX(4,2)
CO TD(5,5) = TD(1,1) * TD(3,3)
CO TD(6,6) = TD(1,1) * TD(4,4)
CO TD(7,7) = TD(2,2) * TD(3,3)
CO TD(8,8) = TD(2,2) * TD(4,4)
CO PH(3,3) = PH(1,1) * PH(2,2) + PH(2,1)**2
VA 1.0 LX(5,4)
CO LX(7,4) = LX(2,1)
CO PH(4,4) = PH(1,1) * TD(2,2)
VA 1.0 LX(6,5)
CO LX(8,5) = LX(2,1)
CO PH(5,5) = PH(1,1) * TD(4,4)
VA 1.0 LX(5,6)
CO LX(6,6) = LX(4,2)
CO PH(6,6) = PH(2,2) * TD(1,1)
```

```
VA 1.0 LX(7,7)
CO LX(8,7) = LX(4,2)
CO PH(7,7) = PH(2,2) * TD(2,2)
ST -.15 GA(1,1)
ST .35 GA(1,2)
ST .70 GA(1,3)
OU ML AD=OFF
```

Explanation of Commands

Kenny and Judd labeled their latent independent variables X and Z, their latent dependent variable Y, and their observed variables accordingly. A low dash joining these labels indicates multiplication. In the covariance matrix CM, most parameter matrix elements are fixed, and so it makes sense to begin with these matrices set to FI (fixed). This program included ETA_Y (latent dependent variable) in the LE command and KSI's (e.g., KSI_X and KSI_Z, latent independent variables) in the LK command in order to minimize confusion between observed variables and latent variables. In the structural equation model, ETA_Y is the latent dependent variable, KSI_X and KSI_Z are the main-effects latent independent variables, and KSI_XZ is the latent-independent-variable interaction effect.

The fixed loadings on the VA command set the scales for the latent variables. The FR GA and FR LX command lines indicate the free parameters relating to the main-effect latent independent variables and their observed variables. The direct effect of the interaction latent independent variable on the latent dependent variable is the *only* additional free parameter in the structural equation—for example, FR GA (1,3).

The CO command lines indicate the constrained elements for the structural equation interaction model. These elements for the interaction latent independent variable are simple products of the loadings of x_1 and x_2 on X and z_1 and z_2 on Z. Since two of those loadings are fixed to 1, they do not appear in the CO command statements (note: parameters that appear on the right-hand side of a CO command line must themselves be free).

The LISREL8 matrix command language program puts the measurement error variances into the matrix Θ_δ (note: the covariances of these measurement error terms are all zero, which is why those covariances do not appear in the CO command lines). On the other hand, the program specifies that the latent independent variables, X and Z, are correlated. Their covariances are indicated by CO PH(3,3) = PH(1,1) * PH(2,2) + PH(2,1) **2. The VA command fixes certain constraints to 1 (note: the loading of an observed variable on its own measurement error is implicitly fixed to 1—for example, LX(1,1) and LX(3,2).

The Kenny–Judd model also requires that certain start values be used, for example, ST command lines. In some cases, an interaction model will require starting values for virtually every parameter in the model. Do not ignore the constrained parameters, either. Just because the "original" parameters have starting values, LISREL8 will not automatically compute starting values for constrained parameters on that basis (note: adding the NS subcommand on the OU command line suppresses automatic starting-value calculations, and this may eliminate some processing error). LISREL8's admissibility check is also not needed when running an interaction model and should be turned off on the OU command—that is, the admissibility check is turned off (AD=OFF). ML is LISREL8's default maximum-likelihood fit function.

REFERENCES

Hayduk, L. A. (1987). *Structural equation modeling with LISREL: Essentials and advances*. Baltimore: Johns Hopkins University Press.

Jöreskog, K. G., & Sörbom, D. (1993). *LISREL8 user's reference guide*. Chicago: Scientific Software International.

Kenny, D. A., & Judd, C. M. (1984). Estimating the non-linear and interactive effects of latent variables. *Psychological Bulletin, 96*, 201–210.

EPILOGUE

We have approached this book from the standpoint that a background in correlation, regression, and path analysis would provide a sufficient basis for understanding structural equation modeling. We have further attempted to provide a nonstatistical presentation of the subject matter. Because of the basic approach taken in the book, we have included several references to software, books, and journals that contain a more detailed discussion of the topics and ideas.

The software packages we primarily examined, namely, LISREL8-SIMPLIS and EQS5, come with numerous data set examples. The examples are easy to follow and serve to further illustrate the topics presented in the book. We hope that after reading this book, you have gained a good applied introduction to measurement and structural modeling. A goal in writing the book was to provide you with a basic understanding of the five areas involved in structural equation modeling, namely, model specification, identification, estimation, model fit testing, and model respecification. The advanced topics were introduced to illustrate the additional capabilities of the software.

We welcome any ideas or suggestions you have regarding the book. If you notice any omissions or errors, please feel free to contact us. Our addresses are:

Randall E. Schumacker
College of Education
UNT Box 13857
University of North Texas
Denton, TX 76203-6857
Telephone: (817) 565-3962
Fax: (817) 565-2185
E-mail: rschumacker@unt.edu

Richard G. Lomax
Educational Psychology, Counseling, Spec. Educ.
225 Graham Hall
Northern Illinois University
DeKalb, IL 60115
Telephone: (815) 753-8461
Fax: (815) 753-9250
E-mail: rlomax@niu.edu

About the Authors

RANDALL E. SCHUMACKER received his degree in Educational Psychology from Southern Illinois University, where he specialized in measurement, statistics, and research methods. At present he is an Associate Professor in Educational Research at the University of North Texas, where he teaches structural equation modeling, psychometric theories, and statistics. He has published numerous nationally reviewed journal articles, and he has presented at international, national, and regional conferences. He serves on the editorial board of several journals and is a member of the American Statistical Association, the American Psychological Association, and the American Educational Research Association.

RICHARD G. LOMAX received his degree in Educational Research Methodology from the University of Pittsburgh, where he specialized in measurement, statistics, and research methods. He is currently an Associate Professor in Educational Psychology at Northern Illinois University, where he teaches statistics, research methods, and assessment. He has published numerous articles in journals such as the *Journal of Reading Behavior*, the *Journal of Educational Psychology*, *Reading Research Quarterly*, the *Journal of Educational Measurement*, the *Journal of Experimental Education*, and the *Review of Educational Research*, and he has served on the editorial board of several journals. He is a member of the American Educational Research Association and has served as Secretary of Division D.

APPENDIX

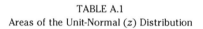

TABLE A.1
Areas of the Unit-Normal (z) Distribution

z^a	Below z^b	Above z	Ordinate u
	Proportion of Area		
0.000	**.5000**	**.5000**	**.3989**
0.01	.5040	.4960	.3989
0.02	.5080	.4920	.3989
0.03	.5120	.4880	.3988
0.04	.5160	.4840	.3986
0.05	.5199	.4801	.3984
0.06	.5239	.4761	.3982
0.07	.5279	.4721	.3980
0.08	.5319	.4631	.3977
0.09	.5359	.4641	.3973
0.10	.5398	.4602	.3970
0.11	.5438	.4562	.3965
0.12	.5478	.4522	.3961
0.126	**.5500**	**.4500**	**.3958**
0.13	.5517	.4483	.3956
0.14	.5557	.4443	.3951
0.15	.5596	.4404	.3945
0.16	.5636	.4364	.3939
0.17	.5675	.4325	.3932
0.18	.5714	.4286	.3925
0.19	.5753	.4247	.3918

(Continued)

	Proportion of Area		
z[a]	*Below z*[b]	*Above z*	*Ordinate u*
0.20	.5793	.4207	.3910
0.21	.5832	.4168	.3902
0.22	.5871	.4129	.3894
0.23	.5910	.4090	.3885
0.24	.5948	.4052	.3876
0.25	.5987	.4013	.3867
0.253	**.6000**	**.4000**	**.3863**
0.26	.6026	.3974	.3857
0.27	.6064	.3936	.3847
0.28	.6103	.3897	.3836
0.29	.6141	.3859	.3825
0.30	.6179	.3821	.3814
0.31	.6217	.3783	.3802
0.32	.6255	.3745	.3790
0.33	.6293	.3707	.3778
0.34	.6331	.3669	.3765
0.35	.6368	.3632	.3752
0.36	.6406	.3594	.3739
0.37	.6443	.3557	.3725
0.38	.6480	.3520	.3712
0.385	**.6500**	**.3500**	**.3704**
0.39	.6517	.3483	.3697
0.40	.6554	.3446	.3683
0.41	.6591	.3409	.3668
0.42	.6628	.3372	.3653
0.43	.6664	.3336	.3637
0.44	.6700	.3300	.3621
0.45	.6736	.3264	.3605
0.46	.6772	.3228	.3589
0.47	.6808	.3192	.3572
0.48	.6844	.3156	.3555
0.49	.6879	.3121	.3538
0.50	.6915	.3085	.3521
0.51	.6950	.3050	.3503
0.52	.6985	.3015	.3485
0.524	**.7000**	**.3000**	**.3477**
0.53	.7019	.2981	.3467
0.54	.7054	.2946	.3448
0.55	.7088	.2912	.3429
0.56	.7123	.2877	.3410
0.57	.7157	.2843	.3391
0.58	.7190	.2810	.3372
0.59	.7224	.2776	.3352
0.60	.7257	.2743	.3332

(Continued)

	Proportion of Area		
z^a	Below z^b	Above z	Ordinate u
0.61	.7291	.2709	.3312
0.62	.7324	.2676	.3292
0.63	.7357	.2643	.3271
0.64	.7389	.2611	.3251
0.65	.7422	.2578	.3230
0.66	.7454	.2546	.3209
0.67	.7486	.2514	.3187
0.674	**.7500**	**.2500**	**.3179**
0.68	.7517	.2433	.3166
0.69	.7549	.2451	.3144
0.70	.7580	.2420	.3123
0.71	.7611	.2389	.3101
0.72	.7642	.2358	.3079
0.73	.7673	.2327	.3056
0.74	.7704	.2296	.3034
0.75	.7734	.2266	.3011
0.76	.7764	.2236	.2989
0.77	.7794	.2206	.2966
0.78	.7823	.2177	.2943
0.79	.7852	.2148	.2920
0.80	.7881	.2119	.2897
0.81	.7910	.2090	.2874
0.82	.7939	.2061	.2850
0.83	.7967	.2033	.2827
0.84	.7995	.2005	.2803
0.842	**.8000**	**.2000**	**.2799**
0.85	.8023	.1977	.2780
0.86	.8051	.1949	.2756
0.87	.8078	.1922	.2732
0.88	.8106	.1894	.2709
0.89	.8133	.1867	.2685
0.90	.8159	.1841	.2661
0.91	.8186	.1814	.2637
0.92	.8212	.1788	.2613
0.93	.8238	.1762	.2589
0.94	.8264	.1736	.2565
0.95	.8289	.1711	.2541
0.96	.8315	.1685	.2516
0.97	.8340	.1660	.2492
0.98	.8365	.1635	.2468
0.99	.8389	.1611	.2444
1.00	.8413	.1587	.2420
1.01	.8438	.1562	.2396
1.02	.8461	.1539	.2371

(*Continued*)

| | Proportion of Area | | |
z^a	Below z^b	Above z	Ordinate u
1.03	.8485	.1515	.2347
1.036	**.8500**	**.1500**	**.2333**
1.04	.8508	.1492	.2323
1.05	.8531	.1469	.2299
1.06	.8554	.1446	.2275
1.07	.8577	.1423	.2251
1.08	.8599	.1401	.2227
1.09	.8621	.1379	.2203
1.10	.8643	.1357	.2179
1.11	.8665	.1335	.2155
1.12	.8686	.1314	.2131
1.13	.8708	.1292	.2107
1.14	.8729	.1271	.2083
1.15	.8749	.1251	.2059
1.16	.8770	.1230	.2036
1.17	.8790	.1210	.2012
1.18	.8810	.1190	.1989
1.19	.8830	.1170	.1965
1.20	.8849	.1151	.1942
1.21	.8869	.1131	.1919
1.22	.8888	.1112	.1895
1.23	.8907	.1093	.1872
1.24	.8925	.1075	.1849
1.25	.8944	.1056	.1826
1.26	.8962	.1038	.1804
1.27	.8980	.1020	.1781
1.28	.8997	.1003	.1758
1.282	**.9000**	**.1000**	**.1754**
1.29	.9015	.0985	.1736
1.30	.9032	.0968	.1714
1.31	.9049	.0951	.1691
1.32	.9066	.0934	.1669
1.33	.9082	.0918	.1647
1.34	.9099	.0901	.1626
1.341	**.9100**	**.0900**	**.1623**
1.35	.9115	.0885	.1604
1.36	.9131	.0869	.1582
1.37	.9147	.0853	.1561
1.38	.9162	.0838	.1539
1.39	.9177	.0823	.1518
1.40	.9192	.0808	.1497
1.405	**.9200**	**.0800**	**.1487**

(Continued)

TABLE A.1
(Continued)

| z^a | Proportion of Area | | |
	Below z^b	Above z	Ordinate u
1.41	.9207	.0793	.1476
1.42	.9222	.0778	.1456
1.43	.9236	.0764	.1435
1.44	.9251	.0749	.1415
1.45	.9265	.0735	.1394
1.46	.9279	.0721	.1374
1.47	.9292	.0708	.1354
1.476	**.9300**	**.0700**	**.1342**
1.48	.9306	.0694	.1334
1.49	.9319	.0681	.1315
1.50	.9332	.0668	.1295
1.51	.9345	.0655	.1276
1.52	.9357	.0643	.1257
1.53	.9370	.0630	.1238
1.54	.9382	.0618	.1219
1.55	.9394	.0606	.1200
1.555	**.9400**	**.0600**	**.1191**
1.56	.9406	.0594	.1182
1.57	.9418	.0582	.1163
1.58	.9429	.0571	.1145
1.59	.9441	.0559	.1127
1.60	.9452	.0548	.1109
1.61	.9463	.0537	.1092
1.62	.9474	.0526	.1074
1.63	.9484	.0516	.1057
1.64	.9495	.0505	.1040
1.645	**.9500**	**.0500**	**.1031**
1.65	.9505	.0495	.1023
1.66	.9515	.0485	.1006
1.67	.9525	.0475	.0989
1.68	.9535	.0465	.0973
1.69	.9545	.0455	.0957
1.70	.9554	.0446	.0940
1.71	.9564	.0436	.0925
1.72	.9573	.0427	.0909
1.73	.9582	.0418	.0893
1.74	.9591	.0409	.0878
1.75	.9599	.0401	.0863
1.751	**.9600**	**.0400**	**.0861**
1.76	.9608	.0392	.0848
1.77	.9616	.0384	.0833
1.78	.9625	.0375	.0818
1.79	.9633	.0367	.0804
1.80	.9641	.0359	.0790

(Continued)

	Proportion of Area		
z[a]	Below z[b]	Above z	Ordinate u
1.81	.9649	.0351	.0775
1.82	.9656	.0344	.0761
1.83	.9664	.0338	.0748
1.84	.9671	.0329	.0734
1.85	.9678	.0322	.0721
1.86	.9686	.0314	.0707
1.87	.9693	.0307	.0694
1.88	.9699	.0301	.0681
1.881	**.9700**	**.0300**	**.0680**
1.89	.9706	.0294	.0669
1.90	.9713	.0287	.0656
1.91	.9719	.0281	.0644
1.92	.9726	.0274	.0632
1.93	.9732	.0268	.0620
1.94	.9738	.0262	.0608
1.95	.9744	.0256	.0596
1.960	**.9750**	**.0250**	**.0584**
1.97	.9756	.0244	.0573
1.98	.9761	.0239	.0562
1.99	.9767	.0233	.0551
2.00	.9772	.0228	.0540
2.01	.9778	.0222	.0529
2.02	.9783	.0217	.0519
2.03	.9788	.0212	.0508
2.04	.9793	.0207	.0498
2.05	.9798	.0202	.0488
2.054	**.9800**	**.0200**	**.0484**
2.06	.9803	.0197	.0478
2.07	.9808	.0192	.0468
2.08	.9812	.0188	.0459
2.09	.9817	.0183	.0449
2.10	.9821	.0179	.0440
2.11	.9826	.0174	.0431
2.12	.9830	.0170	.0422
2.13	.9834	.0166	.0413
2.14	.9838	.0162	.0404
2.15	.9842	.0158	.0396
2.16	.9846	.0154	.0387
2.17	.9850	.0150	.0379
2.18	.9854	.0146	.0371
2.19	.9857	.0143	.0363
2.20	.9861	.0139	.0355
2.21	.9864	.0136	.0347
2.22	.9868	.0132	.0339

(Continued)

	Proportion of Area		
z^a	Below z^b	Above z	Ordinate u
2.23	.9871	.0129	.0332
2.24	.9875	.0125	.0325
2.25	.9878	.0122	.0317
2.26	.9881	.0119	.0310
2.27	.9884	.0116	.0303
2.28	.9887	.0113	.0297
2.29	.9890	.0110	.0290
2.30	.9893	.0107	.0283
2.31	.9896	.0104	.0277
2.32	.9898	.0102	.0270
2.326	**.9900**	**.0100**	**.0267**
2.33	.9901	.0099	.0264
2.34	.9904	.0096	.0258
2.35	.9906	.0094	.0252
2.36	.9909	.0091	.0246
2.37	.9911	.0089	.0241
2.38	.9913	.0087	.0235
2.39	.9916	.0084	.0229
2.40	.9918	.0082	.0224
2.41	.9920	.0080	.0219
2.42	.9922	.0078	.0213
2.43	.9925	.0075	.0208
2.44	.9927	.0073	.0203
2.45	.9929	.0071	.0198
2.46	.9931	.0069	.0194
2.47	.9932	.0068	.0189
2.48	.9934	.0066	.0184
2.49	.9936	.0064	.0180
2.50	.9938	.0062	.0175
2.51	.9940	.0060	.0171
2.52	.9941	.0059	.0167
2.53	.9943	.0057	.0163
2.54	.9945	.0055	.0158
2.55	.9946	.0054	.0154
2.56	.9948	.0052	.0151
2.57	.9949	.0051	.0147
2.576	**.9950**	**.0050**	**.0145**
2.58	.9951	.0049	.0143
2.59	.9952	.0048	.0139
2.60	.9953	.0047	.0136
2.61	.9955	.0045	.0132
2.62	.9956	.0044	.0129
2.63	.9957	.0043	.0126
2.64	.9959	.0041	.0122
2.65	.9960	.0040	.0119

(Continued)

	Proportion of Area		
z^a	Below z^b	Above z	Ordinate u
2.66	.9961	.0039	.0116
2.67	.9962	.0038	.0113
2.68	.9963	.0037	.0110
2.69	.9964	.0036	.0107
2.70	.9965	.0035	.0104
2.71	.9966	.0034	.0101
2.72	.9967	.0033	.0099
2.73	.9968	.0032	.0096
2.74	.9969	.0031	.0093
2.75	.9970	.0030	.0091
2.76	.9971	.0029	.0088
2.77	.9972	.0028	.0086
2.78	.9973	.0027	.0084
2.79	.9974	.0026	.0081
2.80	.9974	.0026	.0079
2.81	.9975	.0025	.0077
2.82	.9976	.0024	.0075
2.83	.9977	.0023	.0073
2.84	.9977	.0023	.0071
2.85	.9978	.0022	.0069
2.86	.9979	.0021	.0067
2.87	.9979	.0021	.0065
2.88	.9980	.0020	.0063
2.89	.9981	.0019	.0061
2.90	.9981	.0019	.0060
2.91	.9982	.0018	.0058
2.92	.9982	.0018	.0056
2.93	.9983	.0017	.0055
2.94	.9984	.0016	.0053
2.95	.9984	.0016	.0051
2.96	.9985	.0015	.0050
2.97	.9985	.0015	.0048
2.98	.9986	.0014	.0047
2.99	.9986	.0014	.0046
3.00	.99865	.00135	.0044
3.01	.99869	.00131	.00430
3.02	.99874	.00126	.00417
3.03	.99878	.00122	.00405
3.04	.99882	.00118	.00393
3.05	.99886	.00114	.00381
3.06	.99889	.00111	.00370
3.07	.99893	.00107	.00358
3.08	.99896	.00104	.00348
3.09	.99900	.00100	.00337

(Continued)

269

	Proportion of Area		
z^a	Below z^b	Above z	Ordinate u
3.0902	**.999000**	**.001000**	**.00337**
3.10	.99903	.00097	.00327
3.11	.99906	.00094	.00317
3.12	.99910	.00090	.00307
3.13	.99913	.00087	.00298
3.14	.99916	.00084	.00288
3.15	.99918	.00082	.00279
3.16	.99921	.00079	.00271
3.17	.99924	.00076	.00262
3.18	.99926	.00074	.00254
3.19	.99929	.00071	.00246
3.20	.99931	.00069	.00238
3.21	.99934	.00066	.00231
3.22	.99936	.00064	.00224
3.23	.99938	.00062	.00216
3.24	.99940	.00060	.00210
3.25	.99942	.00058	.00203
3.26	.99944	.00056	.00196
3.27	.99946	.00054	.00190
3.28	.99948	.00050	.00184
3.29	.99950	.00050	.00178
3.2905	**.999500**	**.000500**	**.00178**
3.30	.99951	.00048	.00172
3.31	.99953	.00047	.00167
3.32	.99955	.00045	.00161
3.33	.99957	.00043	.00156
3.34	.99958	.00042	.00151
3.35	.99960	.00040	.00146
3.36	.99961	.00039	.00141
3.37	.99962	.00038	.00136
3.38	.99964	.00036	.00132
3.39	.99965	.00035	.00127
3.40	.99966	.00034	.00123
3.41	.99968	.00032	.00119
3.42	.99969	.00031	.00115
3.43	.99970	.00030	.00111
3.44	.99971	.00029	.00107
3.45	.99972	.00028	.00104
3.46	.99973	.00027	.00100
3.47	.99974	.00026	.00097
3.48	.99975	.00025	.00094
3.49	.99976	.00024	.00090
3.50	.99977	.00023	.00087

(Continued)

Proportion of Area

z^a	Below z^b	Above z	Ordinate u
3.51	.99978	.00022	.00084
3.52	.99978	.00022	.00081
3.53	.99979	.00021	.00079
3.54	.99980	.00020	.00076
3.55	.99981	.00019	.00073
3.56	.99981	.00019	.00071
3.57	.99982	.00018	.00068
3.58	.99983	.00017	.00066
3.59	.99983	.00017	.00063
3.60	.99984	.00016	.00061
3.61	.99985	.00015	.00059
3.62	.99985	.00015	.00057
3.63	.99986	.00014	.00055
3.64	.99986	.00014	.00053
3.65	.99987	.00013	.00051
3.66	.999873	.000126	.00049
3.67	.999879	.000121	.00047
3.68	.999883	.000117	.00046
3.69	.999888	.000112	.00044
3.70	.999892	.000108	.00042
3.71	.999896	.000104	.00041
3.719	**.9999000**	**.000100**	**.00040**
3.72	.999900	.000100	.00039
3.73	.999904	.000096	.00038
3.74	.999908	.000092	.00037
3.75	.999912	.000088	.00036
3.76	.999915	.000085	.00034
3.77	.999918	.000082	.00033
3.78	.999922	.000078	.00031
3.79	.999925	.000075	.00030
3.80	.999928	.000072	.00029
3.81	.999931	.000070	.00028
3.82	.999933	.000067	.00027
3.83	.999936	.000064	.00026
3.84	.999939	.000062	.00025
3.85	.999941	.000059	.00024
3.86	.999943	.000057	.00023
3.87	.999946	.000054	.00022
3.88	.999948	.000052	.00021
3.89	.999950	.000050	.00021
3.891	**.9999500**	**.000050**	**.00021**
3.90	.999952	.000048	.00020

(Continued)

TABLE A.1
(Continued)

	Proportion of Area		
z^a	Below z^b	Above z	Ordinate u
3.91	.999954	.000046	.00019
3.92	.999956	.000044	.00018
3.93	.999958	.000043	.00018
3.94	.999959	.000041	.00017
3.95	.999961	.000039	.00016
3.96	.999963	.000038	.00016
3.97	.999964	.000036	.00015
3.98	.999966	.000035	.00014
3.99	.999967	.000033	.00014
4.00	.999968	.000032	.00013
4.265	**.9999900**	**.0000100**	**.0000448**
4.417	.9999950	.0000050	.0000231
4.50	.9999966023	.0000033977	.0000160
5.00	.9999997133	.0000002867	.00000149
5.327	.9999995000	.0000005000	.00000027
5.50	.9999999810	.0000000190	.00000011
6.00	.9999999990	.0000000010	.000000006

[a]If z is negative, interchange the "area" columns; for example, if $z = -.10$, then .4602 of the area under the normal curve is below that point.

[b]Percentile points are commonly denoted as $_pz$; thus, the 60th percentile is denoted $_{.60}z$ and equals .253. Commonly used percentiles are given in boldface type.

TABLE A.2
Percentile Points of Chi-Square Distributions:[a,b] $_p\chi_v^2 = _{1-\alpha}\chi_v^2$

v	$p = .01$	.02	.05	.10	.20	.30	.50	.70	.80	.90	α = .05 .95	.98	α = .01 .99	.999	v	Mode	Skewness ζκ	Kurtosis γ₂
1	.00016	.00063	.00393	.0158	.0642	.148	.455	1.07	1.64	2.71	3.84	5.41	6.64	10.83	1			12.0
2	.0201	.0404	.103	.211	.446	.713	1.39	2.41	3.22	4.60	5.99	7.82	9.21	13.82	2		1.00	6.0
3	.115	.185	.352	.584	1.00	1.42	2.37	3.66	4.64	6.25	7.82	9.84	11.34	16.27	3	1	.82	4.0
4	.297	.429	.711	1.06	1.65	2.20	3.36	4.88	5.99	7.78	9.49	11.67	13.28	18.47	4	2	.71	3.0
5	.554	.752	1.14	1.61	2.34	3.00	4.35	6.06	7.29	9.24	11.07	13.39	15.09	20.52	5	3	.63	2.4
6	.872	1.13	1.64	2.20	3.07	3.83	5.35	7.23	8.56	10.64	12.59	15.03	16.81	22.46	6	4	.58	2.0
7	1.24	1.56	2.17	2.83	3.82	4.67	6.35	8.38	9.80	12.02	14.07	16.62	18.48	24.32	7	5	.53	1.7
8	1.65	2.03	2.73	3.49	4.59	5.53	7.34	9.52	11.03	13.36	15.51	18.17	20.09	26.12	8	6	.50	1.5
9	2.09	2.53	3.32	4.17	5.38	6.39	8.34	10.66	12.24	14.68	16.92	19.68	21.67	27.88	9	7	.47	1.3
10	2.56	3.06	3.94	4.86	6.18	7.27	9.34	11.78	13.44	15.99	18.31	21.16	23.21	29.59	10	8	.45	1.2
11	3.05	3.61	4.58	5.58	6.99	8.15	10.34	12.90	14.63	17.28	19.68	22.62	24.72	31.26	11	9	.43	1.1
12	3.57	4.18	5.23	6.30	7.81	9.03	11.34	14.01	15.81	18.55	21.03	24.05	26.22	32.91	12	10	.41	1.0
13	4.11	4.76	5.89	7.04	8.63	9.93	12.34	15.12	16.98	19.81	22.36	25.47	27.69	34.53	13	11	.39	.92
14	4.66	5.37	6.57	7.79	9.47	10.82	13.34	16.22	18.15	21.06	23.68	26.87	29.14	36.12	14	12	.38	.86
15	5.23	5.98	7.26	8.55	10.31	11.72	14.34	17.32	19.31	22.31	25.00	28.26	30.58	37.70	15	13	.37	.80
16	5.81	6.61	7.96	9.31	11.15	12.62	15.34	18.42	20.46	23.54	26.30	29.63	32.00	39.25	16	14	.35	.75
17	6.41	7.26	8.67	10.08	12.00	13.53	16.34	19.51	21.62	24.77	27.59	31.00	33.41	40.79	17	15	.34	.71
18	7.02	7.91	9.39	10.86	12.86	14.44	17.34	20.60	22.76	25.99	28.87	32.35	34.80	42.31	18	16	.33	.67
19	7.63	8.57	10.12	11.65	13.72	15.35	18.34	21.69	23.90	27.20	30.14	33.69	36.19	43.82	19	17	.32	.63
20	8.26	9.24	10.85	12.44	14.58	16.27	19.34	22.78	25.04	28.41	31.41	35.02	37.57	45.32	20	18	.32	.60

(Continued)

TABLE A.2
(Continued)

| | | | | | | | | | | | a = .05 | | α = .01 | | | | | Skewness | Kurtosis |
v	p = .01	.02	.05	.10	.20	.30	.50	.70	.80	.90	.95	.98	.99	.999	v	Mode	ςκ	g₂
21	8.90	9.92	11.59	13.24	15.44	17.18	20.34	23.86	26.17	29.62	32.67	36.34	38.93	46.80	21	19	.31	.57
22	9.54	10.60	12.34	14.04	16.31	18.10	21.34	24.94	27.30	30.81	33.92	37.66	40.29	48.27	22	20	.30	.55
23	10.20	11.29	13.09	14.85	17.19	19.02	22.34	26.02	28.43	32.01	35.17	38.97	41.64	49.73	23	21	.29	.52
24	10.86	11.90	13.85	15.66	18.06	19.94	23.34	27.10	29.55	33.20	36.42	40.27	42.98	51.18	24	22	.29	.50
25	11.52	12.70	14.61	16.47	18.94	20.87	24.34	28.17	30.68	34.38	37.65	41.57	44.31	52.62	25	23	.28	.48
26	12.20	13.41	15.38	17.29	19.82	21.79	25.34	29.25	31.80	35.56	38.88	42.86	45.64	54.05	26	24	.28	.46
27	12.88	14.12	16.15	18.11	20.70	22.72	26.34	30.32	32.91	36.74	40.11	44.14	46.96	55.48	27	25	.27	.44
28	13.56	14.85	16.93	18.94	21.59	23.65	27.34	31.39	34.03	37.92	41.34	45.42	48.28	56.89	28	26	.27	.43
29	14.26	15.57	17.71	19.77	22.48	24.58	28.34	32.46	35.14	39.09	42.56	46.69	49.59	58.30	29	27	.26	.41
30	14.95	16.31	18.49	20.60	23.36	25.51	29.34	33.53	36.25	40.26	43.77	47.96	50.89	59.70	30	28	.26	.40
40	22.16	23.84	26.51	29.05	32.38	34.81	39.34	44.17	47.27	51.81	55.76	60.44	63.69	73.40	40	38	.22	.30
50	24.71	31.66	34.76	37.69	41.45	44.31	49.33	54.72	58.16	63.17	67.51	72.61	76.15	81.66	50	48	.20	.29
60	37.48	38.70	43.19	46.46	50.64	53.81	54.33	65.23	68.97	74.40	79.08	84.58	88.38	99.61	60	58	.18	.20
70	45.44	47.89	51.74	55.33	59.90	63.35	69.33	75.69	79.72	85.53	90.53	96.39	100.4	112.3	70	68	.17	.17
80	53.54	56.21	60.34	64.28	69.2	72.9	79.33	86.1	90.4	96.58	101.9	108.1	112.3	124.8	80	78	.16	.15
90	61.75	64.64	69.13	73.29	78.6	82.5	89.33	96.5	101.1	107.6	113.1	119.6	124.1	137.2	90	88	.15	.13
100	70.06	73.14	77.43	82.36	87.9	92.1	99.33	106.9	111.7	118.5	124.3	131.1	135.8	149.4	100	98	.14	.12

aMode = v − 2, μ = v, σ²_χ2 = 2v. For large v:

$$_p\chi^2_v = v\left(1 - \frac{2}{9v} + {}_pz\sqrt{\frac{2}{9v}}\right)^3$$

where $_pz$ is the normal deviate. For example $_{.95}\chi^2_{55} = 55[1 - .00404 + (1.96)(.06356)]^3 = 55(1.1205)^3 = 77.38$.

bValues not found in existing tables were calculated by George Kretke.

TABLE A.3
Critical Values of r for H_0: $\rho = 0$ [a]

n [b]	$\alpha_1 = .05$ $\alpha_2 = .10$	$\alpha_1 = .025$ $\alpha_2 = .05$	$\alpha_1 = .01$ $\alpha_2 = .02$	$\alpha_1 = .005$ $\alpha_2 = .01$	$\alpha_1 = .0005$ $\alpha_2 = .001$	v [c]
3	.988	.997	.9995	.9999	.99994	1
4	.900	.950	.980	.990	.999	2
5	.805	.878	.934	.959	.991	3
6	.729	.811	.882	.917	.974	4
7	.669	.754	.833	.874	.951	5
8	.622	.707	.789	.834	.925	6
9	.582	.666	.750	.798	.898	7
10	.549	.632	.716	.765	.872	8
11	.521	.602	.685	.735	.847	9
12	.497	.576	.658	.708	.823	10
13	.476	.553	.634	.684	.801	11
14	.458	.532	.612	.661	.780	12
15	.441	.514	.592	.641	.760	13
16	.426	.497	.574	.623	.742	14
17	.412	.482	.558	.606	.725	15
18	.400	.468	.542	.590	.708	16
19	.389	.456	.528	.575	.693	17
20	.378	.444	.516	.561	.679	18
21	.369	.433	.503	.549	.665	19
22	.360	.423	.492	.537	.652	20
23	.352	.413	.482	.526	.640	21
24	.344	.404	.472	.515	.629	22
25	.337	.396	.462	.505	.618	23
26	.330	.388	.453	.496	.607	24
27	.323	.381	.445	.487	.597	25
28	.317	.374	.437	.479	.588	26
29	.311	.367	.430	.471	.579	27
30	.306	.361	.423	.463	.570	28
35	.282	.333	.391	.428	.531	33
40	.264	.312	.366	.402	.501	38
45	.248	.296	.349	.381	.471	43
50	.235	.276	.328	.361	.451	48
60	.214	.254	.300	.330	.414	58
70	.198	.235	.277	.305	.385	68
80	.185	.220	.260	.286	.361	78
90	.174	.208	.245	.270	.342	88

(Continued)

n^b	$\alpha_1 = .05$ $\alpha_2 = .10$	$\alpha_1 = .025$ $\alpha_2 = .05$	$\alpha_1 = .01$ $\alpha_2 = .02$	$\alpha_1 = .005$ $\alpha_2 = .01$	$\alpha_1 = .0005$ $\alpha_2 = .001$	v^c
100	.165	.196	.232	.256	.324	98
150	.135	.161	.190	.210	.267	148
200	.117	.139	.164	.182	.232	198
250	.104	.124	.147	.163	.207	248
300	.095	.113	.134	.148	.189	298
400	.082	.098	.115	.128	.169	398
500	.074	.088	.104	.115	.147	498
1,000	.052	.062	.074	.081	.104	898
5,000	.0233	.0278	.0329	.0364	.0465	4,998
10,000	.0164	.0196	.0233	.0258	.0393	9,998

[a]Column entries for $\alpha_2 = .10$, .05, .02, and .01 for $n = 3$ to $n = 100$ are taken from Table 13 in *Biometrika tables for statisticians*, 2nd ed., by E. S. Pearson and H. O. Hartley (Eds.), 1962, New York: Cambridge University Press.

[b]If the *value* of an r from a sample of size n exceeds the tabled value for α and n, the null hypothesis that $\rho = 0$ may be rejected at the α level of significance. For example, a sample of r of .561 or more with $n = 20$ leads to rejection of the hypothesis $\rho = 0$ at $\alpha_2 = .01$. Use n only for testing Pearson rs.

[c]The degrees of freedom v for a Pearson r are $n - 2$; for partial correlation coefficients, $v = n - 2 - p$, where p is the number of variables partialed out.

AUTHOR INDEX

SUBJECT INDEX